FOOL THE WORLD:

The Oral History of
a Band Called Pixies

Josh Frank has penned numerous plays, screenplays
and musicals. His second book, *In Heaven Everything
Is Fine – The Unsolved Life of Peter Ivers*, will be
published by Simon and Schuster/Free Press in 2008.
He lives in Austin, TX.

Caryn Ganz is the deputy editor of *RollingStone.com*.
She was previously an editor at *Spin* magazine and
MTV News, and her writing has also appeared in
Blender, Entertainment Weekly, GQ and *V*.
She lives in Manhattan.

Visit the book and its authors at
www.fooltheworldbook.com

FOOL THE WORLD:

The Oral History of
a Band Called Pixies

By
Josh Frank and Caryn Ganz

This edition published by Virgin Books 2008

2 4 6 8 10 9 7 5 3 1

First published in Great Britain in 2005 by
Virgin Books
Random House
Thames Wharf Studios
Rainville Road
London W6 9HA

www.rbooks.co.uk

Addresses for companies within The Random House Group Limited can be found at:
www.randomhouse.co.uk/offices.htm

The Random House Group Limited Reg. No. 954009

A CIP catalogue record for this book
is available from the British Library

ISBN 9780753513835

The Random House Group Limited supports The Forest Stewardship Council [FSC],
the leading international forest certification organisation. All our titles that are printed
on Greenpeace approved FSC certified paper carry the FSC logo.

Our paper procurement policy can be found at www.rbooks.co.uk/environment

Typeset by Phoenix Photosetting, Chatham, Kent
Printed in the UK by CPI Bookmarque, Croydon, CR0 4TD

pixie or pixy
n. pl. pixies
A fairylike or elfin creature, especially one that is
mischievous; a playful sprite.

Trompe Le Monde
Combination of *trompe-l'oeil* (adj : creating the illusion of
seeing reality; a visual deception; literally fooling the eye)
and *monde* (n. the world). Fool the world

There is none holy as the LORD:
for there is none beside thee:
neither is there any **rock** like our God.
—Samuel 2:2, Old Testament

I'd love to see someone do their doctorate on the Pixies.
Then we might discover something. You can extract
anthropological and sociological info from everything in
the world. I love sitting round analyzing something to
death. It's never a waste of time. But it's no good talking
to the source. Don't ask me! I don't know! I'm just
writing songs!
—Black Francis, *Melody Maker*, 1990

In memory of Papa Joe Frank
and for all the kids sitting in their rooms, dreaming

CONTENTS

Act Three: Le Monde

Encore

CAST OF CHARACTERS

Steve Albini: recording engineer; former singer/guitarist for Big Black, Rapeman, and Shellac

Johnny Angel: born Johnny Carmen; Boston musician, journalist

Judd Apatow: screenwriter; creator of the television series *Freaks and Geeks* and *Undeclared*

Steven Appleby: cartoonist, contributed illustrations to *Trompe Le Monde*

Chas Banks: former Pixies European tour manager

Andy Barding: former co-editor of the English Pixies fanzine *Rock A My Soul*

Beck: musician

Norman Blake: Teenage Fanclub guitarist

Bono: U2 singer

Steven Cantor: cofounder, Stick Figure Productions

Billy Corgan: former Smashing Pumpkins singer/guitarist; former Zwan singer/guitarist; musician

Jeff Craft: Pixies international booking agent

Kelley Deal: Kim Deal's twin sister; member of the Breeders, the Kelley Deal 6000

Kim Deal: aka Mrs. John Murphy; Pixies bassist; Breeders lead singer/guitarist; Amps lead singer/guitarist

Lilli Dennison: former employee at the Rat; former manager of the Del Fuegos; former owner of Boston club Lilli's

Jon Dolan: senior associate editor, *Spin* magazine

Tanya Donelly: former Throwing Muses guitarist/singer; former Breeders guitarist/singer; Belly founder/former lead singer/guitarist; musician

Perry Farrell: Jane's Addiction singer

Eric Drew Feldman: former Pere Ubu keyboardist; former Captain Beefheart keyboardist/bassist; played keyboards and synths on *Trompe Le Monde*

John Flansburgh: They Might Be Giants cofounder/singer/guitarist

Matthew Galkin: producer, Stick Figure Productions

Marc Geiger: Pixies agent; cofounder, Lollapalooza

Rich Gilbert: Frank Black and the Catholics guitarist; alumnus of several Boston bands including the Zulus and Human Sexual Response

Claudia Gonson: Magnetic Fields drummer/keyboardist; Future Bible Heroes singer

Steve Haigler: mixing engineer, *Doolittle*, *Bossanova*, *Trompe Le Monde*

Joe Harvard: born Joe Incagnoli; cofounder, Fort Apache studios

PJ Harvey: musician

Kristin Hersh: Throwing Muses lead singer/guitarist; 50 Foot Wave lead singer/guitarist; musician

Robin Hurley: former CEO of 4AD

James Iha: former Smashing Pumpkins guitarist; A Perfect Circle guitarist; musician

Paul Kolderie: cofounder, Fort Apache studios; producer of albums by Pixies, Hole, Radiohead

Simon Larbalestier: photographer, contributed pictures to all Pixies albums

Courtney Love: former Hole lead singer/guitarist; musician

David Lovering: Pixies drummer; scientific phenomenalist

Peter Lubin: former A&R representative, Elektra records

John Lupner: studio assistant, *Surfer Rosa*; cofounder, Q Division

Ian MacKaye: former Minor Threat singer; Fugazi singer/guitarist; the Evens singer/guitarist; co-owner, Dischord Records; musician

Shirley Manson: Garbage lead singer

Ben Marts: former Pixies American tour manager

J Mascis: Dinosaur Jr. singer/guitarist

Marc Mazzarelli: aka Mazz, Mente bassist

Ted Mico: former editor, *Melody Maker*

John Murphy: Kim Deal's ex-husband; Mente leader; life-long Bostonian

Gil Norton: producer, *Doolittle*, *Bossanova*, and *Trompe Le Monde*

Stephen Perkins: Jane's Addiction drummer

Liz Phair: musician

Burt Price: former studio assistant, Downtown Recorders

Joey Santiago: Pixies guitarist; Martinis guitarist

Sean Slade: cofounder, Fort Apache studios; producer of albums by Pixies, Hole, Radiohead

Gary Smith: current owner/manager of Fort Apache studios; first person to record Pixies

Kurt St. Thomas: former program director, WFNX, Boston; co-author of *Nirvana: The Chosen Rejects*

Jim Suptic: The Get Up Kids guitarist

Courtney Taylor: The Dandy Warhols' singer/guitarist

Dave Thomas: former Pere Ubu singer

Charles Thompson: aka Black Francis and Frank Black; Pixies lead singer/guitarist/primary songwriter

Paul Tollett: president of Goldenvoice concert promotions, which presents the Coachella Valley Music and Arts Festival

Jean Walsh: Charles Thompson's ex-wife; childhood friend of John Murphy

Ivo Watts-Russell: cofounder, 4AD records

Ted Widmer: Mente guitarist; former member of the Upper Crust

FOREWORD

by Chas Banks, Pixies European Tour Manager

To be honest I don't remember too much about my first meeting with the Pixies. It was *very* early in the morning (it always is when you pick up American bands on their arrival in Europe) and all I knew about them was that they were the support band on the tour and that they were managed by the same guy who managed the headliners, Throwing Muses.

The thing I do remember, though, is how polite they were (Charles even called me *sir*, in the way that American kids do as a mark of respect) and how incredibly excited they were to simply be there. It was totally clear to me that they were going to be easy to deal with, and as a tour manager that's number one on your list of priorities.

Just how easy came as a bit of a shock. During those first few days it became apparent that they were ambitious, focused, and determined to make the best of their opportunity. Of course my attention was on the Muses, so it was two or three shows into the tour before I even watched them onstage and only then because crew members had been singing their praises.

I could hardly believe what I saw and heard. There was an electricity and a power that you just don't normally see for support acts. I've been on the road for most of my adult life and it is very, very rare for a support band to make much of an impression. Most of the stories you hear about support acts "blowing off" the headliner are apocryphal at best and bullshit at worst.

As I watched, I looked at the audience and what I saw was myself as a teenager looking up at the Who. A different band, a different time, but the eternal teenager experiencing what I had seen and felt. The feeling that your world would never be the same again, because you'd just seen the best band in the world. Ever.

The next couple of years were a very fast ride. It wasn't a rollercoaster ride; there weren't enough downs for that to work as a metaphor. It was more like a volcano exploding or a huge storm. The Pixies' ascendancy was nothing less than a force of nature: unstoppable and relentless. Crazy at times, but always ridiculously exciting and fun, too. I wouldn't change one minute of it.

And now, after all those years, the band is back together and better than ever. The really cool part for me is that when I went to see them play last summer I was immediately taken with how many really young kids there were in the crowd, who no way could have been old enough the first time round.

This was no sentimental last hurrah played out to an ageing audience who wanted to relive their teenage years when they still had a full head of hair. Instead, there was a new, (very) young audience, feeling that same feeling that I felt in 1967 when I was 17 looking up at the Who. The same feeling that a young Thom Yorke had the first time he saw the Pixies. The same feeling that one day my grandson will feel for a band that is probably still at junior school right now.

When I saw that they were headlining some of the biggest festivals in the U.K. again this summer, I felt an enormous sense of pride that me and my wife Shirley (who played a bigger part than anyone will ever know) played some small role in the history of one of the best bands in the world. Ever.

Life to the Pixies!

With much love,

Chas Banks, 2005

INTRODUCTION:
A Long Day's Journey Into the White

In the spring of 2001 I called up Frank Black's publicist, Ashley Mathews (whom I can't thank enough, for she is the hidden happenstance architect of the last four years of my life), and said I wanted to write a play about him. A week later I found myself in Los Angeles sitting down to martinis with the man himself, Charles Thompson. It turns out he was a big fan of German cinema, which bought me some much needed street cred since I had staged a Werner Herzog film a few years before called *Stroszek*. All artists take from their peers and heroes, expand upon their work, and make it their own. I was working on my own version of that, I guess, and still am, by trying to sit down with the artists who inspired my work and getting permission to make new works involving their projects.

Charles' career with Pixies and as a solo artist, as well as Kim Deal's, had the profoundest effect on my vision for film and theatre, so while working on an off-Broadway musical in New York for the blue-haired contingency of America I started thinking what would a "rock musical" for my generation look like. It was obvious. It would look like Pixies. And for the next two years I made it my mission to try to show the world these kids' vision. I'm still trying. Suffice to say the band's reunion took me off guard, and gave entirely new meaning to all the work I had previously done.

I am still trying to catch up. The main thing I want to get across is that the book you have in front of you started from the purest of places—the wide-eyed inspiration of a young creative writer but above all else, a fan. I am honored to have had the good fortune of meeting these amazing characters when I did, in the calm before the storm, at the end of the prologue that so many had mistaken for the aftermath.

First let's get something out of the way... If you want Sex, Drugs, and Rock'n'roll, this isn't the book for you. But that's okay because you have your choice of hundreds of others to satisfy your craving for the dirty, demented side of rock. Secondly, for the purposes of this book we are not rock journalists, but rock dramatists. Without the slightest bit of airbrushing, the most subtle truths are often filled with the beautiful drama that is real life. Not all musical tales of rock'n'roll have to be packed with insanity and darkness to be full of inspiration and excitement. A rock dramatist takes those simple moments that whispered change, shapes them into a journey, and brings out the inherent drama that was there all along. Make no mistake, you are about to dig up a hidden history. Hidden under the headlines and glossy photos and a timeline that, as Pixies' first producer Gary Smith said "is paraphrased—leaving out the details in order to create an index of time that is manageable."

So if you want a glitzy, glamorized, mythologized retelling of the story of your favorite band and you want your rock books strewn with journalistic commentary and back-biting stop reading right now—this isn't the book for you. But if you want the truth about the early days of alternative rock and the quiet, subterranean ways in which it changed everything, and if you want it from the mouths of those who lived it behind and in front of the scene, and you want it uncut, with no commercial interruption or overblown segues or product placement—then this is the book for you.

Many journalists have put their talent to use describing the magic of Pixies, the Breeders, and Frank Black. We are not here to do that. Instead of putting words to the music, as you read and follow the movement of the albums and the protagonists from year to year, let us suggest this: if you don't have the albums on hand, go get them. They are great. With each chapter put the album on and listen along as you read the story of the world surrounding the music that would change it forever.

How did this book come to be? I could start with being 15 years old in Potomac, Maryland, attending the high school that Beverly Hills 90210 was based on. The cool, mysterious, agro senior hands me a mix tape, a parting gift as he leaves for better things, me the scared freshman, just getting started in a new town. The mix tape had two sides, one had samples of Robyn Hitchcock and the Pogues and the other side just said "Pixies."

In the winter of 2002 I was going through the research I had collected for a rock musical I was developing about Frank Black and Pixies. I had started about eight months before. Looking through Kim talking about sound, Joey talking about Morricone, David talking about magic, Charles talking about Doug Sahm, it became clear to me that if I wanted to fit all the wonderful words I had collected into a single dramatic work it would be about eight hours long.

My mother calls. I'm sitting in a burger joint in Manhattan's Lower East Side. The manager was a Pixies fan, and knowing I was working on a Pixies musical gave me an open account on burgers and free coffee and let me make the occasional bike delivery for some extra pocket change to pay off said tab in between interviews on my cell phone with people like Pixies European tour manager Chas Banks in Manchester.

I told my mother that I was sitting on so much material, so much time spent hearing stories and there was even so much more I could find, so many more people I could talk to that I didn't even know where to begin cutting. She suggested I compile all the material into one big fat book, so that then I would feel more comfortable pulling out little bits and pieces for a two-hour play. That is how Fool The World began. (Thanks, Mom)

Over the last two years as I waited for funding for the musical to come through, I continued to collect the story of the early days of Boston rock, the American alternative rock invasion of the U.K. and the treasure hunt to find more and more who were involved in the world that surrounded this band—this band that has spent the last four years in my head every hour of every day. I consider myself a lucky guy to have called up Charles when I did, almost two years before anyone had even a glimmer of the idea of a reunion. But somehow, right at the moment, all four members were beginning to think good thoughts again about those days, and to revisit them with fondness. It was apparent to me then that if they all found themselves in a room together as strangers just meeting for the first time, that they would really enjoy each other, would like who they had grown up to be, and maybe even have an idea to start a band together, for the first time, again.

The music of Frank Black, the Breeders, and Pixies is one of the things that drove me first to scrutinize my dreams and ambitions. It made me realize anything was possible—whether it was serenading space aliens who surfed to *Bossanova* or writing rock musicals with distorted guitars. So this journey has been a personal journey and a passionate one, and the fuel that jumpstarted it was the same fuel that fired me up with the chutzpah to call Charles Thompson and ask him if I could write a story based on his life.

So much can be learned from the alternative music scene of the late 1980s. The "do it yourself," movement was really at its peak. For the first time independently created records were making money, landing on the charts, and anything was possible. Artist development was everything, and unlike today, the creatives were nurtured and people felt like they could have their integrity and eat it too. Hopefully a reminder is laced in the text that follows that even today, anything is possible.

A year ago Caryn Ganz agreed to co-write what would become the drama that you have in front of you. Caryn and I have spent the last year reaching out to the farthest corners of a universe, its history, and the splendid array of its alternative rock roots.

> *"Black holes are where God divided by zero."*
> —*Steven Wright*

Because light and other forms of energy and matter are permanently trapped inside a black hole, it can never be observed directly. However, a black hole can be detected by the effect of its gravitational field on nearby objects.

When you look at a black hole, you are actually looking at the energy and matter it is pulling into its irresistible gravitational pull. You can't see a black hole without the energy and matter it sucks in without which it cannot really be said to exist. Without it, it is "a trick to the eye." Thus the drama of *Fool the World* unfolds by taking snapshots of the matter and energy, the people and stories that got sucked into the orbit of one of the heaviest, most gravitational of all bands, a black hole of rock'n'roll called Pixies.

The reader may look at *Fool the World* as an eight-hour musical that never would have made it to the stage: A director's cut of sorts, that not only tells the story of teenagers from different isolated pockets of pre-Internet America; not only the story of a band, but the climate, how it changed, and how four kids started a chain reaction that would effect everyone in rock music from Kurt and Courtney to Bowie and Bono. Everyone has their part in the story, and *Fool The World* does nothing more or less than take their words for it.

Otto von Bismarck proclaimed, "If you want to fool the world, tell the truth." He said it in 1889, when he fooled Prussia into war in order to create a little place to call home. (We know it now as Germany). But a hundred years later, in 1989, it was still not only true but about to be proven, or at least experimented with for the first time in a landscape of sound.

Charles Thompson, Kim Deal, Joey Santiago and Dave Lovering had not spoken about Pixies history, or to each other, for ten years. Large chunks of this book were taken from my interviews that were conducted two years before they met again for the first time—to rehearse for the reunion. That first day of rehearsal was literally the first time all four had been in the same room in all those years.

So take a card from the deck of the kid who could fool the world with a shout by changing it with a whisper, and flip over the newspaper and check the date—it's the 1980s, and although new wave is all the rage and hair bands are taking up space, there is an "alternative"—we just don't know it yet.

In the beginning there were some kids alone in their rooms, and they made something, something different, something simple, something so innocent and pure that it makes you feel dirty. This is the story of the kids who made the music that fooled the world.

—JOSH FRANK, 2005

ACT ONE

BOSTON

1. B.P. (BEFORE PIXIES) (1961–1984)

Kim Deal and David Lovering were born in 1961, one year before the first audio cassette became commercially available and three years before the Beatles made their first epic journey to American shores. Charles Thompson and Joey Santiago were born one year after that cultural landmark, in 1965.

CHILDHOOD (1961 TO 1983)

Charles Thompson (aka Black Francis and Frank Black; Pixies lead singer/guitarist/primary songwriter; born April 6, 1965 in Boston, Massachusetts): Most of high school, grades nine, ten, and 11, I was out here in L.A., and I listened to a lot of '60s stuff—whatever I could get at a used record store. Could be an early Cat Stevens record, could be a Bob Seger record, not exactly hip, cool stuff. Just like, "Hey, this is 50 cents, I've never heard this before, I'll buy it." My father had a bar, so we would hear a lot of stuff on the jukebox. I used to go to the library and get records. My very first guitar was my mother's guitar. And she bought it by stealing my father's tips and throwing them into a closet for a period of months back in 1965 or '66, and bought a Yamaha classical guitar. That guitar went on a road trip with my cousin, then it ended up back in my mother's possession when I was 11 or 12, and I started to play it again.

Johnny Angel (born Johnny Carmen; Boston musician, journalist): Charles' dad was a bar owner/libertarian/tough guy and his mom was more of a hippie, and I think the folk rock hits of the '60s were echoing through his head nonstop.

Thompson: I first lived in L.A. as a baby because my father wanted to go and learn more about the restaurant and bar business. He worked in West Hollywood next to the Troubadour, a nightclub I play at today. He didn't end up liking California—there were a lot of other factors, a divorce—but he came to California because that's where people went. At that time there were a lot of people who were older, coming out of the '60s, '70s, hedonistic lifestyles, sexually promiscuous or involved in a lot of drugs, people that had destroyed their lives, they came out clinging onto Jesus Christ. Southern California Pentecostal culture, it's fire and brimstone but it's more like, *success*, like "God wants you to be successful!" I probably discovered [Christian rocker] Larry Norman when I was 13 because my family had taken up this religious experience, whatever you want to call it. I was going along with it, as my whole family was. I think when you're 13 or 14 you're open to a lot of stuff, and if people say "Hey, Jesus!" you don't go, "Ooh, I'm cynical!" you just kind of go, "Yeah, Jesus, cool!" Larry Norman is a real oddball guy, he's not like what people would think of him, "Ooh, a Christian, what's that going to be about?" He's totally his own thing.

Kim Deal (aka Mrs. John Murphy; Pixies bassist; Breeders lead singer/guitarist; Amps lead singer/guitarist; born June 10, 1961 in Dayton, Ohio): In high school, I hung out with Pat Rohr, this is what I did: We had record albums, he was like three years older than me, and we would sit around. Now I know what we were doing—it's like, what people who love music do—but I didn't know that at the time. I'm like 15, 16, 17, talking about why "Dominance and Submission" is a better Blue Öyster Cult song than "Godzilla" ever was. Just doing shit like that, just pouring over the record collection. Smoking pot. Snowing, constantly snowing, and doing drugs.

Thompson: I used to hang out with some misfits. We weren't the stoner kids, we weren't the jock kids, we were the "we listen to oddball music" kids. I wasn't hanging out at all-ages shows or trying to get into clubs to see bands, and I was buying records at used record stores and borrowing them from the library. You didn't necessarily see a Ramones record at the used record store. You just saw Emerson, Lake and Palmer records. So I didn't know [punk] music but I had started to hear about it in high school. But it was probably a good thing that I didn't know it, that I instead listened to a lot of '60s records and this religious music. It was a different diet. It wasn't mainstream at all, but it wasn't hip, for sure. By the time I did start to make music for real with a band, Pixies, of course I had discovered some things that again, weren't exactly punk. Iggy Pop is not a punk, Hüsker Dü is not punk (they're a post-punk band, they're more related to hardcore), [Captain] Beefheart is not a punk, the Talking Heads are not a punk band (even though they came out of CBGBs, they don't sound like the Sex Pistols or the Damned). By the time I started to write music I heard some punk and punk-influenced things, but it was kind of good that I didn't listen to all these hip records when I was 16. It was good that I was in my own nerdy little world.

Deal: My Mom had this, I think it was two-track, quarter-inch tape reel-to-reel that she'd get me and [twin sister] Kelley to sing to when we were four or five years old. When I was 11 my dad was taking guitar lessons, and the only reason why I know this is because there was an acoustic guitar in the living room and these tablature sheets. I would sit down and look at the tablature sheets, and I learned "King of the Road" by Roger Miller. And he would laughingly say, "Kim, I can't believe you learned that before I did." So that was nice and encouraging to hear that.

John Murphy (Kim Deal's ex-husband; Mente leader; life-long Bostonian): I worked with David Lovering at Radio Shack when I was in high school. He lived in Burlington, Mass, I lived in Wilmington, and we worked at the Burlington mall together. He was a riot, and he really looked at things in a very peculiar way. He always made fun of the customers and did these bizarre things. One time he was supposed to be subbing in for a guy at the store in Stoneham, and it was summertime, and at Radio Shack in the summertime it's dead. He didn't get one single customer, so he set up a little amateur recording studio and made tape loops, put a couple of songs together. He was always a drummer. He was always drumming on something during work.

Thompson: My family moved a lot. Cycled between Southern California and New England. Fifteen times. Just before my senior year in high school we moved to Westport, Massachusetts, which is where I received my Gowanus award for being the Teenager of the Year. You know the Gowanus club? It's like a neighborhood, community service kind of group. They thought I was a good kid or something in high school. We stood out. We were blond and from California and everybody else was very Portuguese and very brunette.

Deal: I was a cheerleader. I don't know if that makes you popular. I'm not embarrassed. People get the idea cheerleaders are mean. You know who the mean folks are? The smart kids, they were fucking pricks. I graduated with honors, I was still smart. These guys were the fucking freaks, they were the ones that were supposed to be so delicate and like, awkward. They were the Dungeons & Dragons crowd. Mean fucks!

Joey Santiago (Pixies guitarist; Martinis guitarist; born June 11, 1965 in Manila, Philippines): Before I met Charles I was listening to classic rock. The Who, Stones, stuff like that. Bowie, Iggy Pop. In fact, the Velvet Underground, too. I had a brother that was like, ten years older than me, so he had *White Light/White Heat* and he had a turntable, so I would just listen to it. I liked it. It was the first piece of music that I heard and was like, "This is doable. I can get my hands around this." Just the simplicity.

Thompson: I remember learning how to scream. The guy who taught me was a neighbor of ours when I was a teenager. He was this guy from Thailand and he ran a T-shirt and florist shop. I used to deliver flowers for him. I was playing the Beatles' "Oh Darling" for him and he said, "No, no, scream it like you hate the bitch!"

Deal: I got like a hundred songs when I was like, 16, 17. I look at 'em and I just think, "Oh, you poor. . ." The music is pretty good but the lyrics are just like, OH MY GOD. We were just trying to figure out how blue rhymes with you. When I was writing 'em, they didn't have anything to do with actually who I was. I started thinking that I'd be published and that I'd write for other people, and they just needed silly, stupid songs with blue and you in it. That's what people sang about. I just wanted to be a songwriter. And I wanted to be a guitar player in a rock band. I didn't want to be a bass player. They always have the tightest pants or something, they seemed moody and weird. And the singer seems like *assholes*. Outgoing, and on all the time. And the drummers, I couldn't play drums. I can now, I really like the drums. If I could do anything I'd play the drums now in a band. I have to find a band who needs my kind of drumming. I have no chops, and most bands still like chops, whatever.

Kelley went to the drive-in movie and saw *Song Remains the Same*. She did acid, I think. She must have been 16, and in her trip she said that she wanted to do that. I think that was the first time [she said that] about rock. Wasn't my idea, it was her trip.

Kelley Deal (Kim Deal's twin sister; member of the Breeders, the Kelley Deal 6000): Not the album, the movie. It was '76, maybe. I said, "I want to do that. I want to be Jimmy Page."

Deal: I wasn't good enough to play guitar to other people's songs. I couldn't really figure out how they went. So it was easier to make up your own songs.

Then we opened for Steppenwolf at this place called McGuffy's House of Draft. And it was pretty scary seeing all the motorcycles in the parking lot.

Kelley Deal: It was really scary. What the hell are we doing here? One acoustic guitar and two vocals.

Deal: But they were so sweet.

Kelley Deal: Plus, I think they liked music. They liked what we liked. Old blues songs we did. Hank Williams.

Deal: Blind Faith. Everly Brothers. And they were cooler to play in front of than like, hanging out with the white T-shirt, blue jeans, Converse kids. You know the NGA kids: No Girls Allowed. Motherfuckers. This is Dayton, Ohio. Nobody would play with us. Seriously, dude. No guy would play with us in a band. It was uncool to have a chick in the band. You could only sing "Hit Me With Your Best Shot." And if you didn't sing it, if the band didn't have a chick, then the guitar player or the lead singer would sing it. He would change the words: "Why don't you put another notch in my guitar case?" I'm serious!

Kelley Deal: It never changed.

Deal: Mainly, I just started writing songs to be published. The songs that I wrote I would never think we would perform. All those country songs and stuff, I just thought that would be a publishing route. Hell, Nashville's close, it's seven hours away. There's a lot of country music around here, the fucking songs are easy to write. We didn't know there was indie rock. It was just spandex here.

Kelley Deal: We moved to Boston. As we grew older we started listening to other music. Just knowing friends who listened to other stuff. Sex Pistols, which I hated, because I like melody and I wasn't an angry 18-year-old British man.

Deal: But see, being in Dayton, Ohio, you have to find your own stuff. There was no zine here. None. I mean, none. The Undertones were on a tape Ron Rider [a friend in Dayton] gave you... rockabilly was kind of popularish about '83, '84, you know, Stray Cats were on MTV and stuff, Johnny Burnett. Dayton is not a place to tour. And the fact that we had a friend who knew people on one of the coasts, and he would make mix tapes, tapes where you love these songs and nobody's heard them and you give them to your friends—that's how you know about things. They weren't on the radio. There were tapes.

Kelley Deal: I'm kind of glad that happened because it forced us to discover our own voice instead of "I want to do that." There was no scene. You made up your own fun.

Deal: It was more like, "I know I don't want to do that." That was the motivation of decisions made. I *know* I'm not going to do that. The role for chicks in Dayton at the time was to sing the Pat Benatar song and shake a tambourine. Maybe a couple of keyboard parts on the other songs. Really cute, real tight skirts and stuff. Just really makes you puke. But you know, the guys were doing the same thing, that made you puke, too. You'd see their package and stuff. Really gross.

Kelley Deal: I guess that's the difference, why did we know it sucked? There was no talking to anybody about it. Nobody. Me and you. Very lonely.

Deal: Madonna came out, it was more '80, '81, that's the school of the gay clubs, and I went to one here in Dayton. They would have women with no tambourine now, no keyboard in front of them, and no backup band. And these girls would come with a tape from the studio. The clubs didn't have the electronic equipment to do the digital pitch-shifting and whatnot, so they could pretty much carry the tune of their club hit. And they would sing two songs dressed really, really provocative. It would be all in fun. Nothing about rock. It's not rock. But nobody said it was, that's the good thing about that.

Kelley Deal: We had our room, and we had mics and our eight-track tape player, our mixing board, effects, we had speakers and amps—we had this whole thing set up when we were 17. Kim made the cords.

Deal: My dad showed me how. He wasn't stoked. I'm making my own cords on the kitchen table, my Dad's helping, splicing the end of cables and soldering the chips to save money for cords. The way we were able to get the equipment was we knew a birthday was coming and we went, okay what are we going to get? We need a board. "Okay, we really want a board for our birthday." Or she'd save her McDonald's money and I'd save my Taco Bell money and we bought a board. When my Grandad [who was a former coal miner] was dying of black lung disease and he was living with us, he was a little bit senile and he had a potty chair. And we used the bottom of the potty chair to put the Yamaha board on.

Kelley Deal: The Aria bass [Kim] used for the Pixies, I went and bought. Dad went with me, and I actually bought it, 60 bucks for that and an amp.

Deal: Then what happened was I got a drum machine, an Oberheim DX, and I would play around with programming the drum machine so it would feel more like we were in a band. And then I got a quarter-inch four-track machine and then I stepped up and pretty soon I had a one-inch eight-track machine, and I had a recording studio in the house in Huber Heights.

COLLEGE (1983 TO 1984)

Thompson: I read an interview with J Mascis, we both went to the same college at the same time and all that. Somebody asked him about me, and he said since I didn't know a lot of punk rock, I was innocent, that I could just do whatever. I think he was right.

J Mascis (Dinosaur Jr. singer/guitarist): My roommate at the time was Charles' roommate the semester before. I think they knew each other from grade school, so he just brought me over to his room to meet his buddy. I remember he said he had an acoustic guitar, he was talking about buying an electric guitar and starting a band.

Deal: I went up to Ohio State University and there's a High Street there, and I cleaned toilets at the Agora [nightclub] in '79, and that was the first safety pin I'd ever seen in a cheek. It was a Halloween party there. Not that that was cool.

Thompson: [Before Pixies I was listening to] an XTC album called *English Settlement* and the first Violent Femmes record. In the mid-'80s RCA started to release two records by the same artist from their catalog into one package. I bought on vinyl Iggy Pop's *Lust for Life* and *The Idiot*. My freshman year in college I really just had my oddball little collection of records, which wasn't a lot, an orange crate's worth of records or so. Up to college, I didn't have a CD player or anything, people weren't listening to CDs, people were listening to cassettes and records.

Santiago: Charles and I had a suite at the college dorm. We'd go to shows, I remember seeing Black Flag and Angst. Initially, I think we just liked each other. I did notice right away that he was playing music. I didn't want any more distractions, but I took my guitar up and we started fooling around with it. He'd write 'em, and I'd throw down my ideas on the guitar.

Thompson: I loved the Cars, and I remember there used to be a song I used to sing around the dormitory there with Joey, I used to sing Cars songs. It's kind of embarrassing now to think about it because I was probably a real dork, sitting around my dorm room singing Cars songs. They were cool to me. Not being a real accomplished guitar player, they didn't have a lot of punk rock attitude, but they had this kind of reserved *gun gun gun gun* kind of thing going on, that I connected with it, I related to it. I was like, oh that's how you do that? You just go (*sings*) "gun gun gun." I started doing it senior year of high school. I'd moved back to Massachusetts and discovered the Cars a little bit, and I started to do that same thing that I heard the rhythm guitar doing. The Cars were very, very influential on me and the Pixies. I heard the way they did their rhythm guitar: muted, and clicky, kind of that new wavey vibe. You can hear that on early Pixies stuff, especially "Is She Weird." That's totally Cars.

We lived in a dormitory, and Joey and I and a couple of our other suitemates rented a house. A professor was on a sabbatical or something, they were out of the country, and that was the house that we found to rent in our sophomore year. Joey moved up to the converted attic. The room I got was directly downstairs from Joey and had a stereo in it with vinyl, so I could continue to listen to my records. I listened to the first two Iggy Pop records heavily, in the dark, in my room. I wouldn't say I was depressed, but I was becoming disinterested in college, trying to figure out what I wanted to do with my life. Probably sexually frustrated. All of those things that a 19-year-old, 20-year-old is going through. But those records were like gospel religion to me. I wasn't a drinker, I didn't take drugs, there was a lot of clarity there.

I dropped out after the first semester of my junior year and went to San Juan, Puerto Rico. I had taped a few of these records to bring with me on a cassette walkman. There was a Talking Heads record called *Little Creatures*, I had a cassette of that, I had a cassette of a Ramones album, and I thought I had a cassette of these couple of Iggy Pop records I was really into, but for some reason I didn't record them right, so they were blank. So that's all I had. A walkman. A Ramones record, a Talking Heads record, and whatever music I heard in Puerto Rico, salsa and meringue.

Santiago: I stopped listening to radio, I like to say after [Elton John's] "Philadelphia Freedom" it just went to shit, I thought. Charles was a DJ at UMass, too. Just for a semester or so. He started listening to more interesting records. He started getting into the Violent Femmes, stuff like that.

Thompson: University is just "Young, dumb, and full of come." That's what I thought when I was in college. It was just like Grade 13—it didn't really feel very intellectual to me. I was really bored.

Mascis: It was horrible. Definitely the low point of my life that I can think of. I stayed three years then I went to college in New York City for two spring semesters.

Thompson: I don't think the songs started getting good until Joey and I dropped out of school. As a matter of fact, some of them are really embarrassing. Some of them are on the Internet now. Some fan who I e-mail once in a while sent me a tape someone had sent him, and he said, "Yeah, it's all these songs you wrote a long time ago," and I was like, "Huh? What's this all about?" And it was a tape I had made myself on a boom box, and it ended up in someone's luggage at the end of their college career, and it circulated around somehow. It was all these really bad songs I wrote when I was a 16-year-old.

After several months in Puerto Rico (where he developed affinities for the Spanish language and rice and beans—the name he later selected for the Pixies' publishing company), Thompson was faced with a decision: go to New Zealand and await Halley's Comet ("It just seemed like the cool, romantic thing to do at the time"[1]) or return to the States and start a rock band. He wrote a letter to Joey urging him to join him in a band upon his return.

GETTING (BACK) TO BOSTON (1984)

Thompson: When I moved to Boston to actually start a band I used to go to a used record store and I had a little boom box, so I used to buy cassettes, and I discovered a couple more Iggy Pop records, and I discovered a Captain Beefheart record, and I discovered a couple of Hüsker Dü records. That was my punk stuff that I got. Hüsker Dü's *Zen Arcade*, *Spotlight Kid* by Captain Beefheart, and the couple of Iggy Pop things again, one of them was kind of demos that had been widely bootlegged called *I'm Sick of You*. Those were the main records that I listened to right before I started a band.

Santiago: Charles and I moved to Boston, we dropped out of school and we had normal jobs. I worked at a warehouse and he worked at a warehouse. We liked to say that I was managing wood for a butcher block company and he was managing buttons on teddy bears and stuff. We were both warehouse managers. We always met halfway for lunch on the pier in Boston. We were like, 20. That's basically what we were doing. In school we were suitemates, but when we moved to Boston we were roommates for just a year. The apartments there were small, so then we got our own apartments. He would just be writing songs all the time on his acoustic guitar. He used to write his lyrics on the subway train, too. So he'd just take a line and go around this loop and write his lyrics.

Murphy: I moved to Ohio, supposedly for six months, and one of the guys that I worked with that I met the first week, his name was Kevin Deal, and that's Kim's brother. One thing led to another and I ended up staying in Dayton for a year and a half. I worked for a defense contractor on their computer systems for the Air Force. Wasn't really my bag, but it paid well, and they paid for me to fly back and forth to home. And I got to meet Kim, so, added bonus.

Deal: So, what year did I get married? Oh Lord. Oh my God. Eighty-fuckin'-four, '85 maybe? He had worked as a computer programmer, writing language. 'Cause Wright-Patterson Air Force Base is in Fairborn, Ohio, so there's a lot of need for that. And my brother was at the same company, or similar company, I don't know, they met. And my brother introduced us. So we got married on Memorial Day, '84, and then we stayed in Ohio and then his transfer—he wanted to go back to Boston—so we moved back to Boston in January.

Thompson: I went *to* Boston. A lot of people think UMass is in Boston, but it's not. It's in Amherst. They have a campus in Boston now, but people think we went to school in Boston and started a band. It's just a technicality, we were in college in the Amherst area, then we dropped out, went to Boston, and started a band.

Santiago: I actually remember one night when I started learning about the job and I was like, "Hey, this job is pretty cool, the way they make these chairs and stuff." I was telling Charles how they made these stupid chairs, "It's kind of neat." He's like, "God, Joey, you're getting real excited. We gotta move on the music so you stop talking about these damn chairs."

Deal: "Hoverin" was a song that me and my fiancé at the time did. I remember I used to copyright the songs by registering with the United States copyright office, but also mailing my cassette tapes off, return mailing it and never opening it. I kept doing that.

Murphy: That was a little trick. Then you have the post office stamp of the date and everything, and if you don't open it, it's proof that it's never been tampered with.

Santiago: It was like, dead of winter, around December, and we really didn't have any plans other than just, okay, we dropped out of school, let's go to Boston. So Charles picked me up, we drove to Boston, and like, hey, we're here. He had sent me a letter in Puerto Rico saying, "We gotta do it, now is the time, Joe, we gotta chase our dreams. This is the time to do it." He was sick of what he was trying to do, being a student and stuff. And I was tired of finding out what I want to do. I know what I want to do, which is music.

I think I wrote him back, and I said, "Yes, now's the time." And this stupid corny thing, starting quoting the Who. I don't know why. We gotta go!

2. ROCK MUSIC—PUTTING A BAND TOGETHER (1985)

As Charles Thompson returned from Puerto Rico and reunited with Joey Santiago, Kim Deal was just making her big move to Boston. All three were looking for the same thing—a band—but they didn't have any clue how they were going to find each other.

Santiago: Right when we got to Boston we said, "Okay, what are we going to do?" We starting watching bands and timing people's sets to see how long it was. We timed ours and it was like, "Ooh, God, we gotta get 20 more minutes or something." And we started putting out ads.

Thompson: I remember even before I got together with the rest of the band I went to see this producer who had an ad in the paper. She was like this older woman, I think she was kind of part of lesbian folk [collective] or something like that. I called her up and I didn't know what I was doing and was like, "What do I need to do to start a band?" I went to go see her at her apartment, and she listened to me play my songs and was very encouraging, and she gave me some starter advice. She said, "I'm probably not what you need right now, go write more songs, get a gig at a club." To this day I don't really remember what her name was, and I wish I could. I always appreciated that.

Deal: I got to Boston in January '85 and I was in a band with Joe and Charles a week later. Because I had the *Boston Phoenix* out.

I was playing at weddings with Kelley, and then I was 24 and moved to Boston with my husband and a week after that I answered that ad. I was working at a doctor's office in Brookline. Dr. Harold Solomon. He let me come in late.

Murphy: We had made an agreement early on in the relationship that after a year and a half I'd like to go back to Boston, and Kim said that would be good for her, too, and maybe she could use that as kind of a springboard for any aspirations she had as far as music went. She took advantage of it right away. We got there in January and I think she was in the Pixies by March.

Joe Harvard (born Joe Incagnoli; cofounder, Fort Apache studios): Kim and John, I knew they weren't really an item anymore, they were already more like friends. And I think the main benefit of that marriage, and I like John a lot, was that Kim came to Boston. It put her where she needed to be.

Murphy: Kim had made a tape with her sister. She used the equipment she had, which wasn't much, electric drums, stuff like that. She had an eight-track, so she hired somebody to help her produce it, and then she sent it around, and that was actually the first publicly distributed Breeders tape. She recorded it in Dayton and produced it in Massachusetts, and she sent it out to all the radio stations just like a regular person would do, and nobody picked up on it at all. She didn't give it much time, but she figured "Well, I'm not going to make it on my own, I don't know anybody," so she started looking at ads. And that's when she saw the famous *Phoenix* ad. I remember her pointing it out to me afterwards.

Deal: I was working, a week had gone by, and I was looking in the *Boston Phoenix* and I saw an ad in the music section as people do, they just scan the back but nobody ever calls, for God's sake. But there was one that I thought was particularly good, and I actually called. It was the only one I've ever answered. And I was the only one to answer their ad, too. The ad [said they were] looking for a harmony, and I liked it because it said, "Hüsker Dü, Peter, Paul and Mary," and it said something like, "Please, no chops." Back in '85 people were all *about* chops.

Santiago: Kim was the only one that answered the ad. Which is probably what Charles wanted. Because he's the one that wrote the ad about "Hüsker Dü, Peter, Paul and Mary." Basically implying we don't want straight-up heavy metal people. She was great.

Deal: I went over to Charles' apartment and he had food out. He was on a Puerto Rican diet, so he had hummus, and celery sticks and carrots, and I thought that was really nice. He had a big hoop earring on, and a preppie shirt. I liked that. Joey was really quiet. I thought Joe was Mexican. Santiago. Sounds Mexican to me. They had a purple telephone. They were living together.

Santiago: She came in, big, huge smile, and enthusiastic, "Okay, let's hear you guys play." I was like, is she auditioning us? What the hell's going on? We just played and she was like, "Okay, you guys are for real." I forgot what we played. We might have had "Here Comes Your Man" at that time.

Deal: There wasn't an audition, believe me. Fuck it, it's Joe and Charles? They're not going to audition me. I heard Charles play "The Holiday Song," I said cool, and I was in. There was not even a "You're in."

Kelley Deal: Joey hadn't decided if he was going to play lead guitar or bass yet. He got to choose first and he picked lead, that's why Kim played bass.

Deal: I told them I could get a bass, they knew I played guitar. I'd been playing guitar ten years. I guess people like to think that about me, that I'm just a bass player. They don't want to know that I had my own studio, making cords. Well, there was nobody to play with in Dayton, so you just did it yourself, you know.

Murphy: She took a chance. She didn't play the bass. She knew she could sing, so that was one thing. She grew up listening to 1970s rock'n'roll, basically, Todd Rundgren and Rick Derringer, plus she really liked country music. But when she answered the ad in the paper she was like, number one, I'm used to being the leader; number two, I don't play the bass. Kelley has one, so I'll get hers if I get in. I think she thought it would be a learning experience, see what these guys are like. She really liked Charles and Joey. I remember her coming home and saying, "I met these two guys, they're really young, they live in this crappy apartment over by BU, but the songs that they have are really cool, and I think I'm going to get in the band." They wanted a female voice, too. Charles has said that they really didn't become a loud band until David joined and started kicking the shit out of the drums.

At first they played alone, that was the strangest part. Charles had this, it turns out, pretty good plan. When they got together in March they didn't even start to look for a drummer until the middle of the summer. They wanted to get the three of them to know the songs so that when they added the drummer they didn't have to figure out the arrangements, they just needed to add that extra piece. It's kind of like the way you do a recording, but he was forming the band that way.

Claudia Gonson (Magnetic Fields drummer/keyboardist; Future Bible Heroes singer): I tried out for them. They had an amazing ad. The thing that was so exciting about their ad was that first of all, it was on the sides of post boxes and stuff. It was just plastered everywhere, it almost looked like street literature. So I stopped to read it because I was like oh, someone's ranting at me about politics. And instead, it was tiny, like four-point font writing, and you had to lean in, and it was like thousands of words long. So you sat there and read it really carefully and it went on and on, and it was beautifully written and incredibly ornate, and had a million, I don't remember if it was influences, I think it was more like, everything. I saw it probably in the Kenmore area, because that's where all the rockers hung out, on the side of a mailbox, which is of course illegal, and read it very carefully, and was really impressed with it. I went, "Wow, this is different."

Rich Gilbert (Frank Black and the Catholics guitarist; alumnus of several Boston bands including the Zulus and Human Sexual Response): I never saw the ad, but I heard about it. That's what you used to do a lot back then in Boston. That's how I got in Human Sexual Response, for instance, when I saw a handwritten flier that somebody had put up in a record store.

Gonson: And then I went to Kim's house where she was living with John in Charlestown, and we sat around in their living room and there were photos of them on the mantle and it was all very domestic. I just sat there and watched Charles play and was totally befuddled by what I was hearing and knew that it had to be something pretty incredible because it was so hard to understand. He was playing really enthusiastically on an acoustic guitar and it was just really mad and kind of countrified. I don't think they had a name yet. Joey and Kim were there. And I didn't play, I just sat and watched them jamming and it was really acoustic and really insane sounding. But they did call me to say, "Do you want to come in, we've got a drum kit now, and you can jam with us?" and I said, "No, I'm going to go to college, instead."

Deal: Joey was scared to walk through Charlestown because he's of color. In the late '80s it was awful. And at that time it had "IRA Rules, IRA Lives" all over it. I don't think anything got physical, but he was scared. Just like, "Ehh, Kim, I hate coming here." But we rehearsed in the basement and then the landlady got a little mad but we still did it anyway, we snuck it when she wasn't around. We played with a drummer. Kelly said no, so we got somebody from Somerville.

Kelley Deal: I went up there and met them.

Deal: Me and Charles split the plane ticket.

Kelley Deal: I went up there because I was a drummer in high school and I took two years of private lessons with this guy, his name is Jimmy Green, he's dead now. He was a Buddy Rich student, so he was really good. And I got really good, I can still read drum music, and I went up there, and I remember you guys played a bunch of the songs and they were great. I remember jumping on the bed. But I had a job in Dayton and I had just got back from L.A., and I didn't want to be in Charles' band, I wanted to be in Kim's band. I've said that in every fucking interview I've ever done.

Deal: And the three of us played in my Charlestown apartment, in the basement. Well, in the bedroom first. I had that drum machine, a Oberheim DX, and a four-track, quarter-inch tape reel-to-reel. But then a drummer started playing with us, so we moved down to the basement. But before we did any shows the guy quit, I don't think we were rock'n'roll enough for him. I think his name was Mike. He went to some of our shows after that, he was a nice guy.

Murphy: They went through a couple of different drummers in audition. One guy, Mikey Dee, died a couple of years back, he had an operation that went bad. He was in the band. They never played live with him, but he was in a couple of practice sessions, and he kind of quit on them. He was in another band and went back to the other band. He was the Pete Best of the Pixies, he used to say that a lot. He was a disc jockey for like, ten years, at WMFO in Medford at Tufts University. He was everywhere, he was in Boston

Rock Opera [a group that presented old and new rock operas on stage], big friends with T Max from [Boston rock gossip newspaper] *The Noise*. Every time you'd see him he was always in a good mood. He didn't play any shows, just practices. That four lineup was the only four that ever played as the Pixies, as far as I know.

Gilbert: Mikey Dee holds the terrible distinction of having the most tragic story of anyone I've ever known. He loved Boston and he loved Boston rock. You'd always see him out and he was really animated and alive and had a ton of energy, and he was a main face in Boston nightlife for a good six or seven years. He had some congenital heart condition, and he went in for an operation and had a stroke. It was so severe that he was basically paralyzed, and he went from being super animated and having a ton of energy to being a guy who spent the next three years basically bedridden. Just terrible. And he finally ended up passing away about two years ago [on July 6, 2003].

Gonson: There's this rumor that the only two people that auditioned for the Pixies besides Dave were me and Mikey Dee, but I'm sure that's wrong. It's sort of funny to imagine that there were only two people who got auditions and we were both such completely inappropriate people. Mikey Dee was kind of a wonderful fixture of Boston, incredibly enthusiastic, and kind of spastic and hilarious, he was a really oddball guy. He did a thousand things. Any town has a handful of people that everybody knows in the scene, he was just famous. There was some moment where I was talking to Mikey and he was like, "I tried out for the Pixies," and I was like, "I tried out for the Pixies!"

Deal: David Lovering was at my wedding reception in Boston. Pinstriped suit. And my husband suggested him when that one drummer quit.

David Lovering (Pixies drummer; scientific phenomenalist; born December 6, 1961 in Boston, Massachusetts): I was going to school in Boston called the Wentworth Institute of Technology. Electronic engineering. And I had worked with Kim's husband, a man named John Murphy, earlier when I was working at Radio Shack, before going to school.

Ted Widmer (Mente guitarist; former member of the Upper Crust): John Murphy helped the Pixies come together. He married Kim and he knew David. It was all through Radio Shack. And then

Murph was basically their roadie and confidante and best friend. For a while it was sort of the four people in the band and then there was John Murphy at all these early shows.

Deal: And to this date, if you ask for the serial number for a two-amp fuse, David and probably John Murphy can give you the lot number, the Radio Shack number, a bunch of geeks.

Murphy: I said, "Well, let me call David." Rush was David's favorite band in high school—he was drum orientated as far as bands would go. I was a little hesitant because Charles' music wasn't Rush. But I said David's cool and he's fun, maybe his musical tastes have changed a little bit, so let's give him a call. I think he had stopped drumming at that point, but he was a good friend, he came right over. I remember him being at our apartment in Charlestown, and he sat down and listened to them. All he had was Kim's electronic drum kit, and they played three or four songs for him, and he was kind of trying to drum with them, and at the end he goes, "Yeah, that's cool, I think I can do this," and he was in.

Lovering: Well, it was interesting for me because when I first went to Kim's place I didn't have any drums, I didn't have drumsticks, I just listened to Charles with an acoustic guitar play the songs. And to me, I mean I wasn't a very worldly—I don't think I heard it at first. I liked it, but it took a little while before it was like, oh yeah, this is really, really good, where I really liked it a lot, I would just think about it all the time, the songs would just run through my head. At first it went right over.

Gonson: About a year later, my band Lazy Susan started to play out shows, and in the fall of '87 I arranged for us to open for Pixies at Maxwell's. They had signed to 4AD and I had assumed by that point that they'd forgotten who I was. I walked in and Charles looked at me and said, "Claudia! Oh my God!" and sort of jokingly poked Dave and said, "*She* was going to be our drummer, but she went to college." I'm sure he was totally bullshitting. I think we would have sounded more like the Raincoats than the Pixies if I had played drums, but it was really flattering.

Gilbert: They're four very unique personalities. But isn't that what makes a great band a great band, though? It's like, when the personalities are all kind of shockingly different but they create that chemistry that creates a fifth or sixth member. That's what makes a great band.

3. IT'S EDUCATIONAL—BOSTON AND THE EARLY DAYS (1985–1986)

In a short space of time, the foursome had arrived at a name, begun writing songs, and played some gigs in their hometown. As Pixies, they came to the notice of some people who were to become pivotal in their career.

Deal: I had a studio in my house already. When we first started, me and Joe and Charles would record in my Charlestown apartment.

Murphy: They practiced in our apartment all the time because the old lady upstairs couldn't hear. It wasn't until they got David that they had to move out.

Deal: Basically, me and Charles did a bunch of stuff. David was living in Burlington and going to school full time, it's like 20 minutes north of Boston. And we practiced at my house, and we used my gear, and I had a car and they didn't have a car. Me and Charles hung out a lot, we put up posters. We were great friends. We hung out together, constantly. Constantly. He was always really fun and nice. Funny guy. I remember him saying that he really has to stop hanging out with the married couple.

Murphy: Oh yeah, they were buds. Charles was at our house a lot, and his place was scummy so we hardly ever went over there. We went to the movies together, and he was at our place. Before he dated Jean [Walsh, his first wife] he dated my other friend Melissa for a couple of months, and we did stuff together as a foursome sometimes.

Lovering: We were all excited about the band and wanted to rehearse and play as much [as possible] 'cause this was all new. I had played in previous bands but it was still all new to me. It was really clicking and everything. And the same with Joe, Charles and Kim. I think everyone was really excited and just wanted to play.

Santiago: Charles had the acoustic or the Tele and I would have the Les Paul. I wanted the Tele first, but he beat me to it. He just respected the way I played, oddly enough. We'd practice and then I would record our practices and go home and write these little parts to fill it out.

Murphy: Joey came up with the name before I met him. Pixies in Panoply was the first name that he wanted, but then they thought that was too long. He just liked the way it sounded, and English isn't his first language, so he just thought it was cool sounding.

Deal: Pixies in Panoply. That was an alternate name. It's armor. Also, Things on Fire.

Santiago: We started getting better and better. There was definitely chemistry there and Charles knew how to direct the drums and the bass and everything else, and let us do whatever we wanted, too. At one point or another it clicked.

Kelley Deal: They practiced in David's garage sometimes, and I will never forget Kim telling me about David's mother. She said, "Kim, you could at least *try*. Get a bustier, and some chunky gold earrings. And I think that would be really good. Get some lipstick on." I only met her once. And she's very well put together. She actually told Kim to wear a bustier.

Deal: Oh, Mrs. Lovering! Oh, Lord. Chunky silver jewelry, chunky silver earrings, a bustier, makeup, some sort of leggings stuff. Jewel encrusted bustier! She was cute. We practiced in her garage, in David's mom and dad's garage in Burlington for a long time.

Thompson: Then we started getting our own rehearsal spaces around Boston, and we rehearsed at various places around town. We rehearsed a lot. I only know because we used to go down to the rehearsal rooms and they were expensive. Boston is expensive now, but it was expensive then, too, and it cost like four, five, six or seven hundred bucks a month, it was like getting an apartment. And they were these crappy rooms, just fucking awful. We had one that had a sewer hole cover in it, that when it flooded the place would fill up with these bugs and it stank like shit.

Lovering: It was a really shitty rehearsal studio. One guy who had a bad drug problem watched the place and he would break in and steal all the equipment. And also there was a Boston sewer cap in our room, this was lower than the street, and the place stunk so bad. It just smelled of sewage, and fleas and flies would be flying around. I had these standard drum cases made of cardboard fiber, and I remember for at least a year after those drums came out of there you could smell the fiber cases and you'd get a whiff of that room. It was unbelievable. But we smoked so much in the room, everybody smoked cigarettes, that it nulled the smell.

Murphy: They got themselves a little practice space over by Fenway Park, and they were in there, I'd say five nights a week after work. David was going to school, Kim was working, Charles and Joey were just fooling around. They sort of practiced around Kim's work schedule, so they practiced for hours and hours every night for a long time, and they were really into it. That was 1986, the year the Red Sox lost the World Series, and I remember going there a lot, dropping her off and going down to Fenway Park and getting a ticket for standing room, watching the end of the game, and then going back to practice and picking them up. I'd go in and they'd just be playing a song, and I'd be like, "That one's cool," or "That one needs some help." I remember "Isla de Encanta," the first time they played it, it was horrible, and by the time I came back after watching the Red Sox play it was awesome—it had completely turned around and Charles had changed the arrangement of it.

Thompson: I remember people used to just go down to their rehearsal rooms and party when they showed up on Saturday night or whatever. We used to go in there every day after we had our work day, in the evenings, just all the time practicing. It didn't seem like anyone else was practicing. So we did practice, and we did actively pursue being in a band very methodically. It wasn't anything genius—we got a poster together, we got a gig, booked a recording studio, just started to do it. And we immediately got a reaction from an audience.

Gary Smith (current owner/manager of Fort Apache studios; first person to record Pixies): They had a song on ERS, I think, a recording of "Down to the Well," it would have been 1986, and on the basis of that they were trying to get gigs and do stuff. Round about that same time they had made that Death to the Pixies poster, which was very provocative and caught everybody's eye.

Murphy: The Death to the Pixies posters, Charles was stripped down, he was naked on his knees, hunched over, but his face was also on the ground, looking up at the camera, and his hand was between the camera and his body with his thumb down. If you looked at it really quick it kind of looked like a fist and that his thumb was his penis. A lot of people thought he was gay. That was part of the reason. He was a completely different person, he was this skinny little boy, and he was emotional and liked to talk, he had qualities that were artistic that people who didn't know him would confuse as feminine. But the poster didn't help.

Kurt St. Thomas (former program director, WFNX, Boston; co-author of *Nirvana: The Chosen Rejects*): They were kind of popping up all over town. I don't know who was hanging them, but they were pretty aggressive. They were all over, and they just grabbed your attention because it was like, what does that mean? Did they break up already? It definitely got people talking about them.

Murphy: It was an excellent poster, it was done on card stock, they were significant in weight and people were seriously stealing them and putting them up in their rooms. They were ripping them off of walls. It was a black background with white lettering and a grayish picture of Charles, and we'd write the upcoming shows with white magic marker on it and just paste them all over the walls. But tons of people ended up with them in their dormitories.

Harvard: I still think those were just a hoot. I mean it's a ballsy move, for a band no one had any clue, who the fuck are they, Charles gets up there nekkid. It was a genius thing. You'd see these things all over the place and be like, what? And to be honest with you, I can't figure out if that's Charles's thumb or his dick.

Deal: Eventually, we went to little places and tried to get demo tapes done. That first one that was passed around probably had "I'm Amazed," "Brick Is Red." That's probably it, maybe one, two other ones. We weren't coming into the regular channels of the cool people with the cool crowd. We had no scene.

Murphy: I think their first show was that September of '86. Joey used Kim's Les Paul in the first few shows they did, then he got his own.

Deal: Our first show was at Jack's. It burned down, you know. Very suspicious fire. *Very* suspicious, like all the valuable inventory just happened to have been moved out, and a fire gutted it. Jack's was in Cambridge. It was a Wednesday night, and Kevin, my brother was there. And John [Murphy]. Jean was there, that was before they went out, that's Charles's [now ex-] wife. I don't even think [friend] John Draper was there. There were probably nine people in the audience. Four of them we knew. Basically, that's how you play. They're just liquor distribution companies, that's where they get their money. You know, the drinking age had just changed from 18 to 21 in Boston, and there were so many bars, Jack's and Chet's Last Call, T.T. The Bear's, and the Rathskeller [a.k.a. the Rat]. If you could bring enough family and friends to the bar and they did a good beer night, you were going to play again. The end, period. Of course, we didn't have any people, but we had some pitchers of beer on the table, and it was a Wednesday night. I think we were the second of three acts, and we got 17 dollars to split between the four of us. We were so nervous I could have puked.

Murphy: David immediately thought it sucked because his friends were saying it sucked. They were expecting Rush, basically. It was four bands on one night, on like, a Tuesday, so you know, you have like two seconds to set up. Charles had two guitars, the electric and the acoustic, but he did at one point break a string and he had to change it or go without it, he was all pissed off about that. But the people who were there to see them were basically friends and family. My friend Melissa from work, my sister and her husband, me, and my friend Jean who turned out to be Charles' wife, they all just showed up because Kim was in a band. Nobody was there to see them from off the street because nobody knew who they were. Obviously no one knew Charles.

Lovering: They spelled the band's name wrong! It was "the Puxies."[2]

Murphy: The ad that I have from the *Phoenix* said "the Pixies" on it, so I don't know where David saw "the Puxies." It could have been another paper, or it could have been on the bill outside, I don't know. It's a good story, though, if it actually happened.

Deal: We were too scared to even give our cassette to the guy who booked bands at the Rat. We had Jean Walsh do it because she dressed so cool. We were just so scared because the Rat was a *really* cool place. Jean looked really cool and she didn't have any trouble: "Here's this tape."

Gilbert: I used to give guitar lessons in Boston, so Jean was a student of mine. There was a period of time where I feel like I gave guitar lessons to one person in every band in Boston. She was already with Charles, but I kind of knew them together, anyway. You would always see them together. She's kind of short and thin and has very white skin naturally, anyway, and she would have dyed blonde hair and dress in black, so it was kind of Goth.

Jean Walsh (Charles Thompson's ex-wife; childhood friend of John Murphy): When [Charles and I] met I think they were rehearsing. They were kind of getting it together, but at that point in Boston it wasn't like, oh my God, you're going to have your own band! It was like, you and what other guys? Everybody in Boston was trying to get a band going. They hadn't played yet. In fact they enlisted me to be their first, I guess they were calling me a manager, but I really wasn't. I used to be this kind of Goth creature, and they thought they looked like nerds. So they had me go and drop off some of their tapes at clubs and try to get them gigs. Which of course had nothing to do with me, it was because their tape was good. But they enlisted me to do that and I remember I realized at one point they were hanging out on the sidewalk watching me outside of some club and I felt like they were checking up on me and I was totally pissed off at them. They hadn't played any shows yet, they did shortly after that.

Kristin Hersh (Throwing Muses lead singer/guitarist; 50 Foot Wave lead singer/guitarist; musician): I didn't know Jean really well. She wore capes.

Harvard: Jean is so cool, I think she would kind of be able to just pop in [when Charles was writing], and was like, "That's a good one, finish that one." She was the perfect person to let you do what you need to do, but at the same time she loved what he was doing, you could tell it. And I always felt like he was more whole when he was with her. She took an edge off of living for him in a way. His focus was on the work so much that her presence allowed that. I'm pretty sure "Subbacultcha" is about her.

Santiago: I met [my wife] Linda about almost the same time Charles met Jean. Early, really early. We broke up a couple of times. That happens almost every time. Now my wife reminds me, "I used to pay for your dinner when you were a really scrawny kid." Thanks, I remember. But she had the credit card, and we were hungry and you didn't want pizza anymore.

Walsh: I was a very longtime, childhood friend of Kim Deal's husband, John Murphy. And from that circle of friends I ended up meeting Charles. I think I met him at somebody's house party on Cape Cod. I definitely liked him from that moment on, but we were buddies for a long time. Just like movie buddies, not like a romantic couple kind of thing. I guess it's kind of corny, but he had this bright light quality about him. He was just so curious about things and interesting. After about six months of being buddies I started to have these feelings that I thought were incestuous—I was like, you don't want to make out with your friends! That's disgusting! That's for people you barely know! So I posed the idea that we would somehow become involved with a very crass note to him at one of the Pixies' earliest performances that said, "I want to have your abortion." I gave it to him and then I ran out of the club. Then he of course called me the next day and was like, "Well, I think we need to talk about this." And I was like, "Oh, good." And then his words to me were, "I don't need that kind of drama in my life!" and I was extremely despondent for a while. But I guess he decided that he did need that kind of drama in his life, because it was only a couple of weeks after I sent that note that we became a couple. Once we became a couple we were sort of inseparable.

Murphy: The Boston scene back then was you gave your tapes to certain people and you just hoped that they would ring you back, and some clubs would have someone picking the bands out that was listening to the tapes and be really critical, and probably have more influence than they should. And then some clubs, like Jack's where they first played, were like, "You can get 20 friends in here, yup? Okay you're on for Tuesday." We were hearing horror stories about L.A., that you had to pay to play.

Deal: There's a guy that books bands. He's not in every day of the week. All right? He's only in Wednesdays, from two to five. And no, the bartender will not accept the tape for him. "Yeah, I told you, two o'clock, he's not here now. He should be coming in." Well, here's a tape. "I don't take those tapes." So there was a lot of hanging out at bars, waiting. Of course, we don't know what the guy looks like so we're back to the bartender going, "Is that him?" "No, that's not him, that's the manager."

Murphy: There was already somebody who was interested in them, at WFNX or one of those places, and I think that person hooked them up with Ann Holbrook, who was their first manager. She got them a whole bunch of shows, kind of in rapid succession. First every two weeks, and then every week. She loved the music, which was a good thing. She was a scenester to some degree, so she knew quite a few of the people in town for someone who had just started. She wasn't managing anybody else. I liked her, to be honest with you. I think Charles immediately thought she was a pain in the ass, but Charles liked to be in charge. I'm sure he'd tell you that he's a little bit of a manager. Ann was trying to tell him, "Well, this is how we have to do it," and he'd say, "Oh, I don't want to do that, it's a pain in the ass," and she'd say, "No, you have to believe me," and so forth and so on. I wouldn't say they ever were antagonistic or anything, but he didn't have any issue with replacing her. She never really invested anything other than time, and they did pay her, so it wasn't like big love lost.

Lilli Dennison (former employee at the Rat; former manager of the Del Fuegos; former owner of Boston club Lilli's): The first band I managed was called the Loners. Then I managed the Del Fuegos, who were the toast of the town for several years and went on to get some national recognition. My brother was working in the suburbs with David Lovering's mom. She was always asking my brother to ask me to manage his band so it would do something, because all my bands were doing pretty well.

Lovering: We started playing around Boston, we did every gig we could get. It was awful little shit gigs until we started getting a little more frequent gigs at places where we could say we were the house band. There was a place called Green Street Station in

Boston, we played there all the time, and the Rat we played a bunch of times, T.T. the Bear's. We actually slowly progressed up, but at first it was tough, we were just getting any gig.

Walsh: I used to go to all of their shows. I just remember being really excited because I thought their songs were really great. But I didn't necessarily expect it to go beyond being a local band.

Gilbert: The first time I saw them they had a real unique sound, they already had their identity. They were just really good. It was just that simple. They just looked like four people, but that was the thing about Boston, you didn't have to have a look. I just remember specifically that Joey had a little Peavey amp that he would sit on a chair. They all had little amps, they didn't have their Marshalls and stuff back then, so they were just this band with little amps and guitars. They didn't have a lot of gear, and they would just get up and play. And then Charles could do those roars and those screams with his voice that were really dramatic, and Joey would slam his amp against the back of the chair to make the reverb clang, and that was really exciting.

Murphy: Joey used to whack the crap out of his amp during "Vamos." Picked up the amp and moved it around to make it make the sounds. That was them, that was how they got their reputation, underutilized equipment. They didn't start using Marshalls until they recorded *Surfer Rosa* and [producer Steve] Albini said, "We gotta rent some real amps."

Santiago: We just played maybe a handful of shows in Boston and I was browsing around a record store, and I guess the first fan—we didn't have a record out—she said, "Good show!" That was pretty cool. Because you never know.

Tanya Donelly (former Throwing Muses guitarist/singer; former Breeders guitarist/singer; Belly founder/former lead singer/guitarist; musician): The first show that we played with them [was the first time] that I saw them. Kim wasn't there because there was a family emergency for her, so it was just Charles and Joey and David. I remember thinking Charles was amazing and that he's the real deal, being really impressed by the songs. And then the next time we played with them was with Kim, and that was like, oh, wow! That kind of amped it up considerably because it was more of a band at that point, and her contribution, which was enormous, just made it perfect.

Hersh: They were about to play and I was walking out, and a painter friend from RISD [Rhode Island School of Design] stopped me and told me I should watch them. That they had a stupid name, but I should watch them, anyway. And there was nobody there, and I felt kinda bad, so I watched them. They were already great. You could tell they knew what they were doing. They had songs, which is very rare. Kim couldn't play and sing at the same time yet. And she was just coming from her temp job so she was dressed as a secretary with a secretary hairdo and pumps and a dress. I thought that was so amazing! And she was going to go home and change, you know, to look more rock. We were like, this is as rock as you get! This is so cool! She was from Ohio, she never shut up, she just talked constantly, and everything she said was adorable, she was so attractive. Between every song she would walk up to the mic and say, "We're the Pixies!" I was like, shut up! Why does she keep saying that? and then sometimes she would just start talking. Dave would have a heart attack in the back and would just play over her talking so she'd try to catch up. And Joey was terrified, or looked terrified. He had these big, saucer eyes, and he'd stare right at you while he played like you were holding a gun on him. I don't know why he did that, but we thought that was cool, too.

Deal: I was working at the medical doctor's office, and I came from my work to a show in my low heels, my hose, my black skirt, my white shirt, you know. . .and there's mohawks there and stuff. Just to piss them off. Very reactionary, isn't it?

Donelly: Kim would come straight from work, so she had skirt-suits and office pumps on a lot, and her hair all poofty, all poofed up, typical '80s. I just thought that was so interesting, because so many of the people in that scene are trying to look cool, and meanwhile the coolest person there is dressed like a secretary. I have to say, in a day it changed my perception of what was cool.

Hersh: The only confusion was I think we all thought they were women. Kim was obviously a woman, but they all had this kind of shaved-headed, pretty, soft look. And there were lots of lesbian bands at the time, and we always got booked with them, so we just thought the Pixies were another—like maybe they were like angry divorcees or something that formed a band. They dressed kind of asexual and Charles sang really high, and they all wore eyeliner, so it's kind of hard to tell, they were gender free. Well, it didn't take long to figure it out. He started singing about his penis and stuff and I thought, "Wow, right on, sister!" and realized at least some of them were men.

Donelly: I just loved them. I liked the fact that they were all so different and all so eccentric in very different ways. And it's not the kind of eccentricity that sneaks up on you, either, it's just like, wow! Bunch of freaks. David's always doing something with his hands or doing a cartwheel or rigging something up, or fixing something, or breaking something. And Joey's just amazing, the caustic oddities that he comes up with. And Charles is Charles. He's got a quietness to him, he's very comfortable being quiet, which I think puts people off, or makes people uncomfortable sometimes, they read different things—I think people project all different kinds of stuff onto quiet people. He's a great storyteller and really funny person. A sweet person.

Thompson: Too many artists are just too full of themselves, they're so egotistical, and they're just pretending to be valid or something, but really they just want to be famous like everybody else. But the Pixies were not. . .we just are what we are. And there's lots of bands like that. It's not like we're the only one. I think that anyone that's really good has that freedom. I've always felt there are certain acts that allow their true personalities to come through. And that's what's interesting about people. That's why we like each other. It's like, "I like that guy because he's kind of weird, or he's so funny, or he's so serious. Or that other guy, he's a cut-up. I like that girl, she's so silly." Individual personalities! So I think [it's best] when musical acts really allow their personalities to come through the thing, if they're not trying to be so earnest or trying so hard to be famous or something.

St. Thomas: They just sort of had no image. I really liked that, too. It was very much like, "These were the clothes we were wearing during sound check, and now we're still wearing those same clothes." In some ways, at the time, we were kind of coming out of a lot of British bands like the Cure and Depeche Mode and Echo and the Bunnymen, all those bands were very styled, and they had a whole thing. The Pixies just looked like they were wearing whatever they had on. I've always been attracted to those bands.

Deal: Why would somebody have show clothes? It's just crazy. I have favorite T-shirts that I like. Ones I know the sleeves aren't too long and won't get in my way when I'm playing, stuff like that. Mainly it's about function. Like I know certain pants I can bend down and grab a beer if it's on the floor and it won't split or something. I preferred the thinner T-shirt material. And I don't like the ones that are too thin so you can see the bra thing. Because like, I think PJ Harvey played and she had a see-through top on where you could see her nipple, and I swear to God I couldn't take my eyes off of her nipple the whole show, I found it distracting. I didn't want to see the nipple, I didn't want to stare at it, I just couldn't not stare at it. It's hypnotic somehow. And over in Europe there's a lot of times where there's no showering and stuff. You lose combs. I don't comb my hair anyway, who am I kidding. But say you did.

Dennison: I remember they were pretty nerdy. I think that was kind of their thing, too. Nerdy was cool, there were a lot of bands that were nerdy, and they were definitely of the nerdy ilk.

Santiago: I think we more or less probably knew what we didn't want to be, and that was it.

4. DIRTY PLACES—THE RAT, FORT APACHE, AND THE SCENE (1985–1987)

Boston in the late 1980s was a rich breeding ground for offbeat post-punk music. Although a few years later all signs pointed to Seattle as the incubator for alternative rock, during those years in the mid-1980s, there was a place in "the sleepy west of the woody east" where alt-rock's roots were taking hold. Pixies formed smack in the middle of the decade in a city with a thriving underground scene anchored by a gloriously disgusting club called the Rat, where many groups made their first significant mark. From their low-key atmosphere to their willingness to record bands they admired pro bono, the founders of recording studio Fort Apache—Joe Harvard, Sean Slade, Paul Kolderie and Jim Fitting—knew that to capture the sounds of their city, they had to shake things up. It was only natural, then, that Pixies would find their way into the fascinating, filthy corners of town, to the Rat and the Fort, as they felt their way around the scene.

Gonson: I don't think that either the Muses or the Pixies ever felt like they were from Boston. I think that might be a syndrome of bands that are destined to do better, that they just don't feel like they really fit in, in Boston. Because the bands that really fit in, the Neighborhoods, the Lyres—they sold out shows every time they played but they couldn't get attendance outside of Boston. There were all sorts of bands during that era that were more of a scene, like the Turbines, the Oysters, and the Neighborhoods (and the Lyres and the Neats)—they were sort of neo-psychedelic '80s bands. They were great bands, but they weren't really doing anything that was like, bizarre or different.

Angel: Oh, the Pixies were not a Boston band at all. They were there probably because it's a bohemian Mecca in the Northeast. But Pixies were pop. I think that's why they were so much more successful and enduring then any of those bands. At heart, those are really poppy songs. They weren't derivative of anybody, really.

Stephen Perkins (Jane's Addiction drummer): I think the East Coast spoke loud when the Pixies came out. It put a sound on the East Coast for a minute and that was important. The East Coast and Boston, they're all so close to each other. You can drive from Philly to New York to Rhode Island to Boston all in the same day. So from a L.A. point of view, it's an East Coast sound more than just a town coming up with a sound.

The truth is there was a post-punk moment where punk was truly dead. I mean, the attitude was there, the Minutemen were there, Fear, Black Flag, X, they were all there, but nobody else was coming up. Just like Jane's, the Pixies were very environmental, by which I mean they grabbed from their environment. What was happening around them, the sounds, the feel, politically, everything that was rubbing against them, the weather, the coldness—all that stuff goes right into the music and they pulled from their environment instead of listening to someone else's environment and trying to pull from there. Like when a band from Salt Lake City is trying to get a Seattle sound, or a band from New York wants to sound like an English band. And if you pull from your own environment you'll be able to spit out everything that is representing what is around you. I can see how on the opposite side of the country, 3,000 miles away, similar things were happening.

Deal: Some of the heroes in Boston at the time were Del Fuegos, Dogmatics, Human Sexual Response, Throwing Muses, the Lyres, O Positive, Aimee Mann and 'Til Tuesday. They were big then. They were like, on MTV.

Gilbert: At that point Boston had already had four or five manifestations of different scenes, so it probably looked like any city in America that had a rock scene. It was still appealing to a certain amount of social misfits. It was kind of a melting pot. You didn't have to have a specific look or style, you could kind of just be somebody that just didn't fit into the general picture of society.

Hersh: There was garage rock, I think that was the Boston sound right before then, and so everything was a little seeped in that kind of wall of distortion—no matter what you were doing, that was kind of a given. And busy power drums, if that makes any sense.

Harvard: One of the really intriguing things about that whole period was that there's a Boston sound, and none of those guys [Muses and Pixies] have it. The really super-cool thing about that period was there was a moment when the old scene—which was centered in Kenmore Square, which was very much a garage-rock meets British invasion meets punk kind of thing, and overwhelmingly peopled by male personalities and guitar heroes—that dovetailed with this new thing, which was a lot of feminine energy, a lot of women who weren't trying to do what the few key women in the old scene were doing.

Donelly: We didn't fit into anything! Probably most closely with the art rockers, but that didn't even work out for us because we were sort of not weird. We were too weird for the straights and too straight for the weirds. So we kind of ended up just playing on our own a lot or then when the Pixies came along, with them.

Gilbert: The Muses are a funny one. They fell into a camp where people either loved them or hated them. They definitely had a pretty divisive reaction. Because there was kind of no precedent for it in music that was existent in Boston at the time.

Ian MacKaye (former Minor Threat singer; Fugazi singer/guitarist; the Evens singer/guitarist; co-owner, Dischord Records; musician): Music was still regional then much more than it is now. You have to remember this was before there was a nation-wide music outlet, you didn't have MTV, you certainly didn't have ClearChannel, or the Internet for Christ's sake. So basically the music you heard was on your local radio station. And kids were making music in their basements around the country.

Dennison: Mission of Burma was just starting to come up at that point, the Unnatural Acts was a big band around town, the Real Kids, the Nervous Eaters, Le Pest was one of the coolest bands in Boston. The 1980s was kind of a transitional time where people were open to a lot of different styles and not just like, "I'm only into garage punk, or art rock"—it was kind of an us against them deal. So people went out to see all different kinds of bands. Rich Gilbert and Human Sexual Response were almost mainstream at that point, they had a big radio hit, but they used to play around the clubs, too.

Gilbert: I was in a record store and saw an ad for four singers that were looking for a band, and that's how I met what ended up being Human Sexual Response, my first band. It was four singers, three males and one female up front, and then it was backed up by a power trio: bass, drums, guitar. So it was kind of punk, kind of new wave. It was very exciting, you didn't have to fit a genre, you didn't have to fit a style.

Hersh: Oh, they were so great! I listened to Human Sexual Response when I was like, 12! That's what we thought grown-up music was. We didn't find out until it was too late that the rest of the world would never catch up to Boston in that regard.

Gonson: There were other bands that were doing well during that time, like the Lemonheads, but even they didn't really do that well in Boston, they did better nationally. Boston's a really fickle town towards its own. It wants you to be true to it, 100 percent or it might kick you out.

Hersh: Well, that's kind of the Boston scene, too, it was very anti-pretense, and even the bands that went on to be very successful, their ethic was to look and act pretty normal and not act like you thought you were hot shit. Which is probably in response to whatever happened in the music business right before then. Probably a lot of rock stars around.

Angel: Pixies got their own records out so quickly. They went to Europe fast. I don't think they gave a shit if people in Boston liked them, which was really rare for a band from that city.

Gilbert: You know, none of my first impressions of the Pixies are any different than what I have now. David was very friendly and gregarious. Joey was quiet but very friendly and had a really sly sense of humor. And Kim was always just kind of Kim. Charles and I knew each other from like, 1980-whatever, when the Pixies were third on the bill. See, the great thing about Boston then was there was a big mutual support thing among bands. So if there were bands in town that you liked, you generally tried to get on bills with them. I knew that Charles and Joey were big fans of the Zulus, so when the Pixies started playing around they got on a couple shows with us, because at the time we were pretty popular in Boston, and that's how we got to know each other.

St. Thomas: I think the Pixies may have been influenced by the Zulus. Rich Gilbert is amazing and the Zulus were weird and awesome. They had really bizarre vocal arrangements, I could see it rubbing off on the Pixies, there's no doubt about it. They were a big [local radio station] FNX band at the time.

Smith: By the time I'd stopped playing in bands in 1987, the only people who'd kind of broken out were the Del Fuegos. I mean, there were bands like Boston, but it was music that we didn't really care for. Certainly in the world of eccentric rock the Muses were the first band to be on a major, on Sire.

Gilbert: Every city has its personalities that are at the forefront of the scene and [Del Fuegos manager] Lilli was just one of those. She was the girl about town, she knew all these hip people, she waitressed and worked at all the right bars, and then she became a really well-respected booker. She always had a really good ear and really good taste, so when she was behind something you knew it was good.

Dennison: Until the Pixies were kind of a big band they weren't really a big band on the Boston club scene. I was involved in the booking office at the Rat in the mid-'80s, there was a girl who was kind of helping them a lot, and she was constantly trying to get me to manage them. I remember listening to the demo, really liking it, and hearing the songs on college radio in Boston. In those days they played demo tapes on the air and a local band could get a great following together just from people hearing their tapes on the radio. So I remember hearing their songs on the radio and thinking they were pretty cool.

Gilbert: Pixies were just a really good band. I didn't look at them and think, "These guys are going to make such a gigantic impact in the larger culture of music." Because at that point you were always seeing bands that you felt like had that potential if the opportunity was just presented to them. So many bands had so many ideas, and what was going to be the right combination of ideas to crack the global picture, you just never knew what that was going to be. Very quickly, the Pixies built an audience in

Boston of their own, and very quickly they were headlining rooms, and pretty quickly after that they were signed to 4AD, and then they were just out. They all moved out, moved on.

Hersh: I was playing with the Volcano Suns and Uzi, the Five, Dinosaur Jr., so I guess you can put all those bands together and come up with a sound that was definitely a precursor to alternative rock. But when they called us "alternative" then, we were offended. We would ask, "Alternative to what? Real music?" But the shows were in horrible, grungy, wonderful places. Like the Rat.

St. Thomas: I just remember John carrying Kim's bass into the Rat. I don't know if he was their road manager or if he was just a devoted husband, but I remember him being at all those gigs, because I was just like, "That's John Murphy!" He looked very normal. I just thought it was funny because I didn't know her name was Kim Deal, so you'd see him and go, "That's the guy!"

Gilbert: The Rat was the CBGBs of Boston.

Hersh: Absolutely. The Rat's really all I care to remember about the Boston scene because that's where everything happened. The best shows happened there. We wanted to make sure we were playing all the time, and that meant we played in a lot of scary clubs, a lot of gross clubs, a lot of wrong clubs. But the Rat was everything it was supposed to be, and that's such a perfect name for it. It was self-consciously crappy. They tried really hard to make it a sweaty rock club and they succeeded. It was disgusting.

Gilbert: Boston had a plethora of rock clubs between 1977 and 1992. There was a little place called the Club for a while. The Underground only lasted about a year and a half, but it was a pretty important club. It was booked by this guy Jim Kaufman who brought a lot of international bands to Boston that would be playing in New York, so you would see anyone of any importance or influence at his clubs.

Chet's Last Call, Johnny D's in Allston, Maverick's. But headlining the Rat meant you had established yourself in the town. That was the place where your reputation was cemented. It was underground, it was kind of dank, it had a really odd cast of characters who worked there. But there was a period in the mid-'80s where the Rat was really a great place because they had an incredible PA system and an incredible light system, and even though it's just this room that held legally maybe 300, they would squeeze 500 people in there. It could be the best place to see and hear a band. And they had a barbeque restaurant upstairs, the Hoodoo Barbeque, that was like the hip place to eat, and that's where Lilli Dennison worked as a waitress. [David Lovering's ex-wife] Julie Farman used to book the Rat, and all the guys in the Del Fuegos worked at the Hoodoo Barbeque. It was a very incestuous little world. You'd go to a club and you'd go to a party and you'd hang out with the bands, and you'd go to a band's house, and you'd pretty much see the same 250, 200 people. A lot.

Dennison: In different capacities I stayed at the Rat for eight years. I didn't make any money there at all, but I got to see bands every night and get to know people, and that's how I got my foot in the door to start managing bands. It was filthy and there were rats running around. In the late '80s there was a barbeque restaurant on the ground floor of the Rat that I was also involved with. They called us the Algonquin Room because everyone ate every meal there.

Sean Slade (cofounder, Fort Apache studios; producer of albums by Pixies, Hole, Radiohead): Intermedia was the only rock studio in town, and the only 24-track. The very first Aerosmith record with "Mama Kin" was recorded at Intermedia.

Paul Kolderie (cofounder, Fort Apache studios, producer of albums by Pixies, Hole, Radiohead): When the Cars got rich they bought Intermedia and turned it into Synchro Sound. They only made one record there, *Shake It Up*. For as nice a place as it was, it wasn't that up-to-date a studio. Then we started a guerilla studio. It was very rock.

Harvard: I was very good friends with the guys in a band called the Sex Execs, who were a brilliant bunch of guys who had met at Yale. We were the most grossly overeducated recording crew in the history of the world. I went to Harvard, I studied archaeology. And I had a band at the time called the Bones, garagey, real Boston stuff, and I recorded at their house. They were the first people I'd ever seen who could record stuff at their house.

Gilbert: Joe Harvard is awesome. How he got the name Joe Harvard, this is the story I've always heard, but it makes sense: He's from some working class area of Boston, but he had actually gone to Harvard, so they used to call him, as kind of a dig, "fucking Joe Harvard." He's a total character.

Widmer: There was a punk rock scene at Harvard in the late '70s. It was very interesting for about one year and then it flared out and Joe was really involved with it. He was a fixture around Cambridge and throughout the '80s he was this guy that was keeping the Boston rock scene going and keeping it kind of garagey. It was always very garagey, sort of simple '60s sounding bands.

Harvard: I went from Harvard to being a janitor at a dance center because I had no clue what I was going to do. I had been selling a little pot, and I started to sell a lot more pot. And I sold *a lot* of pot. The person I was with became pregnant with twins and she lost them about halfway through. The plan was to get a house for the babies and when it didn't work out, there was all this money. Paul Kolderie and Sean Slade, who were the two principles in the recording end of the Sex Execs, came to me and we had a talk about getting a studio. They had some guy who was putting up the money and then he crapped out and I said fuck it, I'll be like, the money guy. So we got together, it was the three of us and another guy from the Sex Execs, Jim Fitting became the fourth principle, because it was easier to divide the bills by four. So we started the Fort as a collective, we did it for a year as a collective, and then just because things worked out the way they do, there was a little bit of friction. I was going to leave, and it was suggested that a better idea would just be for me to take over the place as the owner since I owned all the equipment, anyway. But we kept the team thing. So I owned the Fort after the first year for another couple of years alone, with us functioning as a quasi-gang, semi-band.

Smith: Lifeboat had been the first client of Fort Apache, we recorded some pretty cool demos there. So January 3, 1987, I left my architects job and went to Fort Apache to be the studio manager because I wanted to have the coolest underground eight-track studio in America—which I suppose we had, but that's not any great shakes, is it? We did it because it was cool and for no other reason. I don't think cool is about what you're wearing or how you subscribe to the current trends. Cool is about transcending your epic and being righteous about it. And so Fort Apache, we wanted to make the coolest studio. It hadn't occurred to me that if people couldn't afford an expensive studio they wouldn't want to come to our crap-ass studio in the ghetto.

Harvard: Paul Kolderie found it. It was a warehouse, like a commercial laundry downstairs, and nobody was upstairs. Huge, old building. So we picked our spot, we built a straight wall. We short-cut it as much as we possibly could, we used moving blankets over the sheetrock, but we did a proper control room wall with the double window. Billy Conway, the drummer from Morphine, framed our control room wall, he's an actual carpenter. The entire Fort was one enormous, 150-foot extension chord with boxes every 20 feet.

Smith: This is the very first Fort Apache, there were two in Roxbury, then there were two in Cambridge. The two in Roxbury followed chronologically, one right after the other, the two in Cambridge we had at the same time. The first Fort Apache was a badly heated warehouse space in an enormous building. There were some lesbian metal workers downstairs, the metal dykes as we called them, they were wonderful people. There was a woodworker named Fox who used to complain that he couldn't hear his power tools because of us. So sometimes he'd make J Mascis turn down his Marshalls because he couldn't hear his power tools. There was the coke/fish people, I don't know exactly what their deal was, but my understanding was they were importing drugs in dead fish and leaving dead fish round about in the building, and it stunk!

Harvard: October '85 we opened up, and I'll never forget, before we had even built the walls I took Jonathan Richman over and we went upstairs and I was sitting on the floor of this space and just sort of like, what do you think? And he was like, "I don't know, it's kind of a bad neighborhood. You really think Boston needs another eight-track studio, Joe?" I said, "You know what, I don't, but I think they need us."

Kolderie: People would come there and go, "Man, this is so cool!" Rock bands usually go to studios and they are all fancy, wood paneled, track lights, gold records on the wall—it's a little intimidating and feels like a dentist's office with gold records [on the walls] in place of tooth decay. But people walked into the Fort and it was like a practice space. It was pretty dirty, big huge empty rooms, and people were psyched and generally it led to more relaxed performances. We didn't tell people how to do things, to turn down, or things the studio people would do to you back then to end up with a half-ass recording. We were in the right place, right time. So we got a rep pretty quickly as the place to go for the rock bands in town. We were also out there in the clubs every night, networking with people, telling them that they should come in.

Smith: It was just like a section of this warehouse that they had petitioned off with two-by-fours and covered with moving blankets, essentially, and it was two rooms with a narrow alleyway that connected the control room to the main performance space. I remember people being in their snorkel jackets while playing the guitar, and I remember people being all huddled up with their arms around themselves trying to stay warm while they were working, so I know it must have been cold, but I don't remember people complaining about it.

Gilbert: The first one was just this long, rectangular room and I loved it, it was great. It looked like a band's rehearsal space, just with taller ceilings. But it was kind of a rough area, so that's why it got the name Fort Apache, based on Fort Apache in the Bronx, the police station in the movie [*Fort Apache, The Bronx*]. You'd always hear about bands getting their vans broken into, tires would be slashed, or their tape players would be stolen out of their cars. It was in Roxbury. It was off on Mass Ave. going down towards the Expressway. It was in this no man's land, there was like a baseball field and you'd take a right there and it was kind of just in the middle of nowhere. It totally had this isolated, outpost quality to it.

Smith: It was dangerous! Sometimes I carried a stick, sometimes I carried a general death-wish and thought, well, at least it won't be my fault. There are many stories about just how rough it was, and the people who came in and stole things, and the drug dealers that lived downstairs, and hibachi full of barbeque chicken that was stolen from the second floor balcony while cooking.

Gilbert: The Zulus were definitely part of the whole Fort Apache scene from the early stages of it. My friend Nat Freedberg had a band called the Flies, and I went in and played guitar on a song they were recording. He was like, "Hey, yeah, these guys are really cool." Because at the time there were no cool studios in Boston. [Studios] didn't seem to understand, creatively, what most Boston bands were about, and so bands oftentimes had a hard time getting good results on tape because there was a real schism between the bands and the recording business.

Slade: We developed a reputation for being able to take two weeks and a couple thousand dollars and make an album for a rock band that actually comes out really good.

43

Harvard: We weren't like scientists in lab coats. If you want to put a friggin' microphone in a toilet bowl, fine, put it in, we had no issues with any of that shit.

Gilbert: Fort Apache changed everything in Boston for a little period of time there. Finally there was a studio that was addressing and catering to this huge creative plethora of bands. Pretty much any band that was good and interesting at the time in Boston was recording at the Fort.

Slade: There was this sound man in the Boston scene, Michael Whittaker, he went out to Cali and started working with SST, and that was when the guys from Black Flag were just starting the label, and he knew Mascis. Mascis had done the first two Dinosaur records at cheap studios and he wasn't happy with the sound. Mike told him about us at our studio and so Mascis went out and got the Big Dipper album and liked it and just called us out of the blue and then he just showed up. That was the beauty of making records in those days. The budgets were so low you never heard from anybody from the record company complaining that they don't hear a single. They were just so happy that you were delivering a master tape for two thousand dollars!

Mascis: I just remember they had a lot of cool guitars and amps and stuff that Joe Harvard had bought. That was kind of a big attraction because they had a lot of stuff you could mess around with. I think everyone could sound a lot better than they had before for not that much money. They were sympathetic to the rock bands around.

Gilbert: They moved to a second location which was actually kind of deeper in a worse area of town, it was over by an area called Field's Corner, which is in Dorchester, and it also was in another commercial building.

Smith: The world in which people lived was different in the music realm. Rock clubs like the Rat and the Channel were filthy and literally rat-infested and there was something about being there that made you feel morally superior, not just because you were suffering for your art, but because it was cool! People didn't care whether it was freezing cold at Fort Apache, it was just cool to be down there in a kind of dangerous place like it was cool to be at the Rat, which was dangerous in some sense.

Gilbert: The Fort was always fun, and they would defer payments if you were short on money. They were really understanding because all those guys were musicians, they all came from bands.

Kolderie: Joe had some money that was. . .he did a little laundering if you know what I mean. He kinda fell by the wayside, he had some personal problems. Drug addiction and stuff. But at the time of the Pixies he was a very big figure. He was a very big man about town at that point and it was very much due to his influence and his friends and connections that our studio got rolling. He had money, he liked rock, and had a band—he was just kind of a bon vivant. He knew how to make things happen. There's one in every town. Joe was king of the scene for a while. But Joe has really bounced back all the way. He's married, he's got a nice kid.

Harvard: The rumor mill when I was leaving the Fort was a bit rife. I'm sort of the Trotsky of Fort Apache. I never happened. I was shooting dope the entire time I went to Harvard, the entire time I was building the Fort, unfortunately. At some point I decided to stop and told everybody. And suddenly I was a pariah, and it was open season on Joe Harvard rumors.

Slade: Once the Fort actually became a business Joe couldn't really handle that, so he brought Gary in because Gary is excellent at that. The Fort never would have expanded or become the kind of famous place it became if it wasn't for Gary. He got us to the next couple of levels. I kind of bristled that Gary came in and kind of acted like the boss—and in a way he was, as he was running the day-to-day biz, but considering the fact that Paul and I and two other guys went and started the damn place and made it what it was.

Kolderie: In order for a scene to happen you need a couple of key artists, a couple of key venues, and then a couple of behind-the-scenes people, managers, producers and engineers to make the records that people are going to hear. So the success of that time in Boston, like New York before and Seattle later, was the right artists and the right enablers. In Seattle it was Kurt, Nirvana wasn't going to happen without him, and at that point in Boston we had Kristin, and then Charles came along, and then Buffalo Tom, J Mascis—you need two or three crucial artists and then you need a place to stir it all up. I know I'm tooting my own horn, but you need a place like Fort Apache.

Slade: All the bands that made records at the Fort would come to our Christmas Parties and we always had a band set-up and all the bands would play. It was a bunch of free food and booze, everyone was sure to turn up.

Mascis: I played with Pixies at a Fort Apache party. Somehow I told Kim that I knew "Gigantic" because I heard it so many times in England when we were touring over there. So we just played that song. I tried to sing the high part at the beginning and stuff. Charles wasn't there.

Harvard: I think we peaked around '90, '91. By then, we had done the [Mighty Mighty] Bosstones, Big Dipper, the Neats, the Connells, the Turbines, Pixies, Throwing Muses, the Ex-Girlfriends, and numbers of informal sessions that never made it to vinyl.

Kolderie: By '91, after we did the Buffalo Tom record, *Let Me Come Over*, we got so screwed on the business deal on that that we said, hey, we got to get a manager. We got a manager and started going on the road soliciting jobs. We went to England and that's how we got the Radiohead job [recording *The Bends*], literally going to record companies and asking for jobs. Once they heard that we had worked with the Pixies and bands like that, once they heard that we were the Fort Apache guys, that totally impressed them.

Slade: I remember a conversation that we had with Thom Yorke and he was like, "I've got a bunch of your records in my collection, I'm totally into it." "Creep" and Radiohead definitely led to Hole. There was a really funny period where we'd get one-off mixes. It would be something that wasn't alt-rock or grunge at all and they'd say, "Can you mix it so it sounds more alternative?"

5. HERE COMES YOUR MAN—GARY SMITH AND *THE PURPLE TAPE* (1987)

Gary Smith caught one of Pixies' sets when they opened up a show for his own band, Lifeboat, and was absolutely blown away. In 1987 Pixies stepped into the Fort Apache studio with Smith for their first real session. Fueled by the highly-caffeinated Jolt Cola, nerves, and excitement, the four Pixies spent six days and nights completing 17 songs. The cassette would become known widely as *The Purple Tape* due to the background color tint. During this time, Smith's energy and passion almost single-handedly pushed the band to the next level.

Smith: There are people who think Christopher Columbus discovered America, like suddenly it was there and nobody was doing anything. The Pixies were playing around town and they were working with Ann Holbrook as their manager. So as much as I would like to take credit for somehow finding the Pixies—like they were living under a manhole and I heard noise coming through the cover—it wasn't really like that.

Ivo Watts-Russell (cofounder, 4AD records): Yes, undoubtedly, Gary discovered the Pixies.

Smith: I was at the Rat with the Throwing Muses. We were going to go to dinner with some record company dude, and I wanted to stay for sound check because I could hear something was going on, on the stage. When the Pixies did their sound check it became apparent to me that there was something very special.

Deal: Gary seemed like a real nice guy! I guess we ended up opening for his band, a band called Lifeboat, and I think it was their reunion gig or their last show before they broke up. And he was really complimentary about our show, that was nice.

Hersh: Gary is an angel, always has been, always will be. I think he's the invisible man when it comes to the Boston scene back then and yet he was just the engine behind it all. I'm not sure either of us bands would ever have been heard without him.

Harvard: I readily admit that my role in the Pixies saga was minute in terms of time and input, but if you look at the timing part of it, was pretty important just as far as being able to open the door when the door needed to be opened. All I had was the key. I didn't think about opening the door, I didn't knock on the door, that was Gary, but I was holding the keys at the time.

Hersh: My band opened for Gary's in Newport, Rhode Island in 1985. And we were watching them sound check, and then Gary asked if he could put his amp on a milk crate, and then he said, "Or would that be silly?" and we all snapped around and were like, "Silly! He said silly!" Only cool people use that word! And after watching our set that night, which is another thing only cool headliners do—watch the opening band—the wheels were in motion. Because he had heard us once and immediately was scheduling demos and our move to Boston.

Harvard: He played the Muses and I listened to it, and I was like, I'm not getting it, it just sounds like someone gargling or something. They hadn't played many shows at all, and I went and saw them play and they did a song called "Hate My Way" which made me cry. It was so beautiful, and they were so fucking powerful, and I went, okay, well, maybe there's a chance that Gary's got better ears for modern rock than I do.

Hersh: We were working out of Providence, we were tiny, we were like 15, 16 years old. We were doing very well as an arty little band because of [colleges] Brown and RISD, and were playing to about 800 people every weekend in Providence and thought we were rock stars. That was as far as we had ever planned on going, and Gary convinced us to move to Boston, which had an actual music scene, not just an art scene. He was less take-charge as much as he was a facilitator. But he got us all jobs at [architecture firm] Moshe Safdie and helped us find an apartment, began scheduling demos in Roxbury for us.

Smith: It's hard to remember what motivates you at different points in your life, particularly when you're in your 20s. It's like you're out on your own and everything's happening around you. It was a really interesting era, I was just excited to be alive, and to be in the city, and finding the extraordinary in the ordinary was what moved me. Sing For Your Supper, I don't know how many I did, a dozen maybe. I had people come over to my house, I made dinner, and while I was cooking they were putting stuff down.

Hersh: I remember Sing For Your Supper mostly because we were so hungry. I don't really remember playing, but I remember the eating part. I was probably pregnant and starving. It was a two-track, and you just sat on his bed and played whatever the hell you wanted while he made dinner.

Harvard: This might sound snotty or something, but I'm not 100 percent convinced that the Pixies would have gotten where they got had it not been for the synchronicity involved in Gary seeing them when he saw them, and them being in the same town that the Muses were.

Smith: I like music that isn't full of received ideas. I like music that makes me think again about what I was hearing as opposed to things that reassure me that what I'm hearing is what I'm used to. That's why I liked Throwing Muses. But none of my friends liked Throwing Muses. The first time our band played with the Muses everyone was like, "You have got to be kidding. You're just saying you like them so that you can feel superior to other people who know that they suck." I didn't believe that, but I came from a different musical epoch, which was somewhere between the Clash and R.E.M., chronologically speaking. Hearing the Pixies was like, there's another band that's way out. Because I like pop bands, I like songs that resolve. But I like pop songs that somehow shook me up and didn't just follow a formula, and what I heard in sound check that day was that. It was just like, "Holy Jesus, what is going on here!?"

The Muses and the Pixies were both bands where they were regular people but when they were doing what they did with music they became something else, they channeled something that was otherworldly. It only took 30 seconds of, I think they played "Vamos" in sound check. I saw that guy screaming and I was thinking to myself, "Look at that fresh-faced. . ." He had the cleanest complexion and blond hair and he was thin—maybe he wasn't thin, but he was a well-proportioned young man—and he just looked like a nice guy, not like some drug-addled Iggy Pop guy, not like some Nick Cave guy or Nick Drake guy or some guy who you could already tell was outside of the mainstream. He was a guy! He went to college and shaved in the morning and he had a pink face from being a clean, blond-haired kid, and then he was screaming at the top of his lungs! And it wasn't like people screamed back then, people didn't scream. Kristin Hersh screamed. Who screamed? Hüsker Dü? No, they didn't. They made a racket, but they didn't actually go "Balahahaha." People just didn't do that. And to see that happening like some kind of scene from *The Exorcist* coming out of this very fresh-faced kid, it just made me stop and not go to dinner with the dude, whoever it was we were going to go to dinner with. And the Pixies were cute! I'm also a sucker for cute, and I don't mean musically cute, they were an attractive bunch of people. It's hard to believe that now, but that's the truth. There was something about them, they seemed like regular, normal people, and yet they were doing this thing that was from another planet. It's just like Throwing Muses, they're regular people. You go to lunch, you talk about stuff, they're engaged in the world, they can have conversations about math, or about literature, or about what's in the chicken salad today, and then they got on stage and turned into like, Shanen.

I watched the whole sound check, and I went up to Charles and said, "Can we talk?" After their set I just hung around in the dressing room. They didn't know who I was. I suppose they were 21 or 22 and I was 29, of course I felt like a lecherous old man. And I told them about the Throwing Muses thing, because I had done this project with Throwing Muses that had eventually gotten them signed to 4AD and it made the [*Village Voice*] Pazz & Jop polls. It was a self-released cassette and it was next to Bruce Springsteen and Madonna in these Pazz & Jop polls, which is pretty intense. I used that as leverage, just trying to say, "Look we did this thing and then they got signed." It wasn't like I expected them to pay me, really. I wanted them to pay me and I wanted them to be paid something, but that wasn't why I was going back to the dressing room. I was going back because I had to be near what they were doing.

They were nice, they were pleasant. I remember trying not to scare them like I was trying to have a piece of them or wanted to pick them up. So they seemed nice enough, but to some extent were standoffish, the same way the Blake Babies were standoffish when I went to them. It was very much the same kind of thing—what do we need a producer for? I said we should get together and talk about the idea of working together and then I had a meeting with Charles. He came with his brother, and he described me to his brother as a Communist, as I recall. I'm not sure what in conversation had made him think that about me, but I definitely was way to the left, socially, and he wasn't, as a matter of fact. And we met at some restaurant which was above my band's practice space, and I think where they practiced. It was called the JD First Complex and it was down by Fenway Park, across the street from Star Market. So we went to this restaurant, we had a brief conversation about what could we do together, what was the value of working together.

Shortly after that, I invited Charles to do one of these Sing For Your Supper things, and he said he would, which was great. I think after that I had the whole bunch of them over to play music, too, but the one that he did somehow survived the various movings from apartment to apartment and then ended up coming out on one of those myriad Pixies collections. He's an intense guy. As normal as he was then, he is a high-strung sort of fellow, and he gets excited. It's like he comes to a boil, and this is what I remember: That night when he was doing the recording in my apartment he was teaching me his songs and as he got to the chorus he would get excited and he would stand inches from my face with an acoustic guitar and say, "And now it's going to go BLAHHHA," and he would do this chorus to the point where you could see his uvula, and I was just like, "Oh my God, I can't believe this is happening in my apartment!"

Hersh: I listened to that tape because Gary gave it to me and he was saying, "Should I work with them?" It was kind of an intense experience to sit there by yourself and play songs that you've just written that are still kind of flying out of you. And he was whacking the guitar, using it as a percussive instrument, and you know, singing in Spanish—obviously, it was just messed up. He didn't have that Charles thing yet, he sang really high and he screamed like a woman and that just sounded really honest and immediate. If you haven't built up a shell yet, then what comes out of you is going to be pretty fucking balanced, gender-wise. In music there's definitely a masculine and a feminine and it has nothing to do with who's a man and who's a woman and who's gay and who's straight. And if a songwriter is really using their most honest voice it comes out as person instead of man or woman, and that's what this tape sounded like. Listening to that tape, I got to know songs that didn't appear on Pixies records until the last couple of records, so by that time they were really old songs, and I just preferred Charles' version. Later when I heard the songs with the Pixies I just thought, "They're playing all over it! Get out of the way!"

Smith: There were so many songs, and they were so fast. They were short songs, all of them, and I loved that. He didn't have all the words down, and he'd be mumbling in that way that people mumble before they have words, and it was all just very, I think, moving. . .I was moved by the situation of how invested he was in the music and how recently he had come to be a musician, officially. That seemed impressive to me, because it's those people who are able to do that sort of channeling, it's coming from somewhere else, really. It does actually happen where either it's your adrenaline going into your brain and giving you powers that you did not formerly possess, or something happens to people who are able to do that, who don't sort of coldly craft their material but somehow have it arrive on a wave of inspiration. And that is entirely what happened during the time when I was hanging with those guys. They were just really inspired.

And they were strangers, except for Joey and Charles, the other ones didn't really know each other. It was very odd. And maybe that is sometimes a cause for inspiration. If you're suddenly not weighed down by the baggage of your experience with other people. I mean, my band was full of people that I had known since childhood, and we had way too many interpersonal dynamics. It was an extension of your other relationships as opposed to something new and completely fresh into which you can put yourself without inhibitions.

I think by the time he had come to the apartment we had come to some sort of understanding that there would be recording in a proper studio environment. He was coming to my house to give me an outline of what we might be recording. The next thing that happened was we started doing preproduction. We did maybe, six of those practices over the course of a month and a half.

My band played its last show on January 3, 1987 at the Rat. And January 4 I started at Fort Apache. At the first meeting I said I wanted to bring the Pixies in, and everyone was grumbling. Basically, when I came into the studio there were heavy dynamics about how it was being run and suddenly I was the manager and I was the guy who was supposed to run interference. And the general thrust was, well you're going to be the manager, you're not going to be bringing in bands to record because we don't have time for that. And so the first thing I brought in was the Pixies. And they didn't get it. And then after they heard them playing they started to get it. Soon after they arrived for the first sessions, everyone was like, "Can I do a few hours of this?" All of a sudden I had all sorts of help!

Harvard: Gary came in one day and he had the biggest fucking hard-on you can imagine, he was like you've *got* to check this shit out.

Slade: When Gary first played me the Pixies' demos I wasn't that impressed. He wanted someone to engineer the session but he wanted to be in total control and at that stage in the game I really didn't want to take direction from Gary Smith. So I passed on engineering it, but Paul in his infinite wisdom said, "I'll do it."

Kolderie: One day we had our weekly studio meeting and Gary said, "Look, I want to bring this band the Pixies in. They don't have any money but I think you're going to be glad you did it if someone's willing to step up and do it for free." And I was kind of the chief engineer at the time, and I said, "Well, I'll do it." I thought they were pretty good and it was kind of one of those things, like, what the hell?

Harvard: When he played the Pixies tape I was like, this isn't really hitting me hard, but I also knew that the Muses hadn't hit me hard the first time. By then I trusted Gary's judgment, this has happened once before. And basically, he's worked up in a Throwing Muses fashion. And he said, "Look, these guys are a one in a million band. They're the real deal. They've got '*it*.'" Heavily underscored with quotes. He said, "We've got to work out a way to record them, if we don't do it, someone is going to snag them soon." They were playing a couple of nights later and I went to see 'em. And seeing them live, I quote "got it." And they were amazing. They were everything that he had been twitchin' over. And that was pretty much it. It all happened fairly quickly after that because Gary's not one to let the onions lie in the field unplucked.

We did a lot of what I call "artist grants" at the Fort. We did a lot of free shit. If we liked it, we'd do it. We weren't Mother Teresa, but if we dug the band we'd go the fucking mile. So I said, "Well, look, you're officially on the team now, we've all taken personal projects, and we'll call it your personal project. If you can get money, get money. But let's at least try to get the money to rent the machine," because at that stage we were an eight-track studio, we didn't have a 16-track. It was like 350 bucks a week to rent this machine, so I said at least try to get the 350 bucks so we're not paying for the project out of pocket, and 50 bucks for tape. I seem to recall somebody came up with 1,400 bucks after the thing was all done.

Kolderie: We booked six days and we did it as a complete lockout. People were sleeping in the studio, coming and going, but the action stayed constant for six days. And there was a lot what we used to call "tag team engineering," where someone would do eight hours and just lose it and then someone would come in and take over.

Harvard: *The Purple Tape* was done at the original location, Fort Apache South.

Lovering: So we went in, we did 17 songs, and that was the original *Come on Pilgrim*.

Smith: People were coming and going, I was working around the clock, we never left. I had just gotten there in January, all of a sudden it was March and I was supposed to be producing this band. I was on the fast track.

Thompson: It took three days. I borrowed a thousand bucks from my father.

Harvard: They came in, they set up, they took a Death to the Pixies poster, they flipped it over, they stuck it on the wall backwards, and they wrote out the 17 songs as a set list. And then they just *kicked ass* going through them. They plunged through that shit like nobody's business, and I gained a certain respect because they burned on that shit. I really kind of went, okay, not only are they unique, not only are they really fucking exciting, but they got a work ethic.

Smith: It was sort of a communal experience making that record because we didn't have automation, of course, because we were the coolest eight-track studio in the country, and we had just rented the 16-track machine to do these sessions. Because I was actually trying to keep up with the Joneses so I figured I'd get a 16-track machine and that would make me cooler, but we had to use everybody's hands to do the moves on the board because we didn't have automation. I wanted it to be very quiet at the top of the tracks, and that means you have to push all the mute buttons and as each instrument makes its entrance into the recording you would lift your mute button and there it would be, but you wouldn't have tape hiss or stupid fiddling around like musicians do because they're not paying attention. So they would all be standing there with their hands on the board. We worked three days and another three days mixing—the whole experience was less than six days—and so as the time ticked into the night they started to get very tired. And back then I was the sort of guy who only slept two, maybe three hours a night. I thought sleep was a social construct and we'd been duped into wasting our lives in bed doing nothing, so I tried to actually foil that. So they would wake up and go put their fingers on the mute buttons in their snorkel jackets, and then they would let go of the mute buttons, the song would start, and they would lie back down on the floor with the blankets that they'd brought from home, like their Dr. Denton's [footed pajamas]. And that's the way the session went, which was cool, because they were very much engaged and important to the project, aside from just playing their instruments.

Kolderie: The atmosphere in the studio was pretty tense for *The Purple Tape*, but it was fun. I remember it kind of being like a long dream and at the very end of it we were all kind of dead tired and I was splicing the final mixes all together to make the master for the cassette—yes cassettes—and I remember getting three songs into it and thinking, "Shit, this is good."

Smith: There's a lot of glass in mill buildings, ceiling to floor multi-paned glass windows, and so it was very live out in the great, big, empty, hardwood floored room, and my goal was to make a record with no reverb. I had come from the modernist architecture tradition, the Bauhaus style, and I felt like there was a need for truth and clarity in things that the '70s had been really unfortunate in ignoring, and so I didn't want to use digital reverbs, I only wanted to use live rooms. So I shoved the bulk of the work out into that space where there was absolutely no heat, in part to get the sense of the room, and in part to put people ill at ease so it wasn't easy for them to give a lame or studied performance.

Deal: You got to put a lot of Jolt Cola in Fort Apache. Lived on the Jolt. It was a new product that just came out. And we did it in like, really two and a half days, because the last day was done with mixing and making cassettes.

Lovering: And from Friday night on, through Saturday, to Sunday when we left it just got colder, and colder, and colder. It was fun, it was the first time, really in I guess you'd call it a professional studio. So it was really nice. We knew all the songs from playing clubs and playing for a period of maybe six or seven months beforehand.

Harvard: There was a heater, but because the place had been a sweatshop, it was one of those enormous heaters in the ceiling, and there were a couple of ancient radiators from Alexander the Great's time, but when the heat came on it was like *clang clang*. In the beginning when we just couldn't get around it, it was so bitterly cold in Boston that we had to have it on, there were a number tracks that had what we called "the organic percussion." Once in a while it would end up being in time, but frequently not. Finally we had to grin and bear it so we got some electric radiators and turned off the radiator heat. The Pixies were freezing their asses off, as I recall.

Kolderie: When we recorded *Come on Pilgrim* we were all kind of in the same boat. They were new at being a band, and they didn't know if they were supposed to be doing anything in particular or not, and I was new at being a studio engineer. And we kind of needed each other to figure it out. It was sort of like, hey if that's your song, and it's a minute and a half long, sounds good to me, why not, sure. Kim was a little volatile. At one point she got kind of drunk and started freaking out about the kick drum sound. I remember her screaming at us, "You call that a kick drum! You call that a fucking kick drum sound?!" and we were like, "Um, yeah," and she was like, "Ahhh, fuck you!" and stormed out. She was up and down. But mostly it was a nice time. David and I were kind of friends from the scene, I would see him around town. Joey never talked. He was very quiet except when he played.

Smith: It was a couple of days a very long time ago. I remember being very tired and delirious by the end of it. I'm not much of an engineer to be perfectly honest. I can do it in a pinch, but I never really liked it, I feel too nervous like I'm going to fuck something up. And I did! I do remember erasing a very important section of "Vamos." We had gotten to the end and I had gotten excited, and I just popped everything on record and whoosh, it was all gone! And we had to call Paul, and Paul came in and he set it all up and I think they played the end of the song and we just punched them in, like the entire band playing the entire song, we just punched in for the last, I don't know, five bars, eight bars.

Kolderie: At one point I went home to sleep for a few hours and got a frantic call from Gary at like, six in the morning: He had just rewound the master tape too far and erased one of the mixes of "Vamos," the last 30 seconds of it, so I had to come back and remix the last 30 seconds and splice it back on.

Smith: I just remember people being cold, I remember people lying on the floor and sleeping, I remember listening to "Levitate Me" while Charles came up with all the lyrics and people making suggestions about it. He just was out in that great big space with some stereo mics around to try to pick up the sound of the room, and him just going into "Levitate Me" like he'd always known the song. I remember being frozen in time watching the needles move and thinking this is not one of those situations where some day I'll realize this guy is really good. It was like, right there I said to myself, "Holy mother of Jesus!" It's incredible what was going on. To me it never really matters whether anybody else gets it, if I think it's good that's what matters to me, and I was just totally swept away with the force of what he was doing, and that's what I remember the most. I remember seeing the needles and seeing the red record light on and seeing the other band members standing around me and feeling like I was at the signing of the Declaration of Independence or something.

Murphy: On "Levitate Me," the chorus at the end where it's like, yelling—Charles was asleep, and they did their recording in 72 hours of rolling time, freezing cold, so while some people were sleeping they were still working. Somebody came up with the idea and Dave and Kim were the ones doing the vocals to that while Charles was sleeping, and then when he woke up they played it for him and he was like, "Oh that's cool, let's keep it." Charles gave credit to everybody in the world who wrote that song, too. His girlfriend Jean came up with a couple of words, he threw her a songwriter credit.

Kolderie: Charles was friendly back then. I remember just being blown away by the method in which he used to write his lyrics. Once I asked him what "Ed is Dead" was about and I remember him telling me, "Oh, it's about this girl, this weird kinda girl, she was retarded and didn't have any friends and she would ride her bike around with a transistor radio strapped to the handlebars blasting music." So that's why there are lyrics like "With music on her bars." So I said, "Okay, I understand that, but what does it have to do with Ed being dead?" And he said, "Well nothing, I just liked the way it sounds." And that blew my mind. It's like, here is this guy that's writing these songs and they are really catchy, but it has no meaning really whatsoever. The hook of it is completely unrelated to what starts you off on the journey of the song and at one point they are just going "E – I – D!"

Santiago: It was very primal. I couldn't believe it. Goddamn, he was really screaming it out. I didn't expect it. He's singy-songy. I was trying to leave the studio at Fort Apache and he was recording so I shouldn't shut the other door because I didn't want to make a door slam during the tape. He was in the warehouse with just headphones. I couldn't hear the music and all I saw was him in the headphones in front of a microphone screaming. There was nothing to reference the music on. It looked crazy, in a good way. Holy Christ, you know. He's never cancelled a show because of his voice. He's got strong vocal cords.

Smith: I believe I had heard them do "In Heaven (Lady in the Radiator Song)" in practice once. It was weird and quirky and so was the movie [*Eraserhead*, which it came from] and it obviously had a very dark component that seemed not out of line with the rest of the material. It had that fantastic screaming section, which Charles excelled at.

Thompson: If anything is a big influence on me, it's David Lynch. He's really into presenting something but not explaining it. It's just, "This is an image, this is an idea, isn't it cool?" The way I understand it, that's the only way to be surreal. To be not so connected with it, except that it came from your brain, somewhere way back *here*.[3]

Kolderie: It was so early on in my career, that the hindsight is 20/20 and then some. At the time it was hard to imagine that it would do what it has done. But I definitely remember hearing when "Subbacultcha" went by thinking, "Man, this is good."

Murphy: The "Allegre" part that David yells at the beginning of "Isla de Encanta"—I don't even know if he's pronouncing it right—it was a PBS TV show for kids, I think it was *Viva Allegre* or something like that. He just thought it was funny because it would be in Spanish.

Smith: We never called it *The Purple Tape*, by the way. We didn't call it anything. We called it the record, and we didn't even call it demos. To be perfectly honest, my take on it back then was we'll go get a record deal with this, and if we don't, we'll put it out ourselves. Before a single inch of tape had rolled, that was my position. I felt like you make your own opportunities, you don't wait for these losers to come tell you you're good. You build yourself, and frankly that is something that's going to have to happen again nowadays because nobody's getting signed.

Kolderie: A lot of those songs that we recorded didn't come out 'til later—"Subbacultcha" didn't come out until the fourth record—but it was there from the beginning. They didn't really write much after that initial burst of about a year where they wrote just about everything they ever did. But by the end of *Surfer Rosa* there wasn't really any new stuff ever. They had "Dig For Fire" but we didn't record it on that first thing and they didn't want to do "Here Comes Your Man." They called it the Tom Petty song.

Smith: There was some reluctance to do "Here Comes Your Man" because it was too pop, there was something too straight about it. I came from a jangly pop background, so I was all for it.

Lovering: I remember when everybody left and Gary and I were putting all the equipment in his van that we were gonna drop off at the rehearsal space. And we were really tired, we had been up for a couple of days, it was all freezing cold winter, snow outside, and we're driving out and his van breaks down. Oh, it was horrible.

Smith: Oh yeah, that's true. It was a real metaphor for my own personal exhaustion. My van was the van that my band had driven around the country in, and when my band broke up just before I worked with those guys, I inherited the van for a fee. I also inherited all our loans. It had seen the world.

Murphy: Charles and Gary mixed it on their own the following weekend, and I remember when it was all said and done I said, "This is great." I was playing it for my family and everybody and saying, "This is them, they really sound good, somebody knows somebody and maybe they might get a record contract!" Charles sent it to a million places, he wrote all these letters, "Please consider our tape."

The Purple Tape has purple-tinted liner notes, and the cover shot shows a naked man running in front of some buildings. The band's name is listed as Pixies, not the Pixies, and there's no official album name printed on the record anywhere.

Smith: [The name] was definitely a matter of discussion. That question happens with a lot of bands that don't want to be called "the" something or another, but usually they end up being called "the" something or another. Like "the" Throwing Muses. It was Throwing Muses.

Deal: That's David Lovering [the naked man on the cover]. I guess Gary Smith took that picture because we wanted a tape. Because what you did back then was consign it. Go to like, Newbury Comics and stuff. So you have your tape and the store would agree to put it in the store and you don't get any money unless they sell it. And they get a little piece of it.

Smith: David ended up running in place at Fort Apache in front of a fake black backdrop. I snapped a ton of photos of him doing that, and the word was, "If I look embarrassing, tell me to turn, or you turn away." And then I cut a mask, and it didn't come out the way I wanted it to. I was working at the architect's office so I had access to the architect's account at Charette, it was a photo reprographics house. I masked two images, one was the projects behind where the studio was. I don't know why we chose those two images. Pixies in urban landscapes, I think there being some conversation about the wee people in urban landscapes or something like that. They had a plan that each one was going to be naked on a subsequent project of some sort. I think Kim was next and that's why it never happened. They got onto a real label, and that was the end of that. But there was an hour of David Lovering jogging in place and me taking pictures of him. It was mildly perverted. And then he had some idea about taking pictures on a chair. I have all these contact sheets, half of them are of him sitting on a chair in weird positions with his hands on the floor, looking dead.

I found a box of cassettes in my barn recently and there were a lot of Pixies tapes in there. I'm sure they were the rehearsals, I haven't really listened to them to find out what's on them. One of the things that I took out of storage are the original Pixies tapes, which are right across my desk right now. And I hadn't really looked at them since then, they went into a vault and that was the end of it.

[Reading track sheets from original Pixies recording session] 3/12/87... here are the track sheets. Leonard Norman acoustic number, it doesn't even say what it's called. And then there's one that's just called "The New One" and then there's a bit of red crayon and an arrow, and it says "Levitate Me." Reel 1—this is what became known as *The Purple Tape*: Holiday Song, I'm Amazed, Rock A My Soul 1, Rock A My Soul 2—I don't know what the difference is—Isla de Encanta, Caribou, Broken Face, I've Been Tired, Build High, Break My Body, Ed is Dead, Here Comes Your Man.

And then Reel 2: Down to the Well, Subbacultcha, Nimrod's Son, Vamos, there's a couple of versions of Vamos, it looks like. In Heaven, which is the Lady in the Radiator Song, The New One, and another take of Isla de Encanta, and then another one that says New One, under which it says Leonard Norman acoustic number, and the track sheets are here. There's things that say "check bass sound" then there's things that say "stretchy part." This one says "skiffle, it's Build High" and it's not written in my penmanship, oddly enough. Here it says "Hair Comes Your Man" and there's an afro drawn on top of the word *hair*. I think maybe what I was doing was giving them the track sheets and saying, "Okay, tell me what this one's called," and they'd write them out.

Harvard: They had done the Charles thing [the Death to the Pixies poster], and there's the one of the drummer, David, jogging. He looks phenomenal. He was a babe magnet, Kim was the heartbreaker.

Smith: I was laying out the type for the cover of *The Purple Tape* in my apartment. I had typed up some things and I remember saying, "How are you going to be known? What is your name going to be?" To that point, to be perfectly honest, I don't think he had ever uttered the words *Black Francis*, at least in my presence. I'm sure he'd said it to his father, and nobody else in the band seemed to blink an eye, so maybe they already knew. And I was thinking, is it Charlie? Chuck? Is it Charles K. Thompson IV, what's it going to be? And he said, "Black Francis." And I was like, "Where the hell did that come from?" His father had said that would be a good stage name, or he and his father had somehow together decided that would be a good stage name. I remember saying, "Are you sure? I'm going to put it on here. It's going to be printed." He was like, "Yeah, I'm sure," and there it was. Immediately following that decision Kim said, "I'm going to be Mrs. John Murphy, then." I said, "Are you sure?"

Murphy: I know she was doing it as a goof on feminism, but it made me proud. A lot of people didn't think it was true, either, like it was a made-up name. But I was the roadie, so she needed me.

Deal: I worked in a doctor's office, mainly typing, I love to type. I was in the doctor's office in January, in Brookline, at Dr. Solomon's office. And that's why I ended up calling myself Mrs. John Murphy. Because one of the women called up and her name was Ethel Goldstein. "Oh, hi, Ethel," 'cause I got the chart, and she goes, "My name is not Ethel, my name is Mrs. Harold Goldstein!" Like, by calling her Ethel was to demean her, it gave her more value if I called by her husband's name. So I wanted to be Mrs. John Murphy. Not just Kim.

ONE POSSIBLE FUTURE:

ONE POSSIBLE FUTURE:

ACT TWO

U.S. vs. U.K.

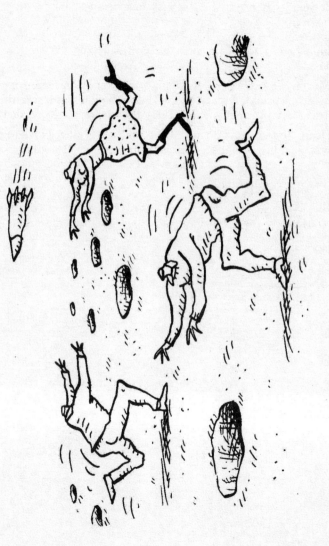

6. C'MON PILGRIM—SIGNING UP WITH 4AD (1987)

Smith's previous work with Throwing Muses had led the Rhode Island act to a record deal with the English label 4AD, known for its dreamy synth-pop. Now Gary Smith was approaching Muses manager Ken Goes to see if they could convince 4AD to release Pixies music as well.

Murphy: It wasn't until they recorded *The Purple Tape* that Ann Holbrook sort of was dusted off for [manager] Ken Goes. They recorded that in March of '87, so Ken probably took over in summer of '87 when they were trying to get Ivo, 4AD to sign them.

Harvard: Ann Holbrook was a very, very sweet girl who worked as a DJ, I'm pretty sure at ERS, the Emerson radio station. She was tremendously well-endowed physically and that drew a certain amount of attention from pigs like me. My read on the situation was she just stepped aside because bigger and better things were happening for them. When they booked time, she was the interface that we had when I was talking to people about the session, and it was Ann who was popping in. I know she was hustling to get them gigs and shows.

Smith: I was trying to get Ken to pay attention because I wasn't a manager. Ken was managing Throwing Muses. Somehow he had taken the tapes that I had made in '85 and gotten them the deal with 4AD, so I figured, well, there's a connection here. I don't know whether 4AD wants a band like the Pixies, they like stuff that wasn't loud rock, they liked the Cocteau Twins. But I thought Ken actually is a manager, maybe he can make this happen. And he sent it to some people and they all said no. At first he didn't want to do it because he just didn't get it. He admits to it now. He didn't really hear it until other people started hearing it.

Hersh: I sat Ken down and made him listen to a Gary tape. I said, "You have to listen to this. They sound a little bit like the Violent Femmes, but they're not derivative"—and I know he didn't know what the Violent Femmes sounded like, anyway. So he just listened to 30 seconds and said, "Eh, this is a Violent Femmes rip-off."

Watts-Russell: The Pixies were so lucky that Throwing Muses were in the same town, for a number of reasons.

Donelly: Our manager became their manager; our producer, Gary, became their producer; our label became their label.

Dennison: Hooking up with Ken Goes was a great move on their part because he already had his connections with 4AD and that is what totally worked out for them. My handful of regrets in life is that I didn't end up managing the Pixies when I had my chance.

Smith: And so then I started giving tapes to people. Ken was one of them. We made, I think, 500 copies, I probably have an invoice somewhere because I file everything. I started sending the tapes around, and the band that I had been in had toured extensively and I had met tons of cool people. Then I sent what they called the G-card, which was the insert of the cassette. They had extra of those printed and used them as postcards, and I just wrote "This is the next big thing" and I sent it to all the people I had met on the road because I kept a very elaborate address book of all the people who let us sleep on their floor, or who we had opened for, or who opened for us.

Watts-Russell: I think I only knew recently that the Pixies actually sent demo tapes out to everyone before I got one.

Deal: I kept my rejection letters. They were from SST, Elektra, everywhere. I was working in an office so I was able to use the mailing system.

Murphy: Yeah, they're like, "No, thank you, we listened, we don't like it." Luckily Gary really, really loved them, because he kept pressuring Ken to give the tape to Ivo, and Ivo really liked it, which was cool.

Hersh: We had signed to 4AD long before we even played with the Pixies. We had been making demos since we were about 15 years old and we had quite the press kit by the time we were 17. I was living in an apartment called the Doghouse in Rhode Island and sending out press kits and demos all day long. But it probably wasn't me that sent stuff to 4AD because I'd never heard of them when Ivo started calling our apartment. Normally, that's not what a label guy would do. I didn't know who he was, Ivo was a weird name, and I assumed he was just some local guy putting on an English accent and pretending to have a record label. Because the girls in my band were really hot, Tanya and Leslie [Langston] were gorgeous, so there were always men calling our apartment. I just figured he was trying to get one of them on the phone and I kept answering. So I'd politely excuse myself and get off the phone and try not to answer it the next time it rang. But he was saying, "Well, I don't sign American bands," so I didn't really have any reason to stay on the phone with him, anyway. And then eventually he called and said, "All right, I'll sign you." I was just like, fine, asshole!

Watts-Russell: The very first connection with the States was enough to put me off for a very long time. It was with Modern English, it had the single "I Melt With You" on it, we licensed that through Sire and had just a dreadful experience. Until that point I had nothing to do with a major label, nothing to do with any other label, it was to do with me, to do with exploring, doing it innocently, and then suddenly I was exposed to the anonymous noncaring mega-corporation, and I loathed it. I was 27, I was old enough to be wiser, but I've always been pretty naive. I got drawn into the business an idealist.

Donelly: Ivo didn't want to sign us originally because he wanted to keep the label English, but he did want to make sure that we were well-placed, so he flew over here and met with labels on our behalf and tried to find somebody, and when he couldn't find anything that he thought was appropriate he just signed us.

Watts-Russell: I heard the Muses demo in the post—99 percent of things I got involved in were from being handed a demo—sent to me from Boston, Ken Goes, I guess. It was very different for the label, an amazing energy and originality. Tanya, all of them, lovely people, they were kind of the trial run for the Pixies in a lot of ways.

This is the one that gets confused with the [first time I heard] Pixies, but I was literally stuck in traffic and I took the Muses tape with me and by the time I got back to 4AD I had listened to it four or five times and I was really excited and I called Ken right then.

Donelly: It is true. I remember always thinking that's sort of a backhanded compliment. I was trapped. Trapped with you! Well, it's like, if you're trapped with something you're going to like it eventually.

Hersh: We were teenagers and we had never really heard of 4AD. They just had the best offer. We were talking to independents and majors and all of the offers at the time were "A gazillion records, we can drop you whenever we want." All I wanted was one record so that we could tour on the back of something, and that was 4AD's deal. And it continues to be 4AD's deal—you just sign for every record you make with them, which is unbelievable. The only problem was we were only available on import in the States. And everyone thought we were English. And all the other bands on 4AD were *extreme* English. Suddenly we realized we were in the company of bands like the Cocteau Twins and Dif Juz—they're all real gauzy and beautiful and ethereal and we just so weren't.

Deal: Goth rock was big back then. 4AD, a lot of it is based on the Goth rock period of time, Bauhaus. There were a lot of Goth rockers who loved Ivo Watts-Russell. Most of the people who went to our shows when we first got out of the State didn't know who we were, they knew we were on 4AD. After the show, people would come up and ask us, "What's Ivo Watts-Russell really like?"

Marc Geiger (Pixies agent; cofounder, Lollapalooza): If you knew Ivo, and you knew his taste, even though I think the label had an ethereal trademark—because the artist Vaughan Oliver was so distinct graphically that it lent itself to sort of the ethereal, beautiful sound of Love and Rockets, the Cocteau Twins—his taste was very pure, but it wasn't genre-specific. Pixies really fit the pureness of it because he was looking for greatness.

Hersh: We were playing like, country-punk, and we were *so* goofy and dorky, so American, that whenever we played a show from then on we were just like, "And the Pixies also have to play." At least put us in a better light. We were playing with bands that we didn't really go with. It was fun to be in Boston and be playing with the Volcano Suns and Dinosaur Jr. and Uzi and the Five, that was great, you'd play with five or six bands a night and no one seems to be headlining. Then we were just buried in noise. But when we were actually headlining a show, it was just confusing if we didn't have a band like the Pixies to play and make us look cooler.

Donelly: The Birthday Party was the only band I'd heard of when we signed to them. And Bauhaus a little, from college radio. But I don't think we really knew how strong their aesthetic was until we realized that we'd messed it up.

Hersh: We were very lonely over there and that's why we were so desperate to get the Pixies to sign with Ken and record with Gary and sign with 4AD, because everybody over in England is English! We involved ourselves with the Pixies just because we were so damn lonely!

Watts-Russell: I think the reason I was in Newport when Ken gave me the Pixies tape was to try to [have a] face to face [conversation with Ken]. Throwing Muses' one-off record got a lot of attention and suddenly Sire was interested in them. I felt like, well, I can't control an American band's career from England. If they want to sign with Sire, that's fair enough, but for God's sake, I knew they wouldn't sign with them in England because we all got on, and fuck it, we were a good label! But they were going to sign to Sire in the rest of the world and I just knew it would be a mistake. Sire/Warner Bros. in Europe is like the pop label, nonsense. So that is why I was over there in America, failing in convincing Ken or the group not to sign to Sire, and out of that I got the Pixies tape.

I guess Ken had picked me up from the airport, and Ken handed me a tape that David Narcizo from the Muses had given him. He had told Ken that he thought he should manage them. Dave really liked it, handed it to Ken, Ken wasn't sure and handed it to me and it all had a positive result, he ended up managing them.

I absolutely adored it from day one, because my day one was marching around New York with it in a Walkman. It was very exciting. It was the obvious things, Joey's guitar playing, and the Spanish aspect to it. Throwing Muses were the first American band that we worked with. The most obvious thing to do next wasn't to go and sign another American band, especially one managed by the same person. And also the "rock'n'roll" thing, I was interested in the label developing in a less definable way. And my girlfriend at the time, Deborah Edgeley, did the press for us and I said, "You know, I really like it but I don't know if this is what I want us to be doing," and she said, "Don't be so fucking stupid. This is brilliant, we have to work with them!"

Kolderie: Ivo jumped right on it, he had some money. That guy started a label and did as good as you can do. He put out some of the most important records of the late twentieth century. A really good instinct for not only what was commercial, but also really good. He's really mellowed a bit; he was a pretty snotty Englishman for a number of years there.

Slade: Ivo was a real crusty English chap. I assume he's mellowed.

Geiger: To this day, I think Ivo is one of the most innovative A&R guys in the world and I wish he would come back to the business. He's intense.

Thompson: They were in England. All I knew was that they were in London, and it sounded cool to me. It sounded exotic to me. We didn't give a hoot. What do we do? "Hey, will you guys work with this guy Albini? He's really cool." Yeah, sure! When do we begin? "Hey, we're going to use our art guy to do the records." Sure! Whatever! Let's go! "Hey, can you re-record 'Gigantic' and 'River Euphrates' as a single?" Yeah, let's go, where's the studio? Sounds good! Europe! Woo-hoo! Let's go!

Harvard: I'm not sure to this day that the Pixies realized just how extraordinarily easy it was for them in relation to what other bands go through to get signed and get established. They came out of the box, they got grandma Gary there, the ultimate one-man support team. He's making calls immediately, and if you think about the road to music business success as something like Westward Ho, the Muses had cut the trail. It was like, they took that famous double play—Tinkers to Evers to Chance—it was Gary to Ken Goes' management to Ivo at 4AD for them.

Watts-Russell: Charles, David, and Joe, I met first. I was in Boston and they were playing and Kim wasn't there because a relative had just died, a brain aneurysm, and she had to go to a funeral somewhere. So the first time I saw the Pixies was without Kim, it was as a trio. And you know, it was good. Even then it was good. Kim is such an important part in the initial impression of the Pixies, though. In those early days, she sang back up on a lot of songs, and her big smiling face on stage is still a sight to behold.

Kolderie: I remember after we did the Pixies record Ivo came to town and wanted to see where we did the recording. He showed up and he was appalled, like, "No, this can't be it." We were like, no, this is where we did it. And he said, "Okay, I've seen enough."

Lovering: Oh, it was unbelievable. But the most amazing part of it was it was so exotic that we're on 4AD. And I didn't know much about 4AD, and I heard about how much of a cult label it was. "Ooh, we're not just on an independent label we're on a British, cool label!"

Watts-Russell: They were friendly, enthusiastic, polite, people who were just genuinely [thrilled] that somebody was going to put their record out. I don't think they knew much about 4AD at all. The only thing I truly remember from my first meeting with three of them was Joey saying—I was flattered to think that he thought I had the power or ability—"All I care about is that you make me famous in the Philippines because the chicks are really pretty." That's probably the most I ever heard Joey really say.

Deal: No, never heard of 'em. Well it wasn't really a deal. It was a one-off. And it was import. It's not like it was actually sold in America. But they did put it out. In vinyl form.

Thompson: Back then they used to call it a "p and d" deal. It's a pressing and distribution deal. You used to record your own record using your own money, and you'd find a little indie rock label somewhere, and you'd get the label to press it up and distribute it, so that's what we did. We recorded a demo with the intention of releasing it as a record. We recorded the demo, they took about half of the material and put it out as a sort of mini-LP.

Watts-Russell: My opinion of the tracks on the original tape was that there was too much that was just not that good, there was a certain smoothness to that recording. I picked eight songs minus "Here Comes Your Man" because I really liked "Here Comes Your Man," but it felt too obviously commercial and I didn't know what we were doing with them. It's not like I was rushing over to America all the time to go, "And here's the Pixies, I think this is quite good I'll go back to see them play." We didn't have that sort of money, so it was just a question of well, look, I'd like to put these eight songs out. I felt that those eight songs were a bang in your face, left you wanting more, and I thought that the recorded versions of the other songs that were on *The Purple Tape* were not that great. And I think it's lucky because the next recording they did, was *Surfer Rosa* with Steve Albini, and he kind of raised the benchmark in terms of the power and rawness that the Pixies could have.

Smith: I was pissed. I thought this collection of 17 songs was special. And that they should all be served up at once because that's how you would get a sense of how colossally important this band was. And then they cut it to bits! They went on to put out the songs on different records, different types of production. That was a lot of their work as it turned out, they mined that material for years. And Ivo, he thought he did the right thing, he wanted it as a teaser, he thought they would do greater things and they did, I suppose. But to my mind, hearing that unadulterated body of work, as pure as it was, as rapid fire as it was, was the most important thing about it. I didn't care what else they did, why didn't they write new songs, do something else—that was the recording that we had made! But they didn't really see it that way, they were just like, "A record deal! Yippee!"

Watts-Russell: As it turns out, it was lucky that I did do that. Imagine if I had not, and we had released *The Purple Tape*—every record thereafter would have been different. It did not take the world long to realize that Charles, once he kind of got through a batch of material, didn't really have any, so he ended up sort of writing it in the studio.

Smith: [During preproduction] I think there were some other songs that we mixed. One is a song called "Watch What You're Doing" which never came out, which I just recently discovered sitting on a shelf in my house. It was composed not by them, but by the fellow from whom Charles had swiped the lyric "Come on, pilgrim, you know He loves you!"—Larry Norman.

Thompson: I discovered Larry Norman's records probably because either I went to a concert and I saw him, or there used to be a music store that I would go to when I was 13 or 14, it was a

Christian bookstore, the Carpenter Bookstore in La Meda, California. In one room they had the books and in another room they had the music store, and they had records and guitars. I had a job at a pharmacy next door, so I would go and hang out there, I bought one of my first guitars there at the religious bookstore. I don't think Larry Norman was necessarily respected by religious people. He's too weird. He had more of a rebellious rock'n'roll kind of an image. He was like Willie Nelson, he'd come out with this beat-up classical guitar, leather jacket, long hair down to his ass, he was really dry and a little bit sarcastic, and he had a lot of humor in his performances. He used to be in a secular band called People, they had a minor hit called "I Love You" in like '66 or '67. He was a little bit goofy and taking the piss out of convention, and when I was 14 I really dug him. I dressed like him, I looked like him, he was my total idol.

Deal: Larry Norman, Why does that sound familiar? Sounds like a guy who's on a TV show. A Christian rocker? Is he the guy who did the *Come on Pilgrim* thing? You know, I might have heard a tape of him once, saw it on TV or something.

Watts-Russell: The title was a sort of perverse, oh I must have just been being cocky, Billy Pilgrim from *Slaughterhouse-Five*, Kurt Vonnegut book and film. Whatever. It was just a suggestion. I would have not been surprised if Charles had said fuck off.

Deal: I didn't sequence it. And Vaughan Oliver did the artwork. That hairy man. I thought that was Vaughan Oliver. And I don't know if it is or not. I mean I don't think it is actually, but he might have been wearing that hair shirt.

Simon Larbalestier (photographer, contributed pictures to all Pixies albums): He was a friend of mine. It had nothing to do with the Pixies. [The cover photograph of the hairy man and the interior sleeve photographs] was a series of work that I was making based on reading the book *The Temptation of St. Anthony* by Gustave Flaubert. There were all sorts of weird imagery within that. And I produced a lot of work which was inspired by that work, of which those two were particular images. Not the fact that there was a hairy man in the book, but there were references like the fish and things like that. It was very much a part of an experimental period for me, created sets, using friends; it was all very slow and controlled. It was probably very hard for that guy to sit under that hot light because I was very slow to do it. So he was very patient. I didn't work a lot with people, I was much more happy with still lives and landscapes. He is still around, I haven't seen him for a number of years.

Kolderie: For us it was a real key, it unlocked a whole career. I was engineering for Gary a lot then and we were trying to land the gig doing the Throwing Muses' first real album for Sire, it was called *House Tornado*. It was going to be their next major label album and it was a big budget, and the label was kind of like, "Well, who are these guys in the commercial laundry warehouse?" and then all of a sudden Ivo put out the Pixies and it was instantly a real big, hip record. And it came out just at the right time where we could point to this and be like, "Well, look we did this!" And they said, "Oh well, that's great, sure you can do the Throwing Muses."

Watts-Russell: It was an interesting time for 4AD. It was kind of the end of the best period, the purest period, and right before I said let's put this record out we were experiencing this absurd rocket success of this single by M/A/R/R/S, the "Pump Up the Volume" thing.

Geiger: The Pixies were a baby band out of Boston, they had a really nice guy agent named Bob Vlautin for a minute, and as things started to heat up I got a call one day from their manager Ken Goes saying, "We need a more powerful [representative]. This band's happening, will you get into it?" I was already a huge fan, this is just after *Come on Pilgrim* was released. And I said absolutely. He got recommended to me because I did every single band on 4AD. I was a fan and I went over when I was a young agent and spent a lot of time with Ivo. Everybody from The The and Burning Blue Soul to Love and Rockets, I did a lot of Beggars stuff too, Dead Can Dance, Cocteaus—I was doing them all, anyway.

Watts-Russell: Within a matter of six months they got to make another record. If people hadn't responded to the record, I suppose relationships could have soured fast. They were touring their asses off in front of ecstatic crowds after the first record.

NME review by Jack Barron, October 1987: These tales of darklands and deeds are illuminated by smiling tunes veined with quicksilver flashes of guitar. It's this sleight-of-hand, together with a morbid humour which surfaces slowly upon repeated plays, that makes Pixies so addictive...Black Francis is currently without shelter. His biggest fear, as he tells an ardent liberal intent on seducing him, is losing his penis to a horrible disease. Feel free to give him room on your record player, but keep your toilet locked, and whatever you do don't throw water over him. You won't live to regret it.

Reflex magazine review by Jay Blotcher, May 1988: *Come on Pilgrim* offered twisted rockers and ballads, guitar-scarred and coddled, celebrating incest and animals and sex so fine (with an elevator operator). They're charged with a sound as rewarding as scab-picking was when you were a kid. Gleefully reckless. Good nasty fun. The Pixies have the eerie depth of old souls, yet their average age of 22 explains their eagerness to offend, to aurally jar and generally rock people off their mental axis.

Jon Dolan (senior associate editor, *Spin* magazine): *Come on Pilgrim* has this sense of playful, ruined teen dementia. Francis' vocal on "Caribou" is the best punk rock physical comedy since Johnny Rotten. On "The Holiday Song" you get this sense of joy before the void. The big thing about that record (and *Surfer Rosa*) was that Pixies were daringly fusing two diametrically opposed underground rock impulses: American indie-noise and British art-Goth. In the '80s, the whole point of American indie-rock was to be funnier, punkier, more irreverent, noisier, more rocking in opposition to all the fey eyeliner foppery coming out of England. There was some bitterness since American bands deemed themselves too raw to get on the radio or MTV, meanwhile Goth and synth pop were more successful. But there was also a sense of being confrontationally unpretentious. Pixies had the angry mid-American noise thing, the goofy self-loathing of a Paul Westerberg, the poetic pop sense of a Hüsker Dü, but they also dabbled in artistic impulses that were more in line with Brit art sensibilities. This really forecast a cross-pollination that would become alternative.

Courtney Love (former Hole lead singer/guitarist; musician): Fucking are you kidding? *Come on Pilgrim*, I heard it and I was in Minneapolis and I was a scenester and it was all Sonic Youth, Evol, and Richard Kern pictures, Pussy Galore, and all of a sudden there's a pop record—a pop record that is not only approved, but classic. And it was a life saver. I can do that. Yay. Because otherwise, I was surrounded by performance art, frankly.

Watts-Russell: I never experienced anything that immediate, it went so Goddamn fast, so positive. *Come on Pilgrim* got four star reviews everywhere.

Ted Mico (former editor, *Melody Maker*): I was a friend of Ivo's and I was a huge fan of a great deal of what was on 4AD. I heard a demo and thought, "Oh my lord, yes," and the demo ended up on *Come on Pilgrim*. So then Chris Roberts from the *Melody Maker* went off and did the first interview. The Pixies were fascinating people. I remember reading the interview and thinking, "These guys are really strange," and then we looked at their pictures. You sell music magazines to a certain extent on glamour, definitive looks, something that's trenchant and eye-catching and pops off the stands, and when we got the pictures of the Pixies they were not exactly in that mold. In fact, they broke the mold. I remember having a massive row with the editor over it. There was a faction of the paper that thought it'd be a disaster to have people who look like plasterers on a cover, and then there were those who thought this was the thing that had to happen. And of course it happened, everybody started to get interested. One of the first things I remember reading about Kim was in the Chris Roberts interview—she gave some profound comment, and then she had to leave and Chris said, "What are you going to do now?" and she said, "First I'm going to piss like a racehorse, then I'm going to dance like a black woman." And really, honestly, that was a quintessential Kim Deal quote.

Dennison: When the record came out and it was so intense for everybody, and all of a sudden everyone was like, huh? They were opening up shows two months ago. They were doing something really special that only a few people were hearing at the time.

Kolderie: I remember that "The Holiday Song" started getting played in discos, no kidding. You could dance to it. I mean, it wouldn't make it these days on the dance floor, but they were playing it in dance clubs. They were doing things people just had not seen—the quiet to loud cocktail, Joey would go up there and kick the shit out of his guitar, huge reverb explosions—they came at you. Charles was screaming at you. We went down to the Palladium after the record came out and they were blasting it out of the speakers on the dance floor. And "Isla de Encanta" was picked up and put into the movie *Married to the Mob*. Within a few weeks all this stuff was happening. It just seemed to get to the culture really fast.

John Flansburgh (They Might Be Giants cofounder/singer/guitarist): They opened for They Might Be Giants at the crummiest of clubs in Boston, in Jamaica Plain at Green Street, and I remember it well. They definitely blew us away, they were just absolutely transcendent. I guess they had just signed the deal with 4AD, and they were very excited about that. They vibrated at a completely different frequency than any other band, they just were at this velocity that was just different than any other band that I had experienced. The quality of the songwriting and the general kind of ultra-vivid approach that they had was so immediate and grabby.

Thompson: We went on our first tour with the record not even being released in this country, in the United States. So we went to West Virginia.

Deal: We really didn't have a manager at that moment. But we got a tour booked. So we rented a cargo van, you know, no seats, and David ingeniously found a way where we could push all our cargo to the back. See the problem with cargo vans is that once you put your cargo in, there's no place to sit. So David built a plywood thing and was able to brace it in so we could actually sit with the gear behind us on the floor of the cargo van.

Lovering: We rented a van, and I put a board across the back seats and put a mattress in there. Actually, the equipment went in, too. There was nowhere to sit in the back. You could have a person driving, a person sitting there, and you'd just lie on an air mattress in the back.

Deal: We had a CD player. Charles' wife gave it to him for a present, we brought it in the van on the first tour. I was just like, "Wow, I heard about these." I remember thinking, "Wow, it skips a lot" because it didn't have the shock thing going on yet. I still don't like CDs. I think they sound funny—thin and weird.

Lovering: We would drive around, we did little tours down to, maybe North Carolina, something like that.

Deal: Well we had played a place in New York, the name of the place was the address of the place. New York City in '87: It was fucking bleak, man. It was black, none of the street lights worked, it was desolate. I would see down this dark block, and it was a line of people with their backs facing the street and their fronts facing the building, with sparks alight, it was all the people trying to shield the wind so they could light up their pipe. I mean, lined up, like 20 people in a row. No cops around, nothin'. It was really crazy. It was wild.

Lovering: I remember the first time we played New York. We stayed in the cheapest hotels. And we learned all the little ploys. You know, you do a gig, if it's a long travel day you'll leave after the show, you'll drive, you'll get to the next hotel early. Not early in the morning, I mean, four o'clock in the morning or something like that. You walk in, say, "I got here really early, is it possible I could check in right now?" So you still have that morning to sleep, you do your gig and you still have that one for that amount of day. And that used to work frequently. We'd also go in and just get one room, and split the bed—split it off and have the box [spring], and then the mattress.

Deal: It was exciting going to New York. 'Cause I remember coming over the bridge—I forgot which bridge it was, 'cause we were coming from Boston—it was the first time we heard the stuff off *Come on Pilgrim* on the radio, I think it was "Isla de Encanta," when we were on the bridge to New York City to play our show. That was exciting, On the college station. We didn't get played on any real radio. But we didn't all go, "Oh, cheers, everybody" we were just like, "Wow!" [*Come on Pilgrim*] was import only. And we played like North Carolina, I remember, Chapel Hill. I think we hit some place in Virginia. People used to come up, when anybody came up at all, and they'd say, "So what's Ivo really like?" Nothing about the music or anything like that. We had 4AD fanatics at our show.

Santiago: We just played the club, drank at the club, and went to the hotel. I don't think we went to any parties at all.

Deal: Charles didn't really drink a lot. Joe went out a lot, but he was always girl hunting. That's fine, 'cause I'm there for the beer, you know. It's cool. I think he was probably bringing me so he gets a little recognition. Just to be there if he needed it. "I'll do my best,

Joe." Meanwhile I'd be at the bar. If it's going well for him, I probably wouldn't see him. If it wasn't going well, he'd probably drink a beer with me. David didn't socialize a lot like that, Joe went out more. And if me and Joe walked into the bar together it might look like we're hooked up, for the people who didn't know that we weren't or something, so that had to be dealt with. We didn't really walk in separately, we just didn't walk in too close together.

7. A GIGANTIC STEP FORWARD—*SURFER ROSA* (1988)

Six months after *Come on Pilgrim* was released Pixies were back in the studio, this time with a polarizing young engineer from Chicago named Steve Albini chosen by 4AD. Pixies knew pretty much nothing about Albini when Watts-Russell recommended him for their first proper album, *Surfer Rosa*.

Deal: Ivo suggested we go into the studio with this engineer called Steve Albini. And I had heard Big Black, "Heartbeat," the Wire cover they do, but that's all I had heard from them. But it sounded cool, so, okay. So Albini came out and we recorded *Surfer Rosa* in 11 days, in Boston, at a place called Q Division. I think it was 11 days. Maybe it was nine days. I don't know. Was it 16 tracks? I don't know, it could have been 16 tracks. . .

Smith: They were booked to do *Surfer Rosa* with Albini in our studio and I was trying to not show my tears and just be the good guy who wanted the best thing for the band. They decided to go elsewhere because I didn't want to give them some super-friendly deal. I wanted to give them our standard studio rate because I had done the other one for almost nothing and they had a record deal! It's one thing to give somebody a good deal because they're poor and they're talented, it's another thing entirely when they have the means and they don't want to spend it. So that led to a brouhaha between Ken and I, and Ken saying, "I just can't have them in there with bad vibes or that kind of an attitude" or something, and then he decided to pull the project. Then I came into the studio one day and Paul was speaking in whispers.

Kolderie: I was just the engineer, I wasn't the producer of *Come on Pilgrim*, Gary was. Everybody was pally-pally and we agreed to do the record on spec, and then Gary turned around and said, "Look, I want a piece of this. I produced the records for free, I paid for the recording sessions myself, and I want royalties." And the Pixies, especially Kim, had a bad attitude about it. I don't want to say too much because it wasn't my business at the time, but things got kinda ugly. Gary actually turned them onto the Throwing Muses' manager at the time, who still manages Charles. So you think the guy would owe Gary a favor. But the negotiations to get Gary points on that first record got very ugly and Kim became sort of alienated from Gary. I've never made any money off that Pixies record. I made $200 for making it.

Smith: So it was all kind of blowing up in my face and I was the asshole who didn't want to give them the deal. Had I given them the deal the second record would have been made at Fort Apache, but instead they went to Q Division, which was another studio in town. So off they went. They didn't take Paul with them, they used some engineer from Q, I suppose, and Albini.

Watts-Russell: The suggestion of Albini to work with the Pixies was from someone who worked for me at 4AD. Just a guy at the warehouse, Colin Wallace, who now doesn't work in the warehouse—he now manages Liz Fraser of Cocteau Twins and works for Rough Trade. So that came from him at 4AD and Gil [Norton] came from me. Colin said, "You should get Steve Albini to do it. The Big Black records sound great." And that was that, really.

Steve Albini (recording engineer; former singer/guitarist for Big Black, Rapeman, and Shellac): Their English record label had approached me about working on their first album for 4AD. Ivo sent me a copy of their cassette. *Come on Pilgrim* had not yet been released, but their cassette was what the songs on *Come on Pilgrim* were culled from. The songs that particularly impressed me were "Caribou'" and "Down to the Well," which was a song that I don't believe ever made it onto a proper record but it had kind of a ghostly quality to it.

Basically, their manager Ken Goes, who had been communicating with me a little bit and coordinating the American side of the relationship, had me come down to a dinner party, I guess you'd call it a cocktail hour, at David's house in Boston and that's where I met the band and we talked about how they wanted to go about making the record. And we were in the studio the next day. We had about ten days or two weeks booked in the studio and to be honest, we didn't need all that time. We could've knocked that record out in a week, in four or five days even, if we were pushing it. But because there was time available we ended up goofing around a lot. We ended up trying more experimental stuff basically to kill time or to see if anything good materialized. This was one of the first times that I'd actually been sort of hired to go elsewhere to be in charge of a session for strangers. I guess that's the key—it was for strangers. And I probably went a little bit overboard in terms of taking charge. I think I got paid something like 1,000 bucks or 1,500 bucks to do that record.

I was the guy that Ivo thought they should work with, and probably their manager had heard my name. Honestly, I think what it boils down to is they wanted to do this record, 4AD said, "We'll do the record, why don't you work with this guy Steve," and at that point if Ivo had said, "Why don't you saw off one of your legs and give it to me?" their manager would've said, "Well, okay, I'll be right there." Because they weren't operating from a position of popularity at that point. They were some unknown band from Boston, right? And they weren't really in a position to say no to these professionals who were acting on their behalf. So if things had come out differently they could have said yes to something that would've fucked them really hard. And as it turns out, Ivo is a good guy and he had their best interest at heart and I was capable of helping them make a good record. But neither one of those things was a given at that point. And I think their blind trust in their manager and their manager's dumb luck put them in that position.

Lovering: It was just the next step for us. Ivo suggested Steve Albini, and we went into an even better studio, it just kept escalating. The progression of the songs, how we went from *Come on Pilgrim* to this new batch of songs—I was really proud of those.

Kolderie: Albini wasn't as big a name as he is now. But it seemed like a good choice and as I was going to be the engineer, Albini called me and we talked for a couple of hours about, "I like this, what kind of gear do you have, what do I need to bring with me when I come out there." But then Ken and Gary had the big falling out over the price and somebody told somebody to go fuck themselves and all of a sudden it was like, "Pixies are not coming in." Then Albini called me and said, "Ah man, I guess we are not coming in, can you give me a recommendation of a good sounding room in Boston?" So I recommended Q Division. And I'm glad I did because they would have never gone there if I had not recommended it, but the sound of that record had a lot to do with where they were and Albini's ability to use it, of course. So I didn't get the record because of the falling out, and I was the house engineer at the Fort so there was no way I was going to go somewhere else. In fact Gary almost killed me for the suggestion, he thought I was scheming to get the project. I had nothing to do with it. But I remember going in for the first playback of the recording and being pretty amazed.

John Lupner (studio assistant, *Surfer Rosa*; cofounder, Q Division): Q Division started in 1986. It was only a couple of years old, and at that point very few people had come from out of town to record with us. It was mostly locals. In a lot of ways our studio wasn't geared towards outside producers and bands. I mention it because I was trying to be helpful to Albini, I tried to give him some advice, and I think I must have stepped over the line. Albini was trying to get a guitar sound, and I think he was looking for a way to run the line to the little amp room. He was asking studio specific advice, and then I guess I crossed the line by asking if it would sound better if he turned up the amp a little, or used this or that mic—it seemed in the same terms to his question, but I guess it wasn't. So he put me in my place, and I was kicked out of the session. I spent the second half of the sessions outside the doorway, waiting in case he did need anything.

Kolderie: Q Division didn't really understand who the Pixies were, they didn't really get it. When I sent the job to them for *Surfer Rosa* I told them that these guys were gonna be big. They didn't understand, and they didn't know who Albini was or anything like that.

Watts-Russell: I don't know if they would have worked with Steve Albini again, but I know Kim swears by him, their personalities seem to really click. He's so good at what he does. It's just ridiculous, his vision for recording naturally is just quite extraordinary, and his ability to record guitars out of fade so you get this extreme left and right pan if you really want your guitar to sound like it's coming out of one speaker. He didn't then want to be credited as a producer. I still think that's his approach, he sees himself as an engineer and as an engineer he is a genius. Our working relationship was always incredibly straightforward. He is the ideal man to hire to work with a band. He tells you how long it's going to take, how much he is going to charge you, and he does it. The albums didn't cost very much money at all. *Surfer Rosa* was ridiculously cheap.

Murphy: Kim worked with him two more times. She liked him. There was a point where he was a big asshole. He's very opinionated, I mean you listen to the recordings, you can kind of tell he's going to be a little over the top. At the time, there was an anchorperson who shot themselves in the head on live TV. As soon as it happened they cut the feed, but Albini goes, "I have the videotape, the cameras kept rolling, I have the whole thing." He's this little skinny guy!

Deal: I picked up Albini and would give him a ride to the studio because I had a car and Joe and Charles didn't have a car. David did but he was coming down from Burlington.

Lupner: Black Francis was wearing some white overalls, I remember, and Kim was wearing jeans and boots. They struck me as a bunch of kids from Amherst, super unaffected, mellow and friendly. It felt like the band vibe was one thing and the producer vibe was completely different, almost comically so. Steve was so hard-edged and the band came across as very soft.

Kolderie: Steve Albini used to really like to fuck with [the studio]. They would stay 'til two or three in the morning and then he would just like leave, and leave all the doors open, lights on, and not lock anything. It really freaked them out.

Lupner: Steve had this big Rapeman poster up, that was his infamous band. We had different sessions in the day and the evening. So this poster was up and the day client was kind of offended by that, and he got pretty bummed out that they ripped it down.

Kolderie: He was a very angry person. He's just one of these guys, this little, short, skinny guy. He wore big boots and tattoos and shaved his head and he was pissed. He never did anything bad to me, if you could relate to him on a technical level he was fine. He was just someone who has a lot of anger. He was very smart, very opinionated. I don't blame him, I mean in a lot of ways I guess the Pixies kind of were pussies. I try not to judge my clients. And Steve at the time was kinda living a hardcore credo, what was what he considered artistically relevant and important. And the Pixies to him were probably the farthest extreme that he could make himself do. I mean, you've heard Big Black records, right? That's the music he makes from his soul. So "Here Comes Your Man"—well, it's aways over to that aisle in the store.

Albini: I think in their earliest stages they were still trying to discern *how* they wanted to play music rather than trying to do it well. I think they were still sort of getting their aesthetic together and it was more scattershot. After a while, after their first couple of albums, there started to be a discernible Pixies style and sound—like there was a degree of density and there was a degree of complexity and there was a kind of a loping verse and then the shouting part. That hadn't really formed yet.

I respect them and I certainly have very high regard for Kim as a singer and I think Charles is a good guy. I have to say, their music never really spoke to me. I never really liked their music in the way that I liked my favorite bands' music—like the Jesus Lizard, Television, Public Image, the Sex Pistols, the Ramones, Suicide, Kraftwerk—unique and brilliant bands that I loved, I never really got that level of interest with the Pixies. It's awkward for me to say it because I feel like in some way I'm peeing on their birthday cake here. I do genuinely like and respect the people in that band. I think David Lovering is a great drummer. I think Joey is an innovative guitar player. I think Kim is probably the best singer *ever* and I think Charlie is a talented and unique guy. But the things that I like about that band, it's not really the music.

Lupner: I sort of felt like there was a real difference in the vibe of the band and Steve recording them. At the time I remember them being very mellow, and Steve was very sharp and sarcastic. I think that from a musical point they were together, but from a sense of humor point. . .One of the things I really remember because it makes it onto the record was the whole "You fucking die thing."

He had us running tape from the beginning, on a quarter-inch two-track, and anytime they were all out in the main room he wanted to be running tape to get snippets to use between songs. It was a concept he was going for to get some studio banter. Basically, what happened was that Black Francis said, "You fucking die," and then Steve knows perfectly well what's going on, but he's kinda playing them in a way by going on the studio mic and being like, "What did you just say to me?" acting like he is being called out, and then Black Francis is totally backing off and being like, "No, no, I was talking to Kim," kind of explaining, you know, she said this and I said that.

Murphy: That was just Kim going out to smoke a butt or something, and she was saying, "I'll be right back," and then just before she left the studio she said, "If anybody touches my stuff"—which is from that movie *Stripes*—"I'll kill ya." And then Charles starts saying, "I'll kill you, you fucking die, if anybody touches my stuff." And then Albini thought he was mad at her, and said, "What's going on?" Charles goes, "Nothing," he tries to explain it. That's why you only hear Charles' end of it, because Albini's talking in the mic back to him, saying, "What are you talking about?" He goes, "Nothing, I was just goofing with Kim," he goes, "Well, what'd you say that for?" and he goes, "You know, I was just finishing her part for her." That's how it worked out. You just don't hear the Steve part of it because it's a one-way conversation because Charles is the only one being recorded. Kim's gone, she left the room.

James Iha (former Smashing Pumpkins guitarist; A Perfect Circle guitarist; musician): I also love those weird snippets on *Surfer Rosa*, the like, "Oh my God!" "All I know. . . all I know is that." Those little stories are so charming but fucked up. It's so irreverent that they would just put those on a record. But it's totally genius because you kind of get their personality besides the music.

Albini: It's on their record forever so I think now they are obliged to say that they're okay with it, but I honestly don't know that that idea would've ever come up if I hadn't done it. There are times when things like that are revealing and entertaining and I kind of felt it was a bit gimmicky on this record.

Lovering: Steve does kind of that Led Zeppelin-y thing by miking the room. You mike all the instrumentation but you have room mics up also. And that gives it a live feel to it. And then you use metal picks, and that gives it the edge. That was kind of his little thing that he did—ambience.

Deal: I think he desires, when he engineers a session, to engineer a band that's playing, and to mike the live performance of that recording, and record the live performance. Not poorly. Have isolation, if it needs to happen.

Lupner: Steve was very picky of how he set up drum mics and he used unusual miking techniques, the way he recorded the room. It's called mid/side, or MS. It's a way of setting up stereo mics in a room to be very realistic. When that record comes on, I often recognize the room more then the song. I worked in that room for 15 years, it has a sound, and that was the sound Steve captured on the album: completely huge but not in a corporate rock huge way, in a "your own house" way. Steve was much more interested in head room than noise. He printed his levels real low. I think it was because he had a good ear for when things were distorting even the tiniest bit. He was interested in a certain kind of clarity. It predates a lot of records in terms of, it's not in any way a lo-fi record because it's so well recorded, but then again it's not conventionally recorded in any way.

Murphy: *Surfer Rosa* I was there a lot. I remember them taking the amps down to the bathroom so they could record the large, large sound for "Gigantic." Albini didn't like the studio sound so they took all the Marshalls and all the cables and they brought them down to this bathroom which was completely made out of cement, and that's where that big echoey sound comes out of it. He didn't want to use studio echo, he wanted to use real echo.

Lupner: There was this bathroom in the back, it was the kind of room that was all cement. There was echo everywhere, we were in a factory building and it was this giant urinal for like, a hundred guys, and we carted a drum kit in there. I can remember there was some definite funniness going on in there, they were playing around, talking into a super reverby chamber. I'm 23 and the guy who is representing Q Division late at night, and these guys are making all this noise in a part of the building that was near the neighbors. Screaming into the mic in the bathroom, "I am the caveman!" So I sweated that. I think that the vocal for "Where Is My Mind?" came from that bathroom, the "Whooooo."

Albini: There was a degree of reserve that everybody carried. Like, Kim has a bouncy personality. She always seems to be having a great time. I don't know if she was or not, but she was constantly smiling and constantly seemed to be having a good time. Joey and David seemed to be having a good time, but I don't know what they would've looked like or sounded like had they been having a terrible time. And, Charles, I could tell was really nervous. I got the feeling that he was also kind of enjoying not just the attention, but also the experience. It seemed, at that point, that they were all committed to the band as a project and that they were all having a good time.

Probably the first time I realized I had anything in common with Charles was he and I both had an affection for this early Christian rock dude named Larry Norman, who I'd been exposed to by this Jesus freak friend of mine when I was in high school. There's a song of Larry Norman's that uses that line "Come on pilgrim" as a sort of a call to Jesus. I recognized it and I asked him about it. It was interesting to run into somebody else who had recognized this guy as an interesting character.

Murphy: In the end of "Where Is My Mind?" the tape runs out. That's why it ends abruptly. The tape actually ran out, and then they extended Kim's vocal past it. The tape started to go *click click click* and they went, "Well, we got most of it."

Lupner: I remember "Gigantic" was recorded through a mic that I never think of as a vocal mic. It was a Sennheiser 421, it has a knob on it for music or speech, and I never even think of that knob except, "Why does this sound so bad—oh, someone accidentally rolled it over to speech"—because it basically pulls out all the low ends. And that's the sound of the vocals in "Gigantic." It was a very weird choice and I would have never thought of it. It was one of the cheapest mics in the studio. It gives it that super intimate quality. I think that the field hockey player story on the album was the story of what "Gigantic" was about. "He was into field hockey players...it was so hush-hush, they were so quiet about it and then the next thing you know..." She was talking about how all the field hockey players were enamored with this guy.

Jim Suptic (The Get Up Kids guitarist): I've heard "Gigantic" is about a penis. I don't know if that story is true, but I like it more if it is. I heard it was about Kim Deal's boyfriend's penis at the time.

Watts-Russell: It was a brilliant three-way marriage: Simon Larbalestier, Vaughan Oliver, Charles, and of course the lyrics. It started with *Gigantic* the EP. Simon's child on the floorboards, and on the other side this glove. I was like, "Simon, why is there a glove on it?" and Simon was like, "Well, the lyrics. . . Gigantic, a big, big glove."

Larbalestier: The baby and the glove, the *Gigantic* EP was one of my favorites. Having a picture of a baby next to a glove and the use of space in the image as the cover of an album set up at Virgin Records among all the other images of the day was really something. He was the baby of a friend that worked at 4AD, simply because it was not easy to get baby models. And I photographed him at my house on my floor and I took eight shots. I was on a step ladder above him. It took about eight minutes. I think people think that the baby was screaming. I think that was the way it was printed, in truth he was eating a piece of bread and laughing. Me and Vaughan were there, and the nanny. It was a fairly uncomfortable experience.

Murphy: I can tell you the "Gigantic" story. Charles came up with the riff but he wasn't really sure what the lyrics were going to be, so he goes, "Eh, well, Kim, why don't you take a shot at it. The only thing I know is that I want to call it 'Gigantic,'" and she says, "Fine." So she comes home with it and she's playing it on the guitar and I said, "Gigantic, okay, maybe it's about a big mall." She goes, "Okay, let's try that for a while," and I'm like, "The mall, the mall, let's have a ball." So I wrote that. It changed to "Hey Paul," because it had to rhyme. And then, a couple of days later she had fixated on this Sissy Spacek movie [*Crimes of the Heart*] about this farm worker, I think he's a black guy, and Sissy Spacek and this farm worker get together—so that's what it's about. An illicit love affair. I came up with the "Let's have a ball," but my friend John Draper, he came up with "Big black mess, hunk of love." He was just writing random things down. She was like, "Help me come up with words," and he wrote down these words and she got them into the song. He was just a friend of mine, was over, hanging out. I think Charles liked it a lot. I don't think they changed anything.

Dolan: "Gigantic" is based almost entirely on a Kim Deal bassline, which is plodding yet cute, ominous but somehow also playful.

The drums sound like they're being played in an airplane hanger, the guitars scrape as tunefully as anything this side of Hüsker Dü. Deal's vocals are close-up and intimate, like she really is letting you in on a sexy secret.

Deal: You know, if you wanted to go in there and say I want a really strong vocal performance so I'm gonna have to meticulously overdub my vocals five times and make sure that all my *s*'s come together—no, that's not gonna happen. Albini's not gonna do that. But you know, he doesn't have to. He's not a producer, he's an engineer. He'll engineer.

Murphy: I respect Albini from a lot of degrees. He never wanted to be called a producer, which is kind of interesting, because he didn't want to think that he was putting his stamp on their music, although he did come up with a lot of the studio tricks. On "Cactus" you can hear them spelling *Pixies* in the break, which T.Rex did in one of their songs, "T - R - E - X," and they were copying it. I was against it, I was like, "No way I'm not doing it," because that's so trite. And I'm the only one who didn't do it. Steve went along with it and liked it. So I'm the only one that never got on the records, oh well. Anybody that was in the studio could have gone in there and done it.

And "Brick Is Red" actually has a verse that they never recorded. You know the first part is instrumental, well, "Brick is red" is the first lyric of the song, it's really, "Brick is red, and Jimmy's dead," I have it on the original.

Albini: I ended up doing a number of experimental edits to bring different instruments in at different times, that kind of stuff. "Vamos" had already been released on their first record and I think they were interested in distinguishing the version that they were recording from that version, so they played the instrumental portion for a really long time, then Joey played a number of crazy little guitar solo fragments and then those were edited together on quarter-inch tape. Some of the fragments were put in backwards, some of them were put in forwards. And then that was played over the multi-track as a guitar solo. So, rather than him playing a crazy guitar solo he sort of *assembled* a crazy guitar solo on tape. That's the sort of thing that I'm sure they wouldn't have done if I hadn't been there saying, "Yeah, well we could do that. Why don't we try that?"[4]

Kolderie: The Pixies' story is a really good example of something that has been proven time and time again: that you do your best work when you don't know you're doing it. What you need to do, and what Gary was totally right about from the beginning, is to get into this zone and you really don't know what you're doing, you have got to not think about what you're doing. The Pixies were a situation that was born out of complete freedom and a healthy lack of self-censorship.

Lupner: Albini was going to mix *Surfer Rosa* somewhere else, and he was unhappy there with it, so he came back and mixed it at Q.

Deal: So then we finished the record and turned it in, and again, it was import only, it was a one-off, and Vaughan Oliver put the lady on there, the flamenco lady, and then they came over, Vaughan, and Ivo, and Deborah Edgeley and maybe [music critic] Simon Reynolds, and I thought it was so cool.

The cover of *Surfer Rosa* is a photo of a topless flamenco dancer standing against a wall that's adorned with a crucifix and a slightly torn poster. For the second time, there are no photographs of the band members on the liner notes, there are no lyrics printed in the sleeve, and Steve Albini's name doesn't even appear anywhere on the record.

Watts-Russell: Again, the title is a lyric within the record ("Besando, chichando con Surfer Rosa Oh my golly! Oh my golly!"), following the pattern of the first one.

Larbalestier: The woman in the picture for *Surfer Rosa* was a friend of a friend. We built the set ourselves because we couldn't find the atmosphere we wanted naturally. That came from Charles, the fact that he wrote songs in his dad's bar, that idea kicked off from that. His dad ran a topless Spanish bar and we sort of loaded that with all the Catholicism. The fish was a direct reference to the hairy man before. The fact that it actually had a wave in the corner was simply a result of the chemical reaction on the Polaroid. It just happened to work nicely with what we were doing. I had been photographing a lot of churches and I was interested in Catholicism and all those things, it fit perfectly—all the contradictions involved. We shot it in the pub opposite the 4AD offices. It was one of the few places that actually had a raised stage. We cast around quite a lot but I don't think that one, many people were Spanish, two, many people could do flamenco dancing, and three, were prepared to be top-less—certainly not with the budget we had going. It was a day's shoot. Must have made 30, 40 negs, one after the other. The atmosphere was pretty charged. There were quite a number of people involved in it so it was more of a sort of theatrical thing. All the other stuff was done entirely on my own. I don't like people being around. It was more of an event that Vaughan was there, Chris [Bigg, his 4AD colleague] was there, and we had an artist. Lots of people from 4AD around. The band was always in the States, they were never there.

The poster with Spanish writing on it—at that time not only was I making photographs but I was also doing a lot of collage work and we built that set almost in the way I built a collage. We just built it in front of a camera so we added posters and area light, and we burned wood or dirtied plaster to create a set around the lens. It wasn't even a room, it was a corner and we basically built that. Everything was given a degree of significance, the broken guitar, the fish, the poster, the cross, it all had an element of meaning in it. What we were after was atmosphere and decay.

Dolan: *Surfer Rosa* blares and stings but it's also pretty and fun to sing along to. Lovering's snare drum is huge and commanding, Led Zeppelin-style. Charles and Kim have to fight through this noise, which makes their songs about violence, Catholic self-hate, and weird love seem that much more alien. Santiago plays surf guitar like a Goth, which became a huge influence on Nirvana a few years later.

Watts-Russell: I remember when I first heard *Surfer Rosa* thinking, "I didn't know the Pixies could sound like the Fall." That was my immediate reaction, in other words, incredibly raw.

Smith: I loved it. I thought it was fantastic, I was really happy that they had made such a forceful, aggressive record. In fact, I thought *Doolittle* was an amazing record, I loved all the records, I loved their music, didn't matter who was making it. That was one of those things where I had been in a band, I felt it important to move from producer to producer so you could stay fresh and have new ideas. I didn't feel these people owed me anything.

Kolderie: I remember Albini was really nasty, not to me, but there were all these people eagerly awaiting to hear it, and he strung up the tape recorder and was like, "All right, lets hear the *hits*!" and then he played "Gigantic." I remember standing next to him and being like, "Wow, sounds real good!" and he was like, "Ah, fuck you." By the end of that record he was so thoroughly sick of them it was almost like a Zen thing. I mean he hated the Pixies, he thought they were such pussies and well, he ended up making their best record.

Mascis: I think he was a little embarrassed by it at that point. He didn't seem too psyched at the time. I always thought the one Steve Albini did sounded way better than all the other ones. I didn't understand why they had Gil Norton produce everything because I never thought it sounded that great.

Steve Albini, writing in FORCED EXPOSURE fanzine #17, 1991: "The Pixies' *Surfer Rosa* LP: A patchwork pinch loaf from a band who at their top dollar best are blandly entertaining college rock. Their willingness to be "guided" by their manager, their record company and their producers is unparalleled. Never have I seen four cows more anxious to be led around by their nose rings. Except that I got to rewrite their songs with a razorblade, thought the drums sounded nice, and managed to get Nate The Impaler on the LP as a cameo. I remember nothing about this album, although I thought it was pretty good at the time. During the recording, a sibling of the sexual partner of a Pixie was lounging around making little fuck me noises, so I took her home and got stiffed. Had to retreat to Byron's "den of satisfaction" and run a batch off by hand. I seem to remember that their Philipino [sic] guitar player was pro-Marcos, but I could be wrong. The album took about a week, maybe two all told. Fee: $1,500.[5]

Watts-Russell: You kind of expect it from him; you don't really take it seriously. If the record had not been as popular and successful as it was, then he would have never had cause to say that.

Santiago: He was two-faced, you know. He's confusing. I would mention him to Charles, he was a great guy, but then later on all these things he said—where did that come from? I thought he was getting along with us.

Walsh: Kind of a dick. I guess I don't really need to elaborate.

Gilbert: I wasn't there, but I imagine there were times when they definitely probably didn't get along, or it just wasn't working. You know, they only did one album with him, and then they did three with Gil Norton.

Albini: I later said some unflattering things about the band in a fanzine and to this day I regret having done it.[6] I think making that Pixies record was one of the formative experiences of my professional attitude and I think I indulged a selfish part of my personality during the making of that record. I don't think that I regarded the band as significantly as I should have. And I felt at the time like I was making a better record for the band. I recognize now that what I was doing was actually warping their record to suit myself. And I think that having gone through that experience and recognize that impulse in myself I've been able to weed it out a little better. Which means that I've gotten better over time at doing things in the band's best interest rather than doing things to amuse myself. And being perfectly frank, there were things that I did while making that record that I did to amuse myself and I don't think it speaks well of me. I think that portrays a weak part of my personality at the time. So I don't know how much they liked their record when it was all over with. And I had limited interaction with them afterwards, partly because I behaved like an ass.

Lupner: If Steve perceived you as the person standing between what he wanted and where he was, he would just kind of tear you a new one. But once that would be all cleared up and he had what he wanted he would just move on and let it go.

Kolderie: But again, I have nothing but respect for Steve, he is a consummate professional and he did an amazing job and I would have loved to make that record with him.

NME **review by Mark Sinker, March 1988:** "Gigantic" sounds like Rickie Lee Jones guesting with Pere Ubu to me. They writhe through the Band and Crazy Horse and (especially) the Fall as if they can hear some kind of history which links them all. They do more than sound like people who went before them—they force the past to sound like them. . . Rock America has given up on Like-Me-Like-Me populism, and some of us are beginning to love it as a result. As they say themselves: Oh my golly! Oh my golly! Rosa, oh oh ohh Rosa! Huh! Huh! Rosa, oh oh ohh Rosa! Huh! Huh!

Q **magazine review by Ian Cranna, May 1988:** What sets the Pixies apart are their sudden bursts of memorable pure pop melody and an intuitive understanding of song dynamics that makes for positive enjoyment. The 13 tracks have short, uncomfortable titles but lyrics that go beyond the usual black nihilism into personal enigma ("Bloody your bands on a cactus tree/Wipe them on your dress and send it to me"—from "Cactus") and, I'd swear, a sense of fun. Not gelling their act together is almost certainly part of the whole point of Pixies, but if they're not careful they could have a bright future in front of them.

Billy Corgan (former Smashing Pumpkins singer/guitarist; former Zwan singer/guitarist; musician): *Doolittle* was like, *the* album, but *Surfer Rosa* was the one that made me go, "Holy shit." It was so fresh. It was like it rocked without being lame. I always liked Steve's drum sound, I didn't always like the looseness of the production, but he does everything really quick and with energy. I thought Steve had his thing. We used to sit in the fucking van and go, "How the fuck does he get that drum sound?" We were very technical so we studied everybody's records.

Watts-Russell: The response to *Surfer Rosa* was times five. The time between the first two was so short, it was all just this mushrooming thing. Nothing but positive feedback.

Lupner: Our big clients at the time were Aimee Mann, 'Til Tuesday, and smaller groups that were making their ways to getting signed or recording their first albums. I just wasn't aware of indie charts and that side of things. So when Paul called up and told us that *Surfer Rosa* was at the top of the CMJ charts, I was like, what's that?

Iha: I don't know how he writes his words, but in "Where Is My Mind?" I love that lyric "I was swimmin' in the Caribbean." The sound of it doesn't sound like what would become typical angst '90s lyrics, they're just so broad, it sounds like some Southern gothic novelist or something, but with a punk rock edge. I won't speak for my band, but a lot of the '90s grunge bands, it turned into that cliché of mope rock or whatever they ended up calling it. Angst rock. People could almost make fun of it. Whereas, the Pixies, you can't nail it down other than it's strong.

St. Thomas: I remember playing it on the air, and I remember people going crazy. We played so many songs off this—we played

"Bone Machine," we played "Broken Face." "Gigantic" was huge for us. "Where Is My Mind?" Those were definitely all in rotation. College radio stations played the Pixies but we were the only commercial station that played them. David Lovering's dad, actually, used to call up the radio station and request the Pixies, which I thought was really funny. He'd usually call at night and be like, "Hey! This is David Lovering's dad, play the Pixies!"

Dennison: Oedipus—He's one I remember when the Pixies first started coming up, he was one of the original punk rock DJs on the Boston scene. He certainly championed their cause early on and helped them get to another level.

Thompson: It had a couple big songs on it, "Gigantic" and "Where Is My Mind?" in particular. "Bone Machine." It was kind of loud sounding. Steve Albini did a good job recording it. It's obvious we weren't there to make some kind of slicko, lame-ass record. We were from a Northeast University town. It wasn't Hollywood and we were trying to get a record deal. It was indie, indie, indie. We were competing with other serious, faux-intellectual, arty kind of bands coming up from New York to play gigs in Boston. And then all the sort of edgy, arty rock bands in Boston trying to get out of Boston. The world we were in was not about "Come on, everybody put your hands together." It was the '80s, it was sort of lame-ass heavy metal on the radio, and that's probably when MTV started to dip, and radio wasn't particularly interesting I suppose, thinking back. All that sort of commercial, corporate stuff we complain about now, it was all just as prevalent back then. The world we were brought up in was all anti-that.

St. Thomas: I thought "Gigantic" sounded really different. At the time, you didn't hear many women singing. People kind of forget about that, too. There was Throwing Muses, and who else? That was odd, to hear a woman singing over some thrashy music. Kim can do no wrong. There's something about her voice that's almost like childlike, and I really, really liked that. Charles would be screaming incoherently, and then she'd sing this little childlike melody, and that was really jarring. I think there's definitely a tension, which obviously we'd find out later that there was a lot of tension between them. It was like a car wreck—once the two of them hit, you had to look at it. There was something really offsetting about that.

Deal: At the end of the summer of '88, before we decided to release "Gigantic" as the first single, we were playing the Roxy in L.A. And I guess it ended up bothering Charles that the song I was singing on would be the first single, I don't know, I can't guess. But [onstage] he's always in the middle, Joe on the right, I'm on the left. And we go into "Gigantic," and he takes a couple of steps back and goes [motions at her to step over]. I have no idea what he's talking about. He wants me to walk over and sing this song on the middle microphone. With the Breeders I always set up on the right. I don't find it particularly one way or another who's singing on the middle mic, never have. For the Breeders I'm rhythm guitar and I like to see the drummer, and I'm always on the microphone so much that it's nice to be able to keep time as a rhythm, because when I'm looking at the front the drummer's right there. And I'm over here [on the side], with the Pixies, and I'm not on the mic all the time, thank God, so I can easily just walk up to David and watch the drummer play. So I just thought, "Oh, *God*" and it seemed like forever, the space was forever, and I'm walking over to the middle mic, I was like all right, I'll sing it in the middle mic, who cares. Somebody wants me to sing it into the middle mic, I'll fucking sing it, I'll sing it backstage, I don't give a shit. And I walk over to the middle mic and my chord stops. It was the most embarrassed I've ever been on stage, ever. I was *so* embarrassed when my chord went *shm*, and I just walked back to my mic and sang. It was so stupid.

Paul Tollett (president of Goldenvoice concert promotions, which presents the Coachella Valley Music and Arts Festival): I did their first Los Angeles show in 1988 at the Roxy. Boo Radleys opened. It was just so great. It was sold out, but only 400 people.

Walsh: I went with Charles the first time he got to meet Iggy Pop. It was at some festival and Charles went to go get a microphone signed by him. That really is Charles' ultimate idol. But I remember the disappointment that we both felt—and I don't think we commented on it because it was too obvious to require comment— I forget if it was in what he signed or what he said, but Iggy Pop was like, "Oh yeah, 'Gigantic!'" Out of all the songs, it was the one that Charles isn't the lead singer on. Sign my microphone, you're my vocal idol!

St. Thomas: I have a fond memory of Joey Santiago putting a guitar up to his mouth and snapping a string in his teeth. He just went *bam*, and a string just snapped right off the guitar. It was early—probably for *Surfer Rosa*. He'd do a lot of crazy stuff like that, flailing about. Joey Santiago rocks!

Thompson: He doesn't have any baggage regarding his guitar playing. He's just like, "I'll play this!" And he can play the most sweet, little, based-on-the-blues scale kind of thing that other guitar players can't get away with. They can play the same solo, the same notes and they wouldn't get away with it. He's the most innocent guitar player. It's like he has no sin.

Robin Hurley (former CEO of 4AD): [Getting an American record deal] was the band's decision and an A&R person by the name of Peter Lubin was the man who signed the Pixies to Elektra. I think it was an acknowledgement by everybody, the band and 4AD, that the band was about to become very successful and we needed major distribution in the States to make that happen.

Peter Lubin (former A&R representative, Elektra records): I didn't know a thing about the Pixies except I was shopping for records at Tower on Sunset, and just like an enormous number of other people, I saw *Surfer Rosa* on the rack and bought it because it looked more interesting than everything else around it. I grew up knowing an awful lot about rock'n'roll and records in general and musicians, but Pixies' music defied comprehension in my brain. So that's what intrigued me the most about them, how completely incomprehensible I thought they were. So I was interested in 'em, and I guess I mentioned to Bob Krasnow, who was running Elektra at the time, "I've been listening to this group the Pixies and they're kind of fascinating because they're so incomprehensible," and he said "PASS." Then they played a gig at the World, on 1st Street and 1st Ave. in the East Village. I think it was in August, and it was scorchingly, devastatingly hot and humid. The club was packed and it was incredibly hot and unpleasant inside. Sweat was rising up off the club, condensing on the ceiling, and dropping back down on us, that's how gross it was in this place. I brought two other executives from the A&R department, so Pixies came out, and they played, and they were wholly inscrutable, as is their stock in trade, and I remember we couldn't wait to get out of the joint because it was so incredibly uncomfortable.

So we're back out on the street, and in classic A&R fashion I turned to my compatriots and said, "I don't know, what do you think?" And one of them said, "Pass" and the other said, "Pass," and I remember saying, "I gotta tell you guys, any band that can get up there and play for 110 minutes and I don't understand note one, that's something I've got to be interested in." I was just as lost coming out of the gig as I was going in. And that's why I called their manager, and I said to Ken, "Look, I guess they're in town, and I would love to get together with them because I'm really interested in them." And he said, "Sure, fine." Now the truth of that is, I was scared to death, because I was really, really intimidated from afar by Black Francis and the Pixies. I was really apprehensive to have the Pixies come and see me because I just thought they're beyond the pale somehow. And then, of course, the appointed hour comes, and Charles and Kim and the rest of them couldn't be nicer, more polite, and more delightful. I think a couple of them sat on the floor because there weren't quite enough chairs. I remember it being very cordial and convivial and friendly, anything but what I expected. I guess all I had to do after that was go back to Chairman Bob and say, "Look, you're wrong about the Pixies, we really should do this," and he said, "That's what you're here to do."

Elektra was the envy of every record label in the industry at that particular moment in time. It was us and Geffen, but we weren't envious of Geffen. And it's because we and Geffen were really the very last of the completely A&R-driven record labels. It was really the most finely crafted roster on the planet Earth and it was just a gift that kept on giving, so we had an incredible run and made a fortune. I think between 1984 and 1994 Elektra practically quadrupled their gross revenues based on Krasnow's philosophy of letting A&R people be A&R people and banking on those judgments and not the judgments of promotion men and marketing guys.

I'm fond of saying that none of my best signings ever had any competition around them. I have some vague notion that A&M was somewhere in the way distant background with some vague interest in doing the Pixies, but in those days it took very little effort to talk almost anybody into or out of anything if you just looked in their direction if you were with Elektra. But there was no competition that I'm aware of. It never was a factor.

Lovering: When we got licensed to Elektra, that was a big deal for us because we were finally on an American, a real label. We're on.

This is a label I used to listen to different things on. So that was cool, it was like a credibility about it. I don't think we were really thinking early on that much of being credible, because we were an independent band on an independent label, you can't sell out. So this was all welcome, it was really nice. We had a publicist working, doing stuff for us. It was a nice ride, so far. We went with Elektra the first day, and their offices are outside [the 21 Club restaurant]. And there's a limo up there. I'd never been in a limo before, and there must have been 17 people in it. Everybody's on people's laps and stuff. It was just ironic.

8. I'M AMAZED—EUROPEAN TOUR WITH THROWING MUSES (1988)

With both *Come on Pilgrim* and *Surfer Rosa* in wide circulation in the U.K. (with limited availability in the U.S.), Pixies teamed up with their friends Throwing Muses for a European tour in 1988. For the fairly inexperienced Pixies—they'd only been together for about two years—it was their first taste of life as a full-time touring band.

Watts-Russell: There's the infamous—quite rightly so—tour that the Muses and Pixies did together in 1988 when the Muses' second album and Pixies' first album were coming out in England. *Come on Pilgrim* had come out and *Surfer Rosa* had just come out that week of the joint tour. Both those bands were together and the whole fucking thing just felt like a merry prankster family—just fuck the rest of the world, but nicely, you know.

Deal: 4AD had a tour booked to open for Throwing Muses. We still didn't have a manager. So in April of '88 when *Surfer Rosa* came out we went over to England. We had a manager then, right before we left, we signed something in the airport.

Murphy: The Pixies and Ken had a huge fight at the airport before they were about to leave, because Ken shows up with this disclaimer or something, and says, "You guys are going to have to sign this." They're all like, "What are you talking about?" They're just about to go over to England for the first time and Ken shows up with this documentation, "You've got to sign this or else there's no tour." He basically had them over a barrel—what are they going to do, get a lawyer at that time? It was a late flight on a Sunday or something. I remember that being really difficult.

Hersh: It was our second European tour. Our first tour we opened for Cocteau Twins, so we just felt like the Beverly Hillbillies. With the Pixies we were a little more in context, and we were part of this little teeny American invasion, what was called "the Boston scene" overseas. We had never heard it called that before, we just thought we lived in Boston and played. We thought it was funny.

Watts-Russell: If the Pixies were coming over to tour by themselves at that point in time, the audience would have been half the size. Throwing Muses were really loved in the U.K., they were the big export, it was totally unusual.

Donelly: As rock as we might have all felt at the time, there was something just very sweet about it. It was a bus-full of kids, basically, which is what we were, but that's how it felt, too—like we were going on a field trip. A field trip with lots of beer.

Deal: It was so interesting, you know. 'Cause I wasn't a trust fund kid, I didn't have my year in Europe after school, so it was really neat to come from Dayton to see England. I mean, I thought Boston was really interesting.

Chas Banks (former Pixies European tour manager): My wife Shirley and I are a team. We had this vehicle, which was specially converted, and 4AD were looking for a way of touring these two bands together. And they were also conscious of the fact that each band had girls in it, so the fact that we were a team made it particularly attractive. You know, if you need a tampon or whatever, it's tough to go to the tour manager, the big six-foot-three guy, and say, "Hey, listen, we need to find a chemists' shop." I mean, Kim would be cool about it, but it did make it easier, the fact that Shirley was there. It's kind of like an aunt and uncle scenario, only we were professionals.

Before that, I'd worked with the Who, Teenage Fanclub, Gentle Giant, the Kinks, Curtis Mayfield, the Replacements, the db's, the Sugarcubes and Björk, Joe Cocker, Van Morrison. Until we went for the interview for the job, I had no idea who 4AD were, I had no idea who Throwing Muses were, and even less idea who the Pixies were. The first time I heard them was three or four shows into the tour when someone said to me, "You know the support band are really good." So I went and checked them out and it was like, wow, they were really good. They were fucking brilliant. The energy level, the commitment, Charles' performance, his persona on stage, the balance, how can you put a finger on it? They were very, very, very exciting. It was a great interaction with the audience and the audience were obviously getting into it. They were really nice kids and they really tried hard. They were so polite, and easy to tour manage, easy to be with. They knew their place, they knew their position. There we were, all crammed into this bus with the equipment in the back, they knew they were the opening act, they knew what they were there to do. No responsibility, no pressure, just enjoying themselves. They were happy. Very happy.

Santiago: Chas Banks is a gentle giant. He took us under his wing.

Watts-Russell: He was fantastic, and I don't think that Ken has any idea how much Chas and Shirley took on that really effectively was Ken's responsibility, but Ken Goes doesn't fly.

Hersh: Chas and Shirley! They were Mum and Dad. Chas is this big, red-headed Viking. He had a big beard, and when we'd come offstage feeling all rockin' and sweaty and he'd pick us up and give us a hug. They were sweet as pie.

Lovering: The first gig was at the Mean Fiddler. And that was shocking. That was the first time that I was just blown away. We had heard that it was doing well in England, people like the Pixies, but it was the first time I'd seen a crowd that was just flipping out. It was the coolest.

Mico: I remember going to the Mean Fiddler to see Throwing Muses and the Pixies supported Throwing Muses. It was their first-ever show [in England], and I remember reviewing that. I have no idea what I wrote. They were astonishing. From the very start it felt like a Mac truck had driven through and taken no prisoners, it was unbelievable. It was one of the greatest shows on earth. We were all expecting wonderful things from Throwing Muses, and nobody really knew what to expect from the Pixies. Certainly they were a tough, almost impossible act to follow.

Deal: I was a gymnast. At the first show, the Mean Fiddler, we did cartwheels on stage, just to piss people off, it's so not punk. People actually went there to see you. On purpose. It was strange to start coming out on stage and people were applauding. Fucking pissed me off. Why are they applauding, we haven't even played yet? Remember, we were doing the bar thing in Boston so much, and so used to nobody ever knowing us. The way I was used to it was you get up and you play, then eventually not a lot of applause, okay? If they're not booing you and talking during your songs and saying "You suck" between the songs, that was good in Boston. You would hate to walk out to applause.

Murphy: That was wild. They'd been playing in the U.S. to a couple hundred people at the most. And when I went to Europe for the first time there were at least a thousand, maybe 800 people—it was way more than what I was used to. It was all because of that first record. Everybody loved it and thought it was genius. Whenever they played the Town and Country there were thousands of people there, all in unison, body surfing, and pogo-ing and whatever they used to call it back then, slam dancing (that was pre-moshing). It was unreal, really. I was soaking wet with sweat in the middle of the crowd because I enjoyed it, I really did. It wasn't just my relationship with Kim, I still think to this day they've gotta be one of my top ten bands of all time.

Slade: They graduated quickly from being no-ones on the local scene to being big stars in England.

Donelly: I definitely feel like we started playing kind of harder and there was some influence from them. We had people just going crazy, knocking speakers over. The whole tour, people were just so excited about the Boston scene. It seemed cohesive to them, so it seemed like we were sort of representing our people. We would say, "There isn't really a scene," but they refused to listen. They didn't believe us. But it felt like one, that's the important thing.

Hersh: From the first time we played with them we requested them at every show. It was purely for selfish reasons. It's hard to watch a band that sucks and then play. You start to wonder why you do what you do, or what music is, or why you're there. But with the Pixies we'd be thoroughly energized by watching their set. We'd play much better when we played with the Pixies.

Jeff Craft (Pixies international booking agent): The Pixies were basically getting better audience reactions than Throwing Muses because they're more dynamic and in-your-face than the Muses were. And by the end of the tour we had to put Pixies on last because they were impossible to follow. Initially, when the tour was first booked, it was a Throwing Muses tour with Pixies as the support. But between the time it was booked and the time that the tour actually happened *Come on Pilgrim* had been released and there was a lot of media interest in the record. And of course once the shows started the reviews were just phenomenal for Pixies. So by the end of the tour it made sense to change the whole thing to a co-billing.

Donelly: We switched billing in Holland. I was relieved because who wants to play after the Pixies? When it was first presented to us by Chas, who was tour managing, we kind of saw it coming, but we had about an hour of feeling sorry for ourselves. Ultimately I think it ended up being a good thing, and crowds were psyched to see us, too. It wasn't like people were leaving after the Pixies. That's a cathartic set, and once you've done that, we had a lot more subtleties and moments of fragility—it was very different, it's a completely different emotion. And also, all of that anxiety of like, "Oh my God! Now we have to play" was lifted.

Watts-Russell: They got flipped when they went from England to Europe because our licensees for the Pixies were promoting the fuck out of it, while Sire for the Muses didn't even know that the Muses didn't have a male singer in the band. It was absurd, so that is why it got flipped, because Warner Bros. were doing their typically disastrous job. Every night Throwing Muses would come on stage and blow the Pixies away on stage in England—that seems to be forgotten by history.

Hersh: The crowds were incredible. That's what happens when you leave your planet and you realize someone else was paying attention. That's what the Boston scene was, at least in England. It was huge. We just kept our mouths shut about not being famous back home. They knew all the words to all the songs. It was just an ocean of sweaty boys, all singing along. We were confused.

Craft: My recollection was that the *NME* very much got behind them. They were the kind of band that would've been more difficult for your average American to have understood. Whereas they seemed to just click immediately—and it wasn't just with England, it was with a lot of Europeans as well. The French got them straight away.

Steven Appleby (cartoonist, contributed drawings to *Trompe Le Monde*): Music in the U.K. at the time of first hearing the Pixies—the scene was boring. Simple Minds, pre-punk I guess in a funny sort of way. The Pixies dealt with taboos and you could listen to the lyrics and not be disappointed. It seemed to me at the time really unusual. I never had heard anybody scream and sing at the same time.

Geiger: Charles was great in the press. He manipulated them, he told UFO stories and said obtuse things, it worked for the U.K. press. The Pixies got more press than almost anybody in the *NME* in the U.K. at the time, but only a few writers picked up on it in the U.S.

Mico: I was features editor at *Melody Maker* at the time. I wrote a lot of features on the Pixies, I interviewed them many times. I found them to be charming and extremely interesting. I think they, like any artist, became mildly impatient with people that kept asking them inane questions. So if you ask inane questions you're going to get short or curt answers. But if you ask Charles about UFO landings or what he would have liked to have invented in the twentieth century or CB radios or something that intrigued him or took his fancy, then you got really interesting things. He had many interesting things to say about many subjects, all of which are in print somewhere.

Flansburgh: Their career was so meteoric. I remember spending a long spell at the Columbia hotel in London where we were on some weird press junket and they were on some weird press junket. Nothing prepared any of us for the fact that we would become national or international acts. I think whatever confidence we had in the quality of what we did, it was at a time when it's impossible to communicate how epically lame the mass culture was. It was really Rod Stewart's world and we were just trying to get a little corner of it. The old rock regime was trying to hold onto its market share. They were really dug in, and there was a lot of things that institutionally went in their favor. And even the few superstar acts that broke out during that time—the Madonnas and other things like that—still had the epic lameness of big '70s rock. There wasn't much that seemed to have the spirit of rock music that I was into. The Pixies didn't behave like rock stars, or at least, in most ways, and it just seemed amazing that they could become so accepted so quickly and not on the back of a hit single. There wasn't a breakout song, they were a good band. I think the image of the band was such a looming question mark. They weren't being sold as faces or young people or fashionable people or sexy people, they were just being presented as unknowable people, which is a pretty savvy way to present a band.

Thompson: We had nothing to compare it to. You write a bunch of songs, you book a nightclub, everybody says "Yay!" and the owner says, "Come back on Friday night, you kids are pretty good." You play Friday night and everyone says "Yay!" and a producer comes up to you and says, "Hey, come record in my studio, you kids are pretty good." You record something, and a manager guy says, "Hey, you guys are pretty good, you want to come to 4AD in London?" and you go, "Yay!" You get there, you're on the covers of magazines, and everyone goes, "Yay!" We had been getting "Yay!" since we walked into a club. So we didn't have the grind that some people go through. There was no real struggle. I'm not saying we didn't work hard, but we were out of there as fast as we could. I suppose had we become a local band who was popular or a regional band—you take what you can get. So any sign of interest from out of town was immediate. It was just like, "Let's go! Let's go to New York." But everyone liked us. Was it surprising to be popular in New York? No. It was like, "But of course. We're the Pixies! Everyone loves us!" It wasn't like we were the best band in the world, but we had a little thing going. People dug it.

Craft: Once the tour was underway and I got to meet them it was obvious that they were very unusual. My impression of them was that they were four completely and totally different people. And that was kind of what made it work. They appeared to have nothing in common at all offstage. In normal situations you would never get four people like that to come together. And I think obviously there was some magic in the air to get those four to meet up because they are so different. And that's kind of why it works. A lot of bands really have to work at how they present themselves onstage, and the magic of what happens when they're onstage is not something that happens spontaneously, it's worked at. Whereas with Pixies, as soon as they get onstage, there is just something you can't put your finger on.

Banks: For starters there's a difference between European bands and American bands. English bands have this thing about being mates, being friends, whereas with American bands it's much more the work ethic being first. But the Pixies were four individuals. You've got to remember it happened very, very quickly. From the day they got together and started rehearsing, it was virtually overnight. There was never a moment when there was no inertia. There was always constant forward movement, there was always something to keep them interested and keep them moving. So they were never forced into a situation where they needed to develop overly personal relationships, they didn't have to try to pal their way through the bad times. But having said that, they were very funny with each other. They used to have a lot of laughs. They had these long bus journeys, and they'd get stoned and talk to each other and they interacted very well. They were really, really close when they were off-duty. It was that difference between it's not work time, they were very disciplined about that. But they had a lot of fun, they'd get stoned, have a laugh, play games, and do bad things.

Murphy: I remember the Muses and Pixies traveled in the same bus and had fun together. They even did little sightseeing things. I remember going to this castle in Leeds at one point. I hung out with Tanya, mostly, and Kim. Coming back after the show was usually when they were more together again and hanging out. We'd sit in the back room and talk a lot, but I don't remember them ever thinking to themselves, "Well, we're going to be the next U2," or whatever, I remember them just thinking, "This is a lot of fun."

Hersh: Chas and Shirley woke us up really early one morning, which is a big deal when you get in at five. We were all sharing hotel rooms and sleeping all over the floor, and everybody else was hung-over—I didn't drink, so I was just sleepy, but [the rest of the band members] were seriously ill, and they all got into the van thinking it must be a long drive. But Chas stopped the van at an aviary and some botanical gardens which were his big treats and everybody was furious. So they all took naps, and I felt bad, so I went and looked at all the birds and the flowers.

Donelly: We were in Berlin and we had just played and we got back in the van and Charles just said, "Let's drive around. Let's just drive around all night." He and I had been listening to *Lust for Life* a lot, like nonstop, just passing it back and forth on the bus, and so we just played "The Passenger" over and over and over, 30 times or something, and drove around Berlin all night. It was really nice and there was just so much camaraderie and peace—it was just a really nice night.

Hersh: We were following Skinny Puppy around, they seemed to play every club right before us. And I don't know what they were doing onstage, but the mic that Charles and I sang into was always covered with blood and so was the floor all around the mic. Charles would be on his hands and knees with a paper towel trying to clean the blood off the floor before I played. It was very sweet.

I remember Charles taking a sharpie and drawing on the dressing room door, drawing a Muses song. He was really high. But he drew his conception of a Muses song, which was like this big pie chart but with all this filigree, and he said, "See, now this would be anybody else's song, but *this* is a Muses song," which I always thought was the highest compliment I've ever been paid as a songwriter.

And I lifted Joey bodily into the van once because some Germans were trying to kill him. All day he'd been talking about hamburgers, they were going to Hamburg, and he wanted to see a hamburger, and he wanted to go to McDonald's and see if they sold hamburgers there. I went to McDonald's with him and he was disappointed that they didn't have hamburgers on the menu, they called 'em something else, and then we played this really scary punk-rock club. Narcizo got trampled by hobnail boots on the dance floor and we were kind of trying to escape. I was in the van first, by myself, when Joey grabbed this Hamburger, this German kid, big, scary kid, and held his face into the van and said, "Look Kristin, I found a hamburger!" The kid got furious, but they were both really drunk, so he started chasing Joey around a pole, but they were each holding onto the other one, so they were just kind of ringing around the rosey around the pole. I thought the kid was really going to beat the tar out of him, so I grabbed Joey and pulled him into the van and shut the door while the kid pounded on the door going, "You stupid Americans! You take our money!"

He was hurling abuse and Joey was just waving at him in the window. He was like, "You can pick me up! Little Kristin can pick me up!" And told that story for years, every time we were together, he'd be like, "You gotta hear this. So I grabbed me a hamburger, little Kristin pulled me into the van!"

Murphy: By the time I was with them they were probably 20 to 30 shows into it, so when I used to see them coming off the stage we went and watched the Throwing Muses, because they were pals, too, they became really good friends while they were on this tour. Different people clicked, like Kim and Tanya clicked, Kristin and Charles, Joey and Leslie, and the two Daves.

Donelly: Kim and I hit it off immediately when we met, but it was on that tour that we started really becoming inseparable. I never had girlfriends like her in high school. She was my first "I'm gonna braid your hair!" kind of friend. "Let's paint our nails!" I'd never had that before.

Hersh: Oh, they were great people. When we toured England and Europe together we were living in a van on the coffee and beer diet, playing these crazy little Belgian towns. And singing on the van every night! We were *babies*, singing "500 Miles Away From Home." I remember Kim going into a bathroom (we called them Pee Worlds) in France, and Tanya and I were following Kim into the ladies room and Kim screamed at the top of her lungs, we thought there was like, a body of a homeless person in there or something. Tanya went tearing in and busted up laughing. Kim had seen the French toilet, which was a hole in the floor with treads next to it for your feet, and like a grating. Kim was just screaming and screaming and wouldn't stop.

Murphy: Tanya was sort of in the same position in the band that Kim was in. Sort of second fiddle from a singing and songwriting perspective. She had that feeling that she had it in her. I think Kristin was a little more democratic about it, because they were obviously more than just bandmates [they were step-sisters, as well]. And Tanya never pushed it, as far as I know, she just sort of said, "I'm happy with one song, two songs on an album, and one day I'll do something different." Whereas I think Kim always felt she had it in her and repressed it on purpose for a long time, which

I've got to give her credit for it. She was always used to being her own person and being in charge, when I first met her.

Banks: It was Charles' band, he was the main man. You never felt when they were on the bus that it was Charles' band, though. He wasn't a bully, he didn't dominate them or say, "We're going to go here." He was very, very polite and treated them all with a great deal of respect. Charles was calling me *sir*. It was a big opportunity for them. There they were in Europe, Throwing Muses were a big band. Overall, they were good kids. It's difficult to sum any of them up in a sentence. Dave was a great drummer who knew what his job was and got his head down and did it. He had a great sense of humor, he was the class clown. Joey was kind of a quiet, shy kind of guy really until he'd had a couple of drinks, like anybody. And Kim was just crazy, she was insane but lovable with it. She had a lot of talent. They were very polite.

Watts-Russell: One thing that you're never going to see, on that tour Kim kept journals and she would pass the journals around. You saw Kim, she'd be writing in them, she'd give 'em to you and vanish. People wrote in them but they also got to read them as well. Just absolutely brilliant, funny, really open—I remember reading some stuff she had written about Charles and at the end of the paragraph she wrote, "Oh my God, if anybody were to read this they would think we were having an affair." But yet this was a book she would pass around and let everybody read. That was early on, when everybody was getting on fantastic. There have been many rumors about what exactly their relationship was at that time, it was just sort of funny too, I never knew if it was a double bluff that she wrote that or a double double bluff. They had a great relationship at that point. She was like nobody I ever met in my life and you just kinda came into her orbit was just so inspired by it. Just an openness and a sense of humor, all you had to do was see her on the stage, high heels, skirt down below her knees and T-shirt with a dreadful painting of a kitten on it. It was the perfect Mrs. John Murphy, just adorable and complicated. Maybe people were drawn to her because she would talk a lot more then anybody else, Charles would talk specifics but Kim would hold court.

Hersh: Kim's gibberish was the best part! She was still doing that in Europe when they didn't even speak English. In Holland she was telling them that their canals smelled like shit in between songs. The not shutting up was great, we loved that about Kim. She was a cheerleader, you know, and she was still a cheerleader. Plus, she was married, which was just so weird. She was a grownup, we were tiny babies and Kim seemed like this lady. I also remember that her ponytail got higher and higher and higher as the tour went on. It started in the back of her head and gradually rose up the back until it was like, cheerleader height, and it kept going until it was at the top of her head like a fountain, and then all the way up to her forehead.

Harvard: I don't think playing in a band with Kim would ever make anybody's job easier. She's a pirate and she's a beautiful, multifaceted pirate. And that's a great thing for rock'n'roll. Not necessarily the best thing for the road manager to deal with when he had to gather everyone up and get 'em in the van.

Banks: By the time we got to Holland, Kim had started to be late. And so I let it slip and slip until the point came where we were all sitting in the bus and still waiting for Kim. She had gotten used to me or Shirley going in and phoning and saying, "We're all waiting for you," but I didn't say anything and I waited for time to go by. So as she came out of the hotel I jumped out of the van and walked to meet her so that I didn't have to have the conversation with her in front of everybody. And I was like, "Kim, they're all there, we're all pissed off because you're late. I don't want you to be the person that we're all pissed off at every day. You can be late, you can take your turn to be late, but don't you be the person who's going to be late every day because otherwise it ain't gonna work." And she said, "Cool, I understand." And that was it. And that took us a long way. It was a long way down the line before she started being late again.

Donelly: [When we got back from Europe] I think Kim and I were both at the point where we were starting to entertain the thought of moving on, but we're both very deliberate people, so it took many years to actually do it.

Deal: We recorded "Gigantic" the summer when we were overseas, when we were touring. At the time I didn't think [it was a big deal to sing lead] but I think maybe it turned into a big deal. I don't think we knew we were doing a single when we went in. I think we just thought we were rerecording for a release. We did "River

Euphrates" over again, we did "Gigantic" over again, and there was a couple more songs we did over again. And then Vaughan did the artwork. And you know there's no names on it, 'cause they're not singles like a Britney Spears, so it wasn't called "Gigantic the Single" or anything, nobody referred to it like that, it wasn't getting played on any radio. People liked it. People sang along even then.

Gil Norton (producer, *Doolittle*, *Bossanova*, and *Trompe Le Monde*): Ivo didn't think there was a radio single on *Surfer Rosa*, so he asked me if I could redo "Gigantic," which is the time first I recorded them, to redo "Gigantic" for the single. I was a bit nervous, actually, just because I was redoing something Albini had done and I liked the band so much. It went really well, well enough that they wanted to do *Doolittle* with me.

Watts-Russell: That was one calculated thing I suggested they do, to rerecord three things from *Surfer Rosa* with Gil. Two were on an EP, "Gigantic" and "River Euphrates," the third still to this day has not been heard, the definitive pop hit version of "Here Comes Your Man." *Come on Pilgrim* was a mini-album so it doesn't really qualify for traditional charts, it just got a good response. The response to that was not as much as the Throwing Muses record. The main explosion was on that tour. That was really exciting. We had never been involved with a group that just virtually took off overnight and were really good—it just got bigger and more exciting. At the end of that tour, both bands came back to England and they had done two nights at Town and Country at the beginning of the tour, and they came back to do two nights at this tiny little pub, the Mean Fiddler, and that was just incredible—the audience just singing the words to every song, I'm talking about both bands. That was really a big part of musical history. And the band, the Pixies, they got on really well. 4AD as a label was kind of staffed up properly, there were six of us—still a small number, but six very fascinating, good people working.

Banks: When a band becomes successful at a rate they became successful, in a lot of ways, it's easy. Most young American kids are inherently ambitious, it's an ambitious society—I've worked with a lot of American bands a lot of English bands and a couple of nationalities in between, but the American bands you do notice their ambition. It's a brighter flame, it's easier to spot, because it's not something you apologize for in America. It's something that's expected of you that you would want to be ambitious and want to be successful. And they all shared that, so it gives them a unifying force. There's a group of you, you're in a foreign country, and you're there striving to do well. It kind of brings you together, you stick together, you're a team, and you're on foreign ground and you can moan about the food and about what you miss and what you don't miss about America. You've got this great unifying influence. There's a lot you put up with. You'll put up with lack of sleep, you've got this excitement of doing well. And they were doing very, very well. So if there are any underlying problems they tend to pale in significance compared with the big problem of how are we going to do this show tonight. So initially, there weren't any problems. It was very exciting. And then later on, problems arose, and there was the famous personality clash, the classic personality clash, and their problems became bigger than the prize, I suppose. And that's what happens. There isn't a band out there that don't have arguments. And if you found a band that doesn't have arguments, chances are they've not been successful, or they're not likely to be successful.

Murphy: Charles thought a lot, like, "Let's go back and make another record," his creative juices were flowing. He introduced songs during the tour, which was pretty cool. He would introduce them and end up playing them. The song "Hey," they were playing on the *Surfer Rosa* tour and it was really on *Doolittle*. And they had other songs that they hadn't recorded yet, officially, but they had already been playing for years. Like "Subbacultcha" was from the first show, that's an old, old, song. And "U-Mass" he wrote before he even met the rest of the band. At the time, he goes, "It's just a riff," and as it turns out it was, but it's a cool song. I just remember them being excited about being in the band and having some success. They certainly weren't like, "We're going to rule the world!"

Dennison: I remember their big show at the Rat, their homecoming show after they came back from England. All of a sudden it was nuts. Everybody wanted to be on the guest list and every radio programmer and writer and everybody was like, "Pixies are the best thing that's ever happened to music!" It kind of came out of left field for all of us who had been around and seen them struggling for a long time. My friend Julie Farman who was booking the Rat (she ended up marrying David Lovering) and I were laughing that night because it literally was one of the biggest shows ever at the Rat. And I was there every night of my life for almost eight years.

St. Thomas: The Pixies played at Jack's a bunch, but I never saw them there. I remember the first time I heard them because I had to make a commercial for them. I remember hearing "Caribou" and thinking it was the weirdest band I ever heard. They didn't seem like a Boston band, they had some weird air about them because they had played in England and other Boston bands hadn't done that. It made them seem very cool.

Hersh: We were like the same band, the same family or something, and after that it was over, it was really over. You know the difference really is they were always rock stars, they were rock stars from day one and they expected people to like them, they expected to be valuable. We just felt like we were on our own planet and that's where we were playing. We were not rock stars. We were not larger than life. We were way smaller than life, and we were playing for ourselves and that was it, and that was appropriate for us.

Banks: Very quickly the Pixies came back and we did a club tour, which sold out, all over the U.K. and Europe, and that was in the van. And then we did another club tour very quickly, within four or five months. Headlining. Sellout shows, everywhere. They made the transition though all the venues in Europe increasing in size.

Santiago: [Things changed] I think when Kim started doing her own stuff.

Hersh: Kim was writing songs on tour, and Tanya and Kim were talking about doing something, but that's kind of what you do, you always talk about songs and projects. But they were also the girls. Leslie and I were the vegetarians, they were the girls, the other ones were the boys.

Donelly: I think at the time it was just kind of like, well, our bands are both kind of taking a break so we're going to do this. It was with everybody's blessing, so there wasn't any tension about it at that time.

I think that Kim not singing as much [over time in Pixies] was fallout from band problems, which happens in every band, and it's that classic thing where you have this group of extremely different personalities which is what makes the music and the band what it is, but that's also what ultimately blows it apart.

Albini: The two of them [Deal and Donelly] got along well and they sort of felt like kindred spirits in this whole circle of bands touring around England.

Murphy: They went to see the Sugarcubes at Axis in Boston and the music between sets was dance music, and Tanya was like, "We can totally do this, let's do a dance album together," because they were drinking and whatever, and they were like, that's a great idea. I think they both realized it wasn't going to work, so Kim said, "Well, I've got a bunch of songs that I've been working on," and Tanya said, "Well, I don't really have any, but I'll help you with them."

Deal: Yeah, we wanted to play. So she would show me her thing, and I would say, "Oh look it, I know this thing." But then we started having songs. Like, "Oh, that's good, you can do this there." "Oh yeah, that's cool." She thought it would be a good idea, she wanted this song to be a disco song. And so we thought, oh we should do a disco song, that would be so fun, so we tried to enlist some people to help us and some people did. David Narcizo helped, and there was another drummer in town that helped too. That was fun. We even went to a rehearsal space—me, and her and Narcizo, to try to come up with this disco song. But we didn't. But anyway that started getting us to think oh yeah, we could do these songs, and these songs. There was a lot of time.

Donelly: It was a way to extend the tour a little bit because we were enjoying hanging out. And so first we were just playing for fun, and then Kim decided that she wanted to do it more seriously. We used to go out dancing every night after the tour and we used to go dancing in Boston. We loved dancing to like, Black Box, Neneh Cherry, a lot of dance stuff—we just would dance to anything. So we just decided we were going to do it, too. I think if we had put a little more backbone into it we could have done it, but it just wasn't happening for whatever reasons. I think probably we weren't quite ready for a concept project at that stage in our lives. So that kind of just morphed into doing the Breeders. And that would actually be mach two of the Breeders, because Kim and Kelley had been called the Breeders when they were teenagers. I didn't even meet Kelley until probably a year after I started hanging out with Kim. So she was not interested at that point, it was only after I left that she came into the fold.

Murphy: And then Kim started talking to another friend of theirs, Carrie Bradley, who was a violinist and singer in another band [Ed's Redeeming Qualities]. So those three formed the crux of the original Breeders, and they had four drummers coming in and helping them do the demos. The bass player on the original demos was another friend of ours, Ray Holiday, but Kim is a perfectionist, so she redid some of his parts. Then they produced this demo and they played one show only with that lineup at the Rat, and it was billed in the *Phoenix* as a Boston girl super-group, and they brought the tape to 4AD because everybody told them it was good, which I did, too. So then when they submitted it into Ivo they were like, this is great, I'd like to do this, but we'll get a real producer and do the songs over again, because they treated it purely like a demo. To this day I think the demo tape was more accessible than *Pod*, the first Breeders CD.

Donelly: [Writing *Pod*, the first Breeders LP] was really fun, just hanging out at Kim's house while John Murphy was at work. After they split he still had [his semi-serious band] Mente, he was still doing stuff around here and I think it was relatively amicable. [Kim and John's breakup] wasn't long after we got home from the big Pixies/Muses tour. I think there was just kind of a shift in what they wanted in life.

Harvard: Once the Pixies were flying, Kim obviously felt the need to do something else and something that was even more enlightened. Because it had more a female element, let's face it, it was more enlightened. And I think they felt the need to push that further than they could in the Pixies where she was one out of four, so they did the Breeders. So Kim had done her demos, she did six tunes, "Lime House," "Doe," and "Only in 3's," and Paul Kolderie who was the best engineer we had at that time, had engineered the Breeders stuff, and in Kim's world, it was too clean, it was too perfect, "I want it messed up." Not surprisingly she would ask me. She said, "I don't want to send it to 4AD this way," so I went in and remixed five of those, and that turned out really well, we had fun. We took it, sent it to Ivo, he actually called me, I had never talked to Ivo, he said, "Joe, this is absolutely magical, beautiful stuff." What happened was Tanya's songs for that second Breeders record became the first Belly record because she left the Breeders right after that.

Donelly: For contractual reasons—because of her contract with Elektra, my contract with Reprise—we couldn't both be the primary songwriter on the record, so the concept was, and it was an extremely idealistic one, was that she would write the first record and it would come out on her label, I would write the second, it would come out on mine. Under hopefully "the Breeders," but if either of them balked at that we would change the name of the band. To something. I don't think that was every really figured out. The whole first Belly record is demoed at Fort Apache under the Breeders, and Kim plays on it, because that's what it was gonna be. So the demos for the first Belly record Joe did with us, and it was me and Kim and it said Breeders on it, because that's what it was supposed to be for. So he produced those and they came out really great. I think I have the tape somewhere, I think Ivo's the only person that has a copy of it, though.

Watts-Russell: I had a good working relationship with Kim. "Well, okay, so you want to record, let's go to the studio in Scotland, we will get Steve Albini out there, it will be fun for you to be out there," done in time off that Tanya had in Throwing Muses before she left. I don't know if she had the best of times with Albini on that record [*Pod*].

Donelly: I loved Big Black, which I think really surprised Albini because he had sort of a warped impression of me when we first met. He told me that if he drank my bathwater he'd probably piss rosewater. He thought I was just kind of girly. We ended up getting along really well and he's a very sweet person. I'm probably going to re-quote Joey right now, it's probably the last thing he'd want anybody to say about him, but I was just so impressed by him in the studio, too, just how decisive he is and he just knows how to get a sound that he has in his head. He also made decisions about cutting down some of the harmonies which we balked at initially, but he was 100 percent right. Some of the parts, it's just better having her single voice, it makes it more effective and sadder and sort of just more focused.

Albini: Kim had some songs and some demos put together with a version of the Breeders that used a slightly different lineup and she asked me if I knew of any drummers that would be appropriate and at that point my favorite band in the world was this band from Louisville called Slint and I suggested that she talk to Britt Walford, the drummer from Slint, who happened to be in Chicago when she was in Chicago. So they got together and talked about it a little bit. And, I think, partly on my recommendation, and partly because I don't think she took the decision very seriously, she had Britt come over to play drums on that Breeders record and I think he made a big difference on that record [on the liner notes, Walford is listed under the pseudonym Shannon Doughton].

I instantly preferred it to the Pixies. Instantly I could tell that it was a unique perspective. And that there was a simultaneous charm to Kim's presentation to her music that's both childlike and giddy and also completely mature and kind of dirty. And I instantly liked that it had the sort of playful nature of children's music and it had this sort of girlish fascination with things that were pretty but it was also kind of horny. That was a juxtaposition that, at the time, was unusual. You didn't get a lot of knowing winks from female artists at the time. But I also think that musically it was quite distinct from everything else that was around at the time.

Pod was a dead easy record to make. I think they had two weeks booked in the studio and we were done in a week, so they sent up a TV crew to film a video and then they had us record a [John] Peel session and they just kept throwing more shit at us. Like, well, you're gonna be there for another week, you might as well do this, you might as well do that. Go ahead, knock out some B-sides.

Murphy: [The Beatles cover] "Happiness is a Warm Gun," that was actually a request from Ivo, he wanted them to do it, that's what Kim told me. Ivo said, "If you could just do this one song. . ." They did a good job on it.

Donelly: I think of all the records I've made, that one is the truest—it's like the truest to the experience of making it, if that makes any sense. It really feels exactly the way it was when we were doing it. We did it quickly, we did it in our pajamas, we actually ended up going down to the pub in our pajamas a couple times.

Albini: I remembered there was a discussion at the time that Kim was getting to make that record was causing some friction within the Pixies. It was an unrelated enterprise. I don't personally see why it would matter but I think it was an affront to Charles that he had had to put his band together and get signed and then be allowed to make a record, where Kim sort of was in that band and by default was allowed to make a record. And a lot of the same people were involved. It was a 4AD record. Ivo was behind it. I was working on it.

Deal: [Later, during a discussion that took place before *Bossanova*] Charles started talking about [how] I got $11,000 to record *Pod*. I guess *Surfer Rosa* cost less or something.[7]

Donelly: I left the Breeders in '91. Because I made *Safari* and then that was it. At that point, Kim had decided to stay on in the Pixies for another record and I had decided not to stay on with the Muses, so I wanted to do my own thing, and that's when I formed Belly. Some time after that Kim decided she wanted to do the Breeders fulltime and sort of tried to coerce me in subtle and not so subtle ways to come back. We had one night, we were in Dayton and she locked us in the bathroom of this bar that we were in. We were talking and getting stuff out, and when we left the bathroom there was nobody in the bar, the bar had closed and the doors were locked. We had to break out of the bar and walk home by ourselves on the highway.

9. RIDING THE WAVE— *DOOLITTLE* DAYS (1989)

Watts-Russell sent the band back into the studio, this time with an English producer who had previously worked with Throwing Muses: Gil Norton, who became something of a mentor to Thompson while relations between Pixies, themselves, were changing. Recording with Norton meant more preplanning, and less spontaneous ideas from Deal, Santiago, and Lovering. The results, however, still stunned critics and fans.

Norton: I did the first Throwing Muses album and they were putting a show on at the Rathskeller in Boston to play me the new material for their next album. Ivo and I were at the show and the Pixies were the support band. They didn't even have Kim with them actually, someone in her family was ill, it was just the three boys, and that was the first time I'd seen them. This was just before *Surfer Rosa*.

Watts-Russell: Gil was blown away by the Pixies.

Norton: I literally was blown away the first time I saw them. I remember being on the back wall, just going, "Oh my God, this is fantastic!" I was so excited. I think I frightened Throwing Muses. I was talking about doing some brass and putting some strings on. Later they went on to do those things, but I think at that time they didn't want to go that far.

Hersh: It was hard. Gil was trying to make us sell out, trying to Britishize us, trying to produce us, and we were fighting the gauzy, ethereal, big production thing tooth and nail. But he's wonderful, we had a great time working with him. We made the record [*Throwing Muses*] out on this farm in Massachusetts. Deep Purple kicked us out before we were done, so the record was never really finished. They called and said, "Kick whoever's in there out, and we don't want to see them." So all of our stuff was thrown out on the driveway. I was ten months pregnant and so was Gil's wife back in England, so every time he'd look at me he'd well up.

Donelly: Producers are all so different, and Gil's a real visionary. Some people don't want that much manhandling, but I think he really crafts things. He's just right in on the ground level of every song, and is very much a part of the parts that are being played. And he's good at song arrangement, he'll take your song and cut it up and paste it back together like Frankenstein.

Watts-Russell: So a switch was made—Throwing Muses went back to working with Gary and Gil took on Pixies. At the end of the day, Throwing Muses didn't respond to Gil's suggestions, whereas the Pixies did.

Deal: That summer we kept practicing in David's mom and dad's garage. And then in the fall of '88 we went and recorded *Doolittle* with the other guy Ivo suggested, a guy named Gil Norton. He's a Liverpudlian, he had done some work with Echo & The Bunnymen.

Norton: We did it in Boston at Downtown Recorders. The studio was great, actually. I remember that we rehearsed in this little room, three bands used to rehearse in there, and it was Juliana Hatfield's rehearsal room. It was just a fun album to do because it was fast and furious and everyone was vibed up for it. *Doolittle* didn't cost that much. I seem to remember it couldn't have been any more than $30,000.

Watts-Russell: *Doolittle* was completely demoed—there exists a demo version of that album that somebody should put out. Two things distinguished the Pixies' albums from each other: production and whether the songs were written. *Doolittle* was probably written between the first two on a buzz and a burn, everything was so exciting it seemed to pour out of Charles. Gil's input onto that record totally shaped it. Shaped their sound from then on.

Norton: For *Doolittle* we had demos, so I'd already got some of the songs. But before [we went into the studio] I sat with Charles with an acoustic guitar for two days in my apartment that we'd rented there and just went through songs and talked about arrangements, about what Charles wanted out of recording this time around, which songs he liked. I got to know how he would react to changing arrangements, which he was very funny about. Charles doesn't really like to do anything twice. If I wanted him to do it again he'd go, "Why, we've already done it once?" So I got to learn a lot about the way his mind works. You've got to keep it really exciting for him and keep him stimulated. If you're doing it twice it's got to be slightly different, if it's longer or a different chord sequence, *something*, so he's not feeling like he's treading water. If he gets bored, you'll get nothing out of him. We did preproduction and recorded in Boston, and then we mixed in Connecticut at Carriage House.

We spent two weeks doing preproduction, because I like doing preproduction, it's a really important part for the band to get to know me and for me to get to know them, and to fine-tune the arrangements. Then we did three weeks of recording, nearly a song a day, and then we did strings when we were mixing "Monkey Gone to Heaven." So it wasn't a very long process of recording, we sort of went in and were very well-rehearsed. Nearly everything went down live.

"Hey" was one of my favorite songs just because everything on that, even the lead vocal, was live, and I had Charles in a little cupboard playing his guitar. It was really tiny, like a broom cupboard, so he couldn't even put his guitar all the way up, he had to have it up at an angle while he was playing the song, and then Joey did the solo live. I was on the edge of my seat all the way through just going, "Go, go, go!" We did a single overdub and a backing vocal with Kim because we couldn't record her vocal in the same room with the drums.

Murphy: Kim and I still lived together for a little while after we got divorced, which was kind of weird—I remember waiting up for her one time to come home from a date. She would bring home the *Doolittle* demos, and I had access to all that stuff because she would play it and leave it around. I remember when they had the demos for "Silver" and she started some of her own compositions that she was thinking maybe Charles would like them, and maybe he'd talk about the band doing them.

Burt Price (former studio assistant, Downtown Recorders): Things seemed like they started to break down a little bit as the recording went on. Black Francis was very serious, Dave and Joe would hang out, laugh, play games have a good time. Kim seemed frustrated. There seemed to be an issue with Kim, I'm not really sure what was going on, I think she was late to a number of the sessions. Gil was very serious, always at the desk working really hard, figuring out tracks.

Watts-Russell: The kind of relationship Kim and Charles seem to have now lasted less than a year, maybe a year. Even before *Doolittle* their relationship had changed, there was some sort of break or something. My take on it was not that Kim was being unprofessional by not showing up. I think she seemed a little bit estranged.

Norton: The strings on "Monkey Gone to Heaven" were inspired more by Kim than me, because we had a grand piano and she had a pick, and she was just picking the strings, and I remember thinking, "That sounds great," it reminded me of plucked strings.

"Debaser," Charles didn't want that on the album. He didn't like it at the time, it hadn't clicked. He was a bit like, "I'm not sure about this song," and I loved it, it was one of the songs I said, "Oh no, you've got to keep this on the album, Charles." We'd start quite a lot of songs, maybe 20, 22 backing tracks or ideas, but on this one, actually, I don't think we did that as much. Most of the songs we tried to do are on the album.

Thompson: "Gouge Away" is about Samson and Delilah. "Dead" is about David and Bathsheba. There were some Biblical things I had gotten into. You can't go wrong with the Old Testament.[8]

Lovering: "La La Love You"? That was one that Charles had written. I can't remember if my voice seemed a little more suited for it. You know, my voice is a little different, so he asked if I'd do it. I had to drink about five beers before I actually did the track and I was having fun with it. But it works. All the ladies like that song, and it's always fun to sing. I've had many people come up to me saying that was their wedding song.

Norton: I think because Dave used to do backing vocals Charles wanted to give him a song, like a Ringo thing. I remember him being very nervous. He was like, "I don't know, I don't know," he'd nearly be sick just thinking about having to sing, and I'd say,

"Jump onto this vocal," he'd say, "Oh, maybe a bit later." And then, when he eventually did get onto the mic it was so fantastic because I couldn't stop him! He was going, "Well, just another run at that one, I'll do this verse again." He went from not wanting to sing a note to I can't get him away from the microphone. He was great, actually, such a showman. It was so apt.

Thompson: ["Monkey Gone to Heaven"] is a reference from what I understand to be Hebrew numerology, and I don't know a lot about it or any of it really. I just remember someone telling me of the supposed fact that in the Hebrew language, especially in the Bible, you can find lots of references to man in the fifth and Satan in the sixth and God in the seventh. I don't know if there is a spiritual hierarchy or not. But it's a neat little fact, if it is a fact. I didn't go to the library and figure it out.[9]

Murphy: "Here Comes Your Man" has an extra verse on it that it never had [before], when they recorded it for *Doolittle*. Charles had to make up that third lyric because they thought the song was too short. The record company said, "This is obviously the hit," so it needed to be longer than two minutes.

Norton: Charles got a little bit frustrated and said, "We have to go down to the record store." We went around the corner and he got me Buddy Holly's *Greatest Hits* off the shelf, and went, "There, look." Two or three minutes for Buddy Holly was a long song. That's the way Charles justified he didn't have to be long, and he's right—you don't have to be long. You don't want to be bored with a song, you know? We weren't doing it for singles, as such. You're always hoping you have singles, but I don't think we worried about it at the time. I always thought "Here Comes Your Man" was a great single, and obviously "Monkey Gone to Heaven." I think everyone thought "Here Comes Your Man" had more of a country feel, so I think people were more surprised with the album. Charles wasn't there when we did the backing track for "Here Comes Your Man," actually, he had to go off for the day. But they'd already done that song—Gary Smith had done a version, and I think it was the third version of it. We had done it before, and then we went back and had all the versions at the time, we listened and we rearranged it again, it was a different arrangement from any of those, the one that's actually on the album. I remember being a bit nervous, obviously it was Charles' song, so I liked having him around when we did it. I remember he came back and he really liked it, so I was pleased.

Watts-Russell: Maybe if Peter [Lubin] had been successful in persuading Charles that the version of "Here Comes Your Man" that was recorded around the time as the "Gigantic/River Euphrates" single should have been released as a single—the version that Gil produced was totally streamlined and ready for radio, but Charles didn't want it out, and it has never been released—maybe if a major label company was able to convince people to take a more commercial route, maybe Pixies would have sold a whole bunch more records than they did. But those steps were just not required back in 1989.

Price: Back then there was a lot of gated snare, 15 microphones on a drum kit, really intense recording, lots of microphones, over-produced sounds, very processed—and the *Doolittle* record is not. It's really upfront, the recording was very basic, there were not a lot of production tricks. That was not the norm for albums at the time.

Lovering: It was more polished. It was the first time we had pre-production. Also, the albums were becoming more frequent—we had less time between touring to do an album and stuff. And Gil was a musician as well as a producer and he helped kind of envision the songs. There might have been a bridge, or maybe a song that could have been slowed down or something, but those couple suggestions really helped *Doolittle*. I would have been happy with *Doolittle* on if we'd had more time, still. Where we could have toured for six months doing those songs before I went into the studio to record them. I'm a slow learner in a way, I can get it but I really feel it's not from really playing it and really feeling it and listening to it, before I can be happy with it myself.

Watts-Russell: In most groups the people who don't write the songs tend to be quieter and you have a slightly different relationship with them. My main memory of David was his insecurity about his drumming and how hard he worked to please Gil Norton in the studio.

Murphy: [They were becoming less excited] when they were mixing down *Doolittle*. Kim would come home and be like, "Ugg, it took us forever to do this one song." They were taking more time with everything instead of just whipping them out. It may have had something to do with Gil Norton, I think he's more of a perfectionist than Steve Albini was, or Gary Smith. Steve and Gary liked the songs and didn't want to fart around with them too much, and to give Gil a little bit of an out on this one, a lot of the songs were new to him and new to the band when he was recording them. So I think it made it more like work. So it wasn't very exciting to record an album, I think, because she was like, "Ehhh, it took forever and I don't know what he's thinking, and we recorded some demos, and this one's in, this one's out, blah blah blah." It definitely went from just all fun to work.

Watts-Russell: Internally, the relationships from *Doolittle* on were not as friendly as they had been. Ego, whatever reasons, there were things going on between Kim and Charles. I don't know the details but after *Doolittle* I think it was Gil who tried to persuade Charles to let Kim do backing on certain tracks. After "Gigantic" she didn't get to sing a lead until, well there was only one more after that, "Into the White." I think relationships were changing—they went from a few days with Gary Smith on *Come on Pilgrim*, *Surfer Rosa* was rattled off in ten days and then after that they demoed *Doolittle*, it probably was only a month that they spent on it, but compared to what they spent before it was a lot. They used strings, click tracks for the first time, David was worked really hard by Gil. He had a more traditional producer approach to stuff.

Kolderie: The last session I did for them was "Into the White," which was a B-side for *Doolittle*. I did "Into the White," "Winterlong," and "Weird at My School." At that last session I did with them they were not getting along too good. Such a change from the *Come on Pilgrim* session where the camaraderie was really there, all for one, one for all. But the session for *Doolittle*, two albums later, they clearly were hating it. "Into the White" they built out of nothing, they came in and constructed it. Charles was walking around the studio just saying words, Joey was trying to come up with a riff. I remember asking Charles, "What are you doing?" and him saying, "Ah, I'm just trying to find a sound, something that sounds good." It was very contentious, he wanted Kim to sing it, she didn't want to. They fought about that. They really didn't know what they had.

Slade: The last session they did at Fort Apache was "Into the White." Paul was the engineer, and Kim and Charles came in and didn't have a song, really. They were using the studio time to kind of force them to come up with something. So what happened was they said they needed some inspiration, so Paul called me knowing that I was always holding, so I came by and rolled a few fat ones and handed them over and then they started jamming out and Kim started screaming "into the white."

Donelly: Gil and Charles were very much a team on those last couple of records. I think Kim and Gil got along really well, for the most part. And I think Gil did the best he could to keep things copasetic. He's a real straight-up kind of person, which I think is good for that, he's a no-bullshit kind of person, and so I think that makes people behave themselves.

Norton: Carriage House is a residential studio in Connecticut. We used to take turns cooking. We used to cook different things every weekend. I did a roast for them. It was quite a little family, really, and they all knew each other really well.

Steve Haigler (mixing engineer, *Doolittle*, *Bossanova*, *Trompe Le Monde*): I recorded Throwing Muses at the Fort with Gary and at the same time Gil Norton was recording *Doolittle* with the Pixies. Gil had worked with Throwing Muses prior to that, and he came over one night to say hi. Gil and I met and we really hit it off that day and he was impressed with what he heard over the monitors for the Muses, so he asked me if I'd like to mix *Doolittle* and I said, "Sure." They were very far behind in the recordings, so when I actually went up to Stanford, Connecticut, Carriage House Studios, there was still half the recording left to do, so I actually ended up recording the rest of the record as well as mixing it. I just remember being blown away by the tracks. The first time I put the tapes up and played them I remember thinking, "This is the coolest shit I've ever heard in my life."

Norton: I knew when I finished it, actually, that it was a bit of a rock'n'roll classic. It just felt like a great rock'n'roll classic album to me, it had all the right ingredients. I thought that when we finished it. I remember everyone left and I had a night in the snow, by myself in Connecticut, my flight wasn't until the next day, and I listened to it and I was quite taken back really, like, "Wow, what happened?" I thought it was so good.

Larbalestier: I heard the music on all of the stuff, but on *Doolittle* we actually had the lyrics, which made a fundamental difference. That just gave it a bit more clarity, it allowed [the art] to be quite specific to the images. It's simple, really. "Monkey Gone to Heaven." I found a stuffed monkey, built the set, *5, 6, 7* were in the lyrics. Everything was dead in this one, the crabs were dead. Again severe, hard, gritty, decaying. The doll in the Petri dish, because we had the lyrics and they were quite specific. The other thing I was quite interested in was the film work of Buñuel, particularly *Un Chien Andalou* [which is referenced in "Debaser"], sort of early surrealist stuff.

Lubin: I remember the band coming up and Charles handing me a white envelope that had a cassette or a DAT in it of *Doolittle*. And I remember putting it on and just being amazed at my own good fortune. "Debaser" is track one, and I had no reason to suspect that the new album would be that comprehensible in the face of the other records. The other ones were more inscrutable, and this one was positively obvious, and deliciously so. And I remember sitting in my chair in my office thinking I was the luckiest A&R guy in the world. Because I thought the thing was just magnificent from start to finish. The day I sent out advance cassettes of *Doolittle*, people were flocking to my office to say, "Dude! You signed the Pixies! This is friggin' great! This is unbelievable"—just the thought that we had them, and I thought, "You know the Pixies?" I don't know, maybe I was sheltered, I thought nobody knew. I remember being enormously thankful and gratified that I didn't have to go around and visit every office and explain what a great thing it was that this was on our label. Not everybody, but certainly enough people from enough quarters of the company were so thrilled and excited that I knew they would do the work for me.

Back in those days alternative radio was a very fledgling format, and you floated a track out to this alternative thing and tried to do well with it there in order to build a base so that you could put a more commercial track out to less enlightened people. So we put out "Monkey Gone to Heaven" first. I think it was a number one Alternative track, but you have to appreciate that an Alternative track in those days was a triumph, but a small triumph. I guess it would be kind of like number one HeatSeeker today. It was considered beside the point in a lot of ways. You could go to mainstream album rock radio and say, "Hey, it was number one at Alternative!" and they'd still say, "Well, we'll see, little man." Elektra had bragging rights around then because we had five number one Alternative tracks that year. "Monkey Gone to Heaven," something by the Happy Mondays, something by the Cure, and Billy Bragg, and They Might Be Giants. We were unbeatable, really.

We did "Monkey Gone to Heaven" and I think there was a video for it, as well, and that went as far as it went, which is as far as it could go on alternative radio and college radio and probably a middling success on album radio. So then, now that you've heated up the marketplace and gotten the attention of radio and retail, then you deliver your big ace in the hole, which we deemed to be "Here Comes Your Man." And "Here Comes Your Man" was blessed with airplay at MTV—you can't underestimate the power of that—and as a result it became an item and we had something of a run with it. I think we always decided to keep "Debaser" in the album, as they say, so it was something that you could enjoy by virtue of acquiring the record. So "Debaser" never did come out as a single track, maybe that could be because the album had been deemed to have run its course.

Larbalestier: The gallery that represented me at the time was putting together a set of work by all the photographers and they decided that it was going to be all about animals. So I went off to do the dog, and when I invited Vaughan to the show, he liked the show and I gave him a Polaroid of it and he happened to be having a meeting with Charles and he showed him the picture and Charles said, "Yeah, let's use that as the single." The dog has passed. Bulldog terriers don't live long, that was 1990, and the dog was four when I photographed it. It was a lovely dog.

Dolan: "Here Comes Your Man" was the most accessible song ever by an underground-type band. The opening chord has an anticipation of something magical and the song just cuts through any indie-rock ambivalence about not sounding "commercial." Gil Norton helped them by bringing the vocals up and turning the guitar noise into something less brutal. Plus, it's a noise band playing a song that was written on an acoustic guitar, so it feels that much more inviting and friendly.

St. Thomas: "Here Comes Your Man" was the song that really almost broke them. I remember thinking that the album artwork was really odd too, with the little monkey with the halo, and the inside jacket is incredible. We really looked at 4AD because they cared about their artists, and they would go out of their way for special packaging and cool artwork and vinyl and B-sides and stuff like that, that the American record companies weren't doing at that time. So there was the attitude that if it was on 4AD, chances are it's probably really cool. Sub Pop had that vibe, too. SST, Twin/Tone kind of had that. That's gone.

Hurley: *Doolittle* and "Here Comes Your Man" was obviously the one that really broke them to a different level. Working for 4AD, that song was like an anomaly in the Pixies' repertoire. I was more involved on the more sort of traditional Pixies songs like "Bone Machine" or "Gigantic," so "Here Comes Your Man" always felt a little out of place in the Pixies catalog. I think Charles and the band sort of felt that as well, and there was always a little bit of caution about releasing that as a single. I think it was released at the right time after the band had already had two or three albums to establish them and their sound so it didn't just seem like they were trying to change direction. It was in the context of an album where the rest of the album was very much the sort of more traditional Pixies sound. It certainly sold a lot of records, but it didn't do what "Smells Like Teen Spirit" did for Nirvana as far as suddenly catapulting them into another stratosphere of sales. "Here Comes Your Man" was definitely the most easily digestible song they did and it certainly did well sales-wise, but it didn't make an enormous difference overnight. I think that's a positive thing.

Andy Barding (former co-editor of the English Pixies fanzine *Rock A My Soul*): I heard "Monkey Gone to Heaven" and I went out and bought *Doolittle* on the day of release. Me and my friend Chris Strange went back to my house after work with this copy of *Doolittle* on vinyl with the beautiful 4AD artwork, nice thick card, little lyric booklet and stuff. We slapped this record on, dropped the needle onto the album and we just could not believe what we were hearing. It was outrageous. "Debaser," side one, track one, is such a fucked up tune, it's eyeball slicing and someone laughing at an eyeball being sliced. We both got the *Un Chien Andalou* reference right away, we both knew the film, but we felt perhaps some people didn't so we felt a little bit clever, and Kim's basslines just came whacking out of the speaker. Those fucking guitars were screaming, and then you've got this idiot singing, "Slicing up eyeballs, ha ha ha ha!" It's like, fucking hell! And then the song finished, and we'd never had so much fun listening to a record, he just said, "Fucking hell! That's amazing! Put it on again, put it on again!"

St. Thomas: "Monkey Gone to Heaven"—it was the greatest thing to see them and everybody was chanting that the "Devil is six and

God is seven." That was huge for us at the radio station, that was the point when it really hit the FNX audience and they became big on the radio for us.

NME review by Edwin Pouncey, April 1989: Cute and mischievous for sure, angelic. . . perhaps, but there's certainly something darker and stranger at play within the Pixies' magical, musical circle. Peel back that little monkey's scalp and you'll probably be both appalled and fascinated at the tumour of evil genius that's squirming there. . .The songs on *Doolittle* have the power to make you literally jump out of your skin with excitement.

Q magazine review by Peter Kane, May 1989: The aptly named Black Francis can justifiably boast one of the most troubled psyches currently at work on the margins of American rock. It's not pretty, but its carefully structured noise and straight forward rhythmic insistence makes perfect sense: a gut feeling that is doubled when it gets within sniffing distance of a tune, as on "Monkey Gone to Heaven" or "Debaser." If the *Come on Pilgrim* mini-album and last year's *Surfer Rosa* were hard acts to follow, then *Doolittle* is a massive 15-track affirmation of mushrooming Pixie power.

PJ Harvey (musician): When I think of *Doolittle* I immediately think of "I Bleed" because that's one of my favorite songs of all time. I love *Doolittle*, I love it. "Tame" and "I Bleed," I mean, I learned to play those back then, I was just in awe of those songs in particular, but Charles' writing is amazing. I don't think I heard *Doolittle* until a while after it came out. I heard *Surfer Rosa* first and that just blew my mind, I went, "What is this?" and obviously immediately went to track down Steve Albini. I can't stress enough what a great writer I think Charles is, and still is. I have such respect for his writing, and the songwriting as much as the sound is what gets me about the Pixies' songs. I just think "I Bleed" is a beautifully structured, very powerful, haunting, scary, and very moving song.

Iha: *Doolittle* was more pop, still corrosive but not as corrosive as *Surfer Rosa*. It wasn't as raw, it was more listenable. Still crazy, but you listen to "Here Comes Your Man" it's a classic pop record where if you didn't listen to the lyrics and you just listened to the melodies and the harmonies it could just be this nice, normal song.

Lubin: It went gold, which, believe me, I thought of as a crowning, masterful, major, freakin' wonderful achievement. To go gold, to me that's still a hell of a lot of records—500,000 people took it to the counter and dipped into their pocket and ponied up for *Doolittle*. I was really proud of that fact, I thought it was fantastic. But Charles refused to lip-sync, which is why in the "Here Comes Your Man" video whenever his vocals come on he simply opens his mouth and shuts it when his vocals stop.

Watts-Russell: A record company responding to the kind of exposure that you get when a video is Buzz Binn-ed is astronomical. The Cure and the Sugercubes had all that MTV exposure, but we got no MTV exposure, and so Elektra didn't have any idea of really what to do. It was a big fucking record company, so they were like, "Whoops, what the fuck do we do?" I mean the "Monkey Gone to Heaven" video, it's the kind of thing that in the last number of years they've gotten exposure for—back then you were still supposed to be lip-syncing.

Norman Blake (Teenage Fanclub guitarist): For news to spread in the U.S. it takes a long time for things to become popular. Here, people will read about them in *NME* or *Mojo*, it will be played on Radio 1 and people will hear it faster. There are fewer outlets over here so it's easier for things to be broken.

Mico: In England things just sort of exploded. It was bizarre, I remember being with them when *Doolittle* entered the top ten. It was a very surreal moment, the Pixies in the top ten in England. It really felt like the lunatics have taken over the asylum.

Thompson: There is a certain dumb rock element to some of our stuff, too. Sure, we're not singing some song about hot lovin' or whatever, but it's still going, "Du-dun-dun, du-dun-dun, du-dun-dun, du-dun-dun," there's some dumbness there, you know what I mean? There's some repetition, some simplicity. There's simplicity in what we do that I think people connect with, too. I mean, "Gigantic" is pretty simple. "This monkey's gone to heaven." That's that whole song. That's it! "Five, six, seven, woo-hoo!"

Flansburgh: I remember we were doing a show at the Ritz in New York, and it was right after the Pixies had blown up in Europe, and I was walking across the dance floor with Charles, and he was like, "You wouldn't believe it, man! Our record is getting played on the John Peel show, it's totally happening!" It was absolutely an un-neurotic response to success. He was just as happy about this niche that they had found in England as anybody could be. I think it seemed like a manageable kind of success, and it was the right thing for them. It just seemed better that way, it wasn't like having some odd breakout hit in the U.S. that would come back.

Thompson: I'm not saying there isn't this intellectual, arty flavor in it, but it's simple. That's one thing the Pixies are good at—being simple. I think because we were somewhat limited by our musicianship at our inception. I'm not some seasoned singer-songwriter, right? Or a fantastic guitar player? And Joey was the most non-virtuoso, unschooled guitar player, and we just said, "You're the lead guitar player." "Okay!"

Murphy: They did most of the recording for *Doolittle* in some house in Connecticut, and that's when Mente started.

Deal: John eventually started his own band and they played at the Middle East. Mente, it's just kind of a joke band, they had songs about [murdered *Hogan's Heroes* actor] Bob Crane, "Body bag, body bag," and Bobby Orr.

Murphy: "Hoverin" is a Mente song that was written in 1978, and Kim covered it twice. Once with the Breeders on a B-side, and once with the Amps.

Marc Mazzarelli (a.k.a. Mazz, Mente bassist): Kim lent us instruments for Mente because we didn't have any and she showed us how to play them. But then John dropped her Les Paul and that was it, we had to give back all the instruments.

Deal: I was out of town, and I let him borrow my Les Paul that I got in the '70s, and it's like a really nice gold top Les Paul, and. . .I can't even say it! He smashed it and broke the neck! On my guitar! I just let him borrow it! And he can't even play guitar, it was more a prop. Oh, that kills me. That really hurts.

Widmer: We played at the Middle East, which actually was a Middle Eastern restaurant with a back room, that's all it was. Now it's a huge rock club called the Middle East but with no restaurant. Basically rock took over a restaurant. The Pixies all came and it was a huge success. I mean probably there were only 50 people there but it felt like a million to us. Kim appeared with us for two songs.

Murphy: We convinced Billy Ruane at the Middle East that if we could play we'd make sure there was a guest appearance by Kim, so that was our first paid performance, out of a bribe. I think it was '88. The Pixies were in New York, and she knew she had our show to do so she flew in the afternoon of the show, flew back the next morning. She spent her own money to come up and be in our show for three songs, I always thought that was cool.

10. VAMOS—ALL OVER THE WORLD (1989)

As soon as the *Doolittle* sessions were finished the band jetted back to Europe for a tour titled "Sex and Death," which included an appearance at the Glastonbury Festival. When they got back to the U.S., although it meant demotion from headliners to openers, they chose to support the Cure on an arena tour. The four Pixies found themselves spending nearly all their time together, which didn't exactly ease tensions when the band was feeling irritated. Despite the fact that the task of writing, recording, and touring kept the group united and enthusiastic, sometimes tempers flared.

Lovering: The Cure, that was our first big tour. The first grand amphitheater, stadium kind of places we were doing.

Ben Marts (former Pixies American tour manager): The first tour I did with them was a combo tour. It was Pixies supporting Love and Rockets. Five to six dates were big arena Cure dates where they added Love and Rockets/Pixies to the Cure, and Shelleyan Orphan was the fourth band.

Lovering: We were opening up for the Cure at Giants Stadium, and I was there early on stage. They got these huge sheets of plywood, laid them all over the field and then put a huge tarp all over everything. This was done the night before and then it rained overnight. So during the night all the moisture warped the boards, bowing the ends and everything underneath the tarp. So I'm on the stage watching and they open up general admission, and just imagine hundreds and hundreds of Goths running in to get in front of the stage and they're going down like flies because they're tripping on all the boards underneath the tarp. It was very surreal.[10]

Marts: Robert Smith actually came into our dressing room and said hello and, "We're hanging out afterwards tonight and gonna have a party," and we thought that was really wonderful. I got the hint from that that Robert Smith was a fan and appreciated both bands being on the bill and wanted to hang out.

Deal: People would come up to me now and be like, "I saw you in '86 or '88" and I think, "Wow, somebody was there, somebody out of the 20 people who saw us in Montreal." They didn't really come to see us, they came to see Love and Rockets, which is fine, we were opening for them.

Gilbert: When *Doolittle* came out, they took the Zulus as their opening act on one of those tours. So we did like East Coast and a whole bunch of Midwest. At that point, it was like a professional tour, and the dates were like, bam bam bam bam bam, seven, eight nights in a row, kind of long distances between, so there wasn't a lot of free time for much hanging out and mischief. It was very work-oriented. There was one night, classic band thing where you know, the promoter afterwards took us all to this club and gave us these mushrooms and they were way stronger than everyone thought they were going to be. But that's band cliché story number 22, the band takes drugs that are way more potent than they expected so instead of being an incredible party, everyone's too fucked up to do anything. They were all pretty youthful, so you have a lot of energy and stamina, and on top of it your career is really soaring, so you can get by, you can get driven by a certain amount of natural adrenaline. You can ingest drugs and play shows and not have it severely adversely affect your performance. At least for a while.

At that point of course their stock had risen quite a bit. We weren't getting any ego from them or any power play type of a thing. They just had a big job to take care of every day, so some days you'd see 'em and hang around with them and some days you wouldn't just because of the nature of the time allocation for when people would be in a venue or not. I never felt like all of a sudden they were different people. It felt very similar and very comfortable, actually.

Iha: I saw them on the *Doolittle* tour, they played the Cabaret Metro, which is a classic Chicago venue. It's like 1,200 people, the sound is really nice, and Happy Mondays were opening. I don't know how long *Doolittle* had been out, but it was acknowledged they had released a classic record, everybody seemed to have that one, and you actually heard it. I remember hearing "Here Comes Your Man" on the radio. There was one station in Chicago that played alternative stuff like that, WXRT, it was kind of VH1-ish but they would play cool, new stuff, too. Everybody was just so psyched for that show, it was obviously a phenomenon. Everybody loved every song and they played great. They played all the hits even though people didn't know they were hits.

Murphy: [On November 21, 1989] The Pixies were playing at Citi, and they were doing two shows. They played the first show, which was all-ages, it started at seven, the second show wasn't until 11, 11:30. So in between sets we hopped in a cab (me, Kim, and Mente's Ted Widmer and Marc "Mazz" Mazzarelli) to go meet Joe Harvard at the Plough and Stars. She sang two or three songs with him, including "I Believe in Miracles," which was the one they did, and then we all went back for the second show. She had three shows in one night, it was pretty funny.

Harvard: Kim I would see a lot, and she used to come down to the Plough and Stars where I did a weekly residency. I had no set band, it was like a clusterfuck every single week. She came in and did an entire set-worth of stuff at the Middle East one night. It was mainly covers because there was no rehearsal. So Kim came and I was doing "You Sexy Thing" by Hot Chocolate, she said, "I could sing that better." I said, "If you can fucking sing that better, Kim, get up and sing." So she started to come and probably five or six occasions she came and sang "You Sexy Thing." And kicked the shit out of it, definitely burned me to the ground. How could she not? She had the voice of an angel, but like an angel who maybe had been a merchant marine.

Murphy: After we were already divorced they were playing the Living Room in Providence, and they had this big box truck and a van. They were switching highways, and the box truck took the exit too fast and tipped over, wrecked two-thirds of their equipment, but they had the show at night. So Kim calls me at work, "You gotta do me a favor," I'm like, "What?" She goes, "Go to Wurlitzer"—that was the name of the music store—"Go to Wurlitzer and rent two Marshalls, okay write this down! We need a Les Paul," and I'm like, "Okay, then what?" and she goes, "Then you gotta bring it to Providence," which is only like an hour from Boston, so not that bad, but I wasn't planning on going that early. She was like "You gotta bring them down, you gotta be there for sound check" which is like, six o'clock—pissa. So I run over to Wurlitzer and max out my credit card on the rentals, "We'll pay you back, we'll pay you back" she kept saying. I jam all this stuff into my 1988 Hyundai, I can barely fit anything, the seat next to me had equipment on it, and I'm driving to Providence at 100 mph, trying to beat them there. I got the equipment there, actually I think I even beat them there, loaded them in, they played a great show.

Marts: The Pixies modus operandi was always here's the set list, we're gonna play the songs, here it comes. Kim always had a fan club because there were two or three songs that she sang lead vocals on and you could always tell there were people who wanted to stand in front of Kim. Kim made more stage banter than Charles and the crowd always reacted favorably.

St. Thomas: I think I was so in love with Kim that I really didn't notice the rest of the band. She's so awesome. You had two vocalists, which I thought was really cool, because that reminded me of X, even though they didn't really sound alike. Joey was so out there. When he'd go into a solo, he'd bend his strings and somehow it would be out of tune, but it sounded dead on. It seems to me that Kim definitely had more of the vibe on the stage, and then Charles would be singing and holding down the ship, same with Dave, and Joey would go into these spazzing guitar solos, and that Kim would basically be just like, funny. I remember being drawn to Kim, thinking she's so cool, just the funny stuff she would do, like wink at people. Charles sang on more of the stuff, so she would just do stuff in between her vocal parts.

Courtney Taylor (The Dandy Warhols' singer/guitarist): Obviously at some point she was the coolest chick in the world, as far as I could tell [the song "Cool As Kim Deal" appeared on the Dandy Warhols' 1997 album *Come Down*]. She has that 1950s chick, "Hey la, hey la, my boyfriend's back" cool. During grunge, chicks weren't cool like that.

Shirley Manson (Garbage lead singer): I was madly in love with Pixies. I always loved the way Kim Deal sang because she had this effortless cool about her voice, and it always had this slightly sort of lazy phrasing that I really, really loved. And her voice just melded so perfectly with Black Francis', it was this incredible feel. And I remember discovering that she was a bass player and just believing that her coolness factor was in outer space as a result. Not only could she sing like that, but she could also play. I just loved the fact that she never really hogged the limelight, she was never looking to take any attention onto herself. She was like the perfect soldier in a band, she was part of a band dynamic and that's what seemed to make her tick and I really respected that about her because there are so few women who are genuinely interested in being a musician and they're not looking for any kind of attention other than that which is created from the music. [Her effortless cool] drew people to her, they were magnetized by her.

Thompson: I think that my personality, and the personalities of other members of the Pixies come through, whether we're playing a gig, whether we're making a record. Especially when we're playing a gig. With Kim, people just love her. She can just stand up there smoking a cigarette and people are just like, "Ahhhh! Kim!" For whatever reason, they love her, because she's being who she is. They can totally tell. People know. They're like, "She's legit." No one asks what's her thing or what she's like, or what's her art all about. Forget about the art. There's this person standing there, and she's totally like, "I'm Kim Deal and this is who I am." She's the same way offstage, and people can tell. It's the same thing with Joey and the same thing with Dave and the same thing with me, I think.

Deal: Onstage Joey didn't say a word, David didn't have a microphone. Those two didn't have mics. I probably talked, maybe Charles was retuning his strings or something. It's fun to piss 'em off. If you're in fucking Toronto, just call it Detroit and it pisses them off. It's easy. But it's not meant to be hurtful. Yeah, so you just say, "Hello, Detroit." Boooo. What? What? I have no idea. They should get it, you know. I mean, do they think that we really don't know where we are? And it freaks people out, it's not like I was doing an act, I was just like, "Hi, how are you?" It freaks motherfuckers out. Because there's this impenetrable wall between band and audience. [The perpetual smile] is just nervousness. I don't smile that much regularly. Probably because I'm so nervous it's just like hey. "Hey." People are staring at you! Hey. Sometimes I'll have moments of being comfortable and then if you look up it's like, "Oh God!" and you look down. Joe, I don't think ever looked up.

Perkins: Dave's a very powerful straight rock drummer, and when you talk to him and look at him you wouldn't realize it. With all the guys, with Joey, you talk and listen to them and then you hear what's coming out of them and it's so dissonant and left of center. You're like, oh wow, these guys look center, but they're left.

Banks: When the Pixies came to town people sat up and took notice. We were the hot ticket. Kids outside begging to get in, amazing. Climbing through windows, the whole nine yards. The great thing about the Pixies was they were the first band that I've ever seen where it was like a two-thirds/one-third split, at times it was even 50/50, with the girls and boys. The girls were down there bopping along and bouncing up and down and moshing, they were doing it and it was totally asexual. But I've never seen so many girls before in that kind of mad physical [atmosphere]. Having Kim in the band, it really helped. There weren't a lot of girls in bands before that, you know. It was very rare. There was an awful lot more afterwards, wasn't there? Don't you think there was a point where every band had a girl? To me, it was one of those tipping points, and that's the thing about the Pixies, they changed so much of what came after them. They opened so many doors for so many people.

Angel: Pixies were great live. I saw them 15, 20 times, and they were rocking every single time. I even saw them under circumstances that were difficult, when they were opening for other groups, and they were good at what they did. There are some bands where it doesn't translate at all. But with them, they did take it up a notch. They were a hard working band. They didn't get out on the stage and fuck around. Kim smoking her cigarette, diddly-bopping and all that shit, that was just part of the act. They rocked.

St. Thomas: One of the big standout shows that I really remember was at the Paradise Rock Club on Commonwealth Avenue. They did their entire set in alphabetical order. I thought it was incredible. I didn't really catch on until about six songs. I was like, "Hold on, 'Ana...'" I couldn't believe how cool that was. They played "Into the White" that night, and that's one of my favorite songs, which was a B-side so it was kind of hard to get. I just thought it was really cool that they played a B-side in the middle of the alphabetical show and the audience seemed to know the song. People were so into it that they knew the obscure B-side.

Banks: We used to do some crazy things to relieve the boredom. Playing the set backwards. I remember at the Kilburn, that was quite funny, where they came on and did the last song, then went offstage after doing one number. They completely reversed the set. Played it in alphabetical order. Played some long shows, as well. Charles used to get some crazy ideas. Some of it was really creative, we used to do rehearsals where we'd try different things, but there was no like, spinning drum risers or anything like that. This is a band that became big very, very quickly, it's not like they had a long history of playing in clubs behind them.

Marts: You put those faster songs that gets the audience pogo-ing or dancing the most, that has a real amazing effect. Those just built it into a frenzy. A lot of times I don't think the kids ever realized it was going on. I don't think people realized what was going on with the alphabetical sets. They did this more on headlining sets than on support dates.

Santiago: Generally, we were happy, just excited to put on a good show. And we learned after a while that you can't do good shows every night. I was just wondering when a good show would arrive. Maybe once a week, twice a week. But it's always exciting when it clicked, very exciting on our end. In general we were pretty happy but very critical of our performance after.

Banks: David has never been excessive with anything, really, I don't think. Neither was Charles. We'd have a few beers, we'd all smoke marijuana on the bus, I mean, man, you're on those buses and you're doing a 16-hour journey, we just used to sit in the back of the bus and smoke a joint and giggle. I'd tell them old stories, and they'd laugh and we'd play games and do stupid things. We were just like on a family outing.

Blake: I remember we played with Pixies in Glasgow and the barrier collapsed in the front of the stage. We got to play our set, but

Pixies only got to do two songs before there was a crush at the front of the stage, people were sort of trying to get to the front and basically the barrier collapsed and Chas had to come out and keep the audience back and tell the audience that the show wouldn't be going on.

They were just massive over here; it's probably difficult to quantify how influential they were on a whole generation of musicians. I think sometimes people forget that. People will talk about the importance of Nirvana or whatever but I think the Pixies had much more of an influence on how music developed, especially in the U.K. Maybe it is more difficult for Americans to quite get how big they were in Europe. They influenced everyone.

Banks: When Charles used to go into "Levitate Me," I personally used to get the same feeling as when Pete Townshend used to play the opening chords to "I Can't Explain." It was music that meant something, that was powerful, that had bite, and just as when I was a kid, just as the Osmonds were around, the Who were around. And just as the Pixies were around, they were like an antidote to the pop scene that was going on.

In Spain they went ape-shit when Charles started doing his Spanglish stuff. The kids, they're just so used to bands singing in English, when someone comes along and they start—it's like half-English, half-Spanish from when he was in Puerto Rico, he called it Spanglish—it's like the kids related to it. They went absolutely crazy when they went into that stuff, they went bananas.

Geiger: There was a huge market disparity—they had broken in Europe and didn't break here [in the U.S.]. So they were playing huge festivals in Europe, big places, but their attitude was always "The hardest-working band in show business." They were very hard-working, they have an incredibly great work ethic. In Europe, you also had an indie chart that was much more influential than the CMJ charts were here at the time. The Pixies were a massive press band, and the press were much more instrumental in a band's growth [in Europe] than they were here, in general. They also worked in Europe from the get-go, whereas R.E.M. and others spent a lot more time cultivating here. The Pixies weren't necessarily sex, and sex does better here. They were more abrasive, and Europe just appreciated their abrasiveness.

St. Thomas: It never seemed like they were just on the bill, and it would always be like, "Yeah, they're in England." It was just like,

"Wow, this is a Boston band in England?" None of the other bands were doing that at the time, absolutely not—they were struggling just to get gigs in Boston or New York. And then we'd get articles from *NME* or *Melody Maker* and they'd rave about the band and you'd be like, "Holy shit, look at this! They're in *NME*, but they're not even in the local paper!"

Barding: Kim said as much [when he interviewed her for *Rock A My Soul*], she said, "No one gets the Pixies back in America." People saw the "Here Comes Your Man" video and they thought the big heads were sort of funny and weird, but they would rarely transfer that into the actual process of buying a record or going to see them.

Angel: In 1989, I was at the big rock station in Boston, WBCN. They were organizing their roster for this event they run every year called the Rock'n'Roll Rumble, which was a battle of the bands. They were talking about bands that were going to be in the Rumble and the Pixies came up. Two of the people at the station said, "Pixies, they'd be pretty good, we've played some of their stuff occasionally." And I said, "Fellas, they're a huge international act. They're not going to play your thing, you know?" And they ignored me like I wasn't there. "I wonder who we would call in the band, if they'd open on Tuesday night." That's how provincial this city is. They have no idea.

Geiger: Radio did not embrace them here. I think the biggest thing was that over here, *Come on Pilgrim*, *Surfer Rosa*, didn't count except at CMJ, whereas in Europe they were seen as absolutely seminal, so by the time you got to *Doolittle*, *Doolittle* was an explosive record for them there, and here that was almost like their first legitimate record. And here, only one of them really counted, which was *Doolittle*.

Hurley: I think there is a more eagerness and openness to accept things that are different in Europe, but certainly the media over there really helps. Back when the Pixies were first putting out records, there were at least two, maybe three, weekly newspapers dedicated to music. And they would put the Pixies on the front cover very early on in their career. Radio 1 would play Pixies music very early so the audience had a much easier way to access and be made aware of what the Pixies were up to, whereas as you know, apart from a few really sort of smart critics over here, you have to get a certain level of success before major media covers you.

St. Thomas: That's the thing, I have this weird perspective on it, because to me they were pretty big in Boston, we played them a lot on the air, people seemed to love them, and they did really well. I guess I never thought about it, but people didn't really know them in other places. As it got into the other records, we'd be five and six cuts deep on these albums. We were playing all kinds of weird shit. We played "Theme from *Narc*" which was in heavy rotation. I don't even know what that's on. It's a B-side, and it's a theme from a video game that they covered the song from. It's a really obscure one, but we played songs like that. They were huge for us!

Deal: The dynamic in the band was not good. It wasn't good at all. It was a long tour.

Thompson: There was a point around *Doolittle* where things got kind of icy. People talked less and less. People hung out on their own more and more. You go into the dressing room and no one's talking. You play a show where the crowd is going crazy, it's sold out, three encores, everything's going great. . .go back to the dressing room and it's cold as ice.[11]

Gilbert: Right around that time was when tension between Charles and Kim was building for sure. And every once in a while you'd get a little sense of that, but at the same time, I never had any specific tales about it. There was one show when they played in Detroit where the PA system was really poorly rigged and Charles just kept getting shocked while he was singing. So 40 minutes into the set he got mad and threw his guitar down and walked offstage and the Detroit audience, they're tough and got super pissed off and started throwing stuff onstage. I remember somebody threw a bottle and it went through Charles' guitar, put a big hole in it. You don't always think that clearly in a performance because your mind is so many places. You've been on the road for a while and you've played a lot of shows, and you're sort of living in this totally weird existence where you're kind of a nomad and you don't have anything grounding you. . . it can just wear people down. But show business is filled with stories of performers doing that. It just happens. People blow fuses in their day-to-day life.

Perkins: One day on tour with your band is like four days at home hanging out with your friends. You have so much to do, so many handshakes, so many different places to be, so much energy you have to give and accept from other people, that cycle. And then you've got to be true to your music and all that.

Thompson: Leonard Cohen's *I'm Your Man*, I bought a cassette of that on the road with the Pixies. They wanted to go party at some stupid beach town in Spain, and I was like, "Drop me off in this town here where there's no people. I'm gonna stay here for the five days or whatever." Get away from the band, get away from the bus, the crew, whatever. Kim and I probably weren't on the best of terms, and I remember I was really annoyed 'cause I got out and I was like, "All right, man, I'm alone. I'm away from the tour. For five whole days." I grabbed my bag, ran to the front desk of this hotel. No one there. No one's staying at this hotel. Everyone else is at this party town, you know, 100 miles down the road. Who comes trottin' out of the bus behind me, decides she wants to do the same damn thing? Kim Deal.

I was like, *fuckin' a*. . .all right. What can I say? "No, you can't stay in this town." Then it's worse. The people at the hotel figure we're probably the best of friends, you know, which we were not at the moment, and this hotel which probably has, like, 500 rooms, they put us right next to each other. I was so pissed off at Kim. I was like, I had this whole town to myself and now you're like next door to me. It's like we can hear each other snoring! I said, "All right, let me listen to this stupid cassette that I bought." Over the course of five days I just submersed myself in that album, listened to it over and over again. I ended up writing a song that week, "Blown Away," which we went and recorded about a week later in Berlin at the same studio where *Lust for Life* was recorded.

Deal: In Stuttgart, I was singing "Into the White," at the very end, when you repeat "Into the white, into the white," and I think that Charles didn't think I was doing it with enough enthusiasm, I don't know. He ended up throwing this acoustic guitar and it kind of knocked my calf and fell at my feet and I turned around and looked at him, and of course he backed up behind Joey. God, what an ass. So stupid. Sometimes you just feel stupid at the mic. Sometimes Joey will just do a really good lead on "Vamos," and really get into it, and some nights he feels awkward or stupid, he won't pick up the Fender Twin and give it a real shake so the reverb cabinet goes *chowa*. So maybe I was feeling stupid and not saying all the "Into the whites" at the end, whatever, I don't know, it's Charles' deal, he was feeling weird and he threw a guitar at me. I was like *what the fuck?* Somebody threw something at me when I was on a microphone, singing *his* song that he wrote the lyrics to! I don't even like singing other people's songs anyway! Ew, ew, ew! And I get the guitar thrown at me. Limply. And then he hides behind *Joey*! It was 'cause I was late for the show. It's the only fucking show I've ever been late to. Like, I was ten minutes late. I got lost in Germany. I didn't like, do it on purpose, it wasn't a Guns N' Roses move. I was extremely concerned, oh my God! I came up to Joe, "Oh my God, I'm so sorry I'm late!" "Don't worry Kim, we love you." Gave me a kiss before the show, it was real sweet. Then fucking fuck throws a guitar at me? Whatever your problem is dude! Back off! That was after *Doolittle*. He was going through something, I guess.

Banks: That was in a country and western club in Stuttgart called the Longhorn. If you imagine a building that from the outside looks like a warehouse where you could store animal feed in it, and when you go inside it was done like a wild west saloon. And at the end was this huge stage. It was just a rectangular shed with a balcony, and all the kids were down below, and that's where it happened. We'd been in Yugoslavia, and Kim had picked up this Yugoslavian guy and he was touring around with her. We arrived at the gig, she did the sound check, she went to the hotel because she had two or three hours, and she said, "I'll get a cab back." Time becomes valuable in those circumstances, and it was wake up little Susie, wasn't it: She'd gone back to the hotel, gone to bed with this guy and fallen asleep. So Shirley phones and the hotel said, "No, she's not in her room." We're getting really anxious now, it's like 30 minutes to stage time, she's not back. Shirley phones again, somebody goes up to the room, bangs on the door and the phone is ringing, eventually Kim answers the phone, she says "Right, I'll be there in ten minutes." That was all she said. Anyway, she was 20 minutes, so the band ended up going onstage late. She couldn't get a cab. It was 45 minutes late, we had to cut 15 minutes off the show, Charles was seriously pissed, we were all pissed off with her. We were all very tight professional people. We did not go onstage late because that's insulting to the audience. And we just all felt let down by it, it wasn't just Charles.

It was an unbelievable show, there's just this level of intensity. And then I can't remember the exact sequence of events, but something happened where Charles thought she had done something and he ended up kicking the guitar, and he ended up hitting her. He hadn't meant it to hit her, because he thought it'd been a bad show—it did go a bit weird in the end—and he stormed off the stage and she came running up the stairs, "How dare you kick your guitar at me!" and they went for each other. Shirley got in the way, Kim ends up kicking Shirley, she's still got a mark on her bloody leg from where she kicked her. You're talking about two basic animal people. Charles is closer to nature than most people. It was like kids in the playground, you know, it wasn't a fistfight. So we calmed it all down and everybody sat in the dressing room. Nobody knows what to do, so I go in, and I said, "All right guys, we've had our first fight, we're all grown up, we're going to get over this, we're going to get on the fucking bus, we're going to go on, we're going to do the next show, we're going to complete the tour, because otherwise, here's what happens when you don't do this: all these guys have to go home, you lose all your money, it's disappointing, all the kids get let down. So, you've had a fight, you don't feel like working together, tough shit, fucking get on with it." I took this hard line. You've got to bear in mind that I'm the older guy, so who's going to do it in the band? Nobody's going to do it in the band. Somebody's got to say come on, team, it's like the coach. So I give them the big lecture, let's shake hands and move on now, the time to sort this out is the end of the tour. An event like that doesn't just happen out of thin air. It was building out of what Kim felt was Charles' bullying or bossy kind of way.

Thompson: It was a screw-up, but in retrospect it seems almost stupid that I got upset over her being late, "This is so unprofessional!" She was late to a gig, you know? Whatever. The gig happened and all was well. I didn't need to get frustrated. I was probably all wound up and everything and there was some tension in the air. But we actually got along pretty well. We may not have always spoken to each other at all times, but we got through it a hell of a lot better than other bands.

11. BLOWN AWAY (AND NEARLY APART)— *BOSSANOVA* BOUND (1990)

When the band returned to the States in 1990 to record *Bossanova*, Thompson, Lovering, and Santiago moved to Los Angeles without Kim Deal. Though she eventually joined her bandmates on the West Coast, recording their third full-length album would be unlike any studio experience the group had had before. But as far as anyone could tell, Pixies were still on their way up.

Deal: So then we came back from Edinburgh in '90, recorded *Bossanova*. After I got fired...well I didn't completely get fired. I was there to get fired.

Banks: [After the Stuttgart incident] they didn't exactly shake hands, but we all got on with it. It was a bit strained, we finished the tour, then they had the big meeting.

Geiger: There were some issues between Charles and Kim.

Watts-Russell: I completely remember a phone call from Kim to our house. I think she might have had a tip off from Michelle Anthony, a bigwig at Sony now who was their lawyer at the time, that something was happening in L.A. Kim called up and was really confused, didn't know what to do, and I was totally useless on the phone. I didn't have anything as quite as constructive [to say] as Deborah, and Deborah just told her get on a plane, get out there. And it's so good that she did, because if she hadn't Kim would have simply gotten a phone call—"You're out of the band." But she went out there and actually got in the same room as them, and it seems no one was really capable of doing it face to face. So she got to stay in the group.

Banks: There were moments of tension but I think in general, to be fair to Kim, she knew what the rules were. What messed Kim up, truthfully, was the drugs and the booze. If she hadn't been involved with all that stuff her mind would have been clearer and she would have been able to see where she stood. Because if you think about it, why did she say, "Will you forgive me, can I come back in the band?" That's where she wanted to be, she didn't want to be anywhere else. All right, she went off and she did the Breeders. The Pixies would have been the place to do those songs, there's no reason why she couldn't have done those, and it would have happened. I think they would have dealt with it, I think they would have worked the way through all this stuff. Because they were so big and successful.

Donelly: Personally, I felt like Kim should have walked away at that point because she was unhappy and she had this other thing going on [the Breeders] that was being received really well. But I think it was just such a shock, and she had made the decision to stick it out and then all of a sudden she was being told that they didn't want her to stick it out. It had gotten to that point in a band's life where everybody's kind of estranged to a certain extent, and I think she was assuming they were all estranged, as well.

Deal: The guys kind of slowly moved out to L.A. and I never did get an apartment out there. Maybe I would have got an apartment if I had known that the next few records would have be done out there and not the East Coast. Joe had just moved from Rhode Island and David had just moved from Boston. It took a while for all of them to get there, we were all like, "Oh, we're going to be based in L.A. now?"

Lovering: We all moved to L.A. because the recording studio was there. And three of us stayed in the Oakwood apartments, that was an experience in itself. Joe and I shared a room, Kim was there. [Comic] Garrett Morris was a neighbor down the way, as well as the band White Lion. The Oakwood is a weird place. In L.A. man, it's another world.

Norton: Charles had moved to L.A. at that point, which we were all a bit grumpy about because none of us liked L.A. I didn't really want to go. Boston, I love, between Throwing Muses and them. We did talk about [coming back East] but he had sort of done that—again, with Charles, he's already done that, he wants to do something different. We actually had a great time out there. We stayed in the Oakwood apartments and me and the band were all in the same apartment block. We all just hung out, we used to go swimming, there'd be like ghetto blasters going on, we'd just have parties all the time.

Hersh: We made records at the same time out here in L.A., we all lived in Oakwood together. We were making *The Real Ramona*, and we were all in the studio so we didn't see each other much.

Donelly: I introduced Julie Farman to David in L.A. because we were out there staying in this big apartment complex and Julie and I had kind of gotten back in touch. We were hanging out and one day, I was a little bit of a yenta then, and I was like, "David come with me, I'm going to meet my friend Julie, she's really awesome." And it worked. They were together for a while.

Norton: We started to record in a place called Cherokee studios, and we had a lot of problems in the studio. Basically at six o'clock in the evening the whole desk turned into a radio transmitter receiver and picked these pirate radios up. So every time we started to record after six we'd have radio all over everything. I said, look, we're losing our flow recording here, so we'll stop for a few days and go somewhere else to do overdubs and then we'll come back and carry on [when the problem was fixed]. But when we came back, every time you'd plug a guitar amp into any of the mains they'd have this incredible hum on it. We couldn't record, it was just ridiculous. So I had this big thing with the studio and they basically were blaming me and saying it's the way you're recording the guitars or something. I was like, it's getting unbelievable now, I can't hack it, so I walked out. So we left the studio and I didn't phone Ivo because I thought he'd freak out and I had nowhere to go. We used to go to this bar, Small's, in L.A., and I was in there with Joey and Rick Rubin was there. He came over and said hello, so I explained to him what had happened, so he just said, "My office is your office" and he got his secretary to start looking to see what studios were available. It was very sweet. And then we moved to Master Control, which was in the Valley. It was a bit hairy for a week, I went completely underground, Ivo couldn't get ahold of me, I wasn't going to speak to him until I could go, "Yeah, we had a few problems, but now everything's fine."

Haigler: Gil asked me again if I wanted to work on *Bossanova*. We mixed it in L.A. at Master Control and Al (Alistair) Clay, an English engineer, recorded most of the stuff. I did the final recordings that still needed to be done and mixed it. Everything was still cool it seemed with everyone. The budget was bigger, the tracks were bigger: 48 as opposed to *Doolittle*'s 24.

Norton: *Doolittle* had done really well, so we sort of could do whatever we wanted, and Ivo was always very sensible. Because *Doolittle* had done pretty well we had a better budget for *Bossanova*.

Santiago: *Bossanova* and *Trompe le Monde* were basically written in the studio for the most part. We had little practice, scheduled two-week practice. Unlike Boston, when we were in the rehearsal place almost every day.

Norton: It was different, most of the songs on there we hadn't got demos for, so lots of them we were writing in the rehearsal room. We'd do these landscapes, as far as I was concerned, they were like sonic landscapes, and I'd make my own little videos up in my head about what the song was about. There'd be a desert, wide open spaces, big cactus plants on some of the songs, or I'd be in space or something. Because we didn't have any lyrics, Charles would come in and go, "This is the verse: na na na na na, this is the chorus da da da da da da da." So you'd have those two bits and then you'd construct an arrangement out of it.

Watts-Russell: The material wasn't written, the lyrics were being written in the studio, it became a different process. How do you produce something when all you have heard was an instrumental?

Thompson: I was writing songs, writing lyrics in the studio, 'cause you know, everything we did was brilliant, so no one was questioning. "Oh they're selling, give us some more of that shit, whatever." So I was writing on napkins five minutes before I sang. Sometimes it's good, sometimes not. That's just the nature of that songwriting.

Norton: "Stormy Weather" is a cover, it's a Neil Young song. "Down to the Well" was an old song that Gary Smith had done a demo for a long time ago, so we had that as a demo. "Cecilia

Ann," that was obviously a cover. It was an old surf song Charles had found. "Dig For Fire" we had a demo for that, as well. That was it, really, we had those, the rest we worked up. But I mean, there's 14 songs on *Bossanova*, but we probably would have recorded 22 backing tracks. Quite a lot of them we wouldn't finish off. We'd start them off get them up to a certain point, and if they didn't have lyrics, they'd just get left.

"Dig For Fire" was the first time we used a drum machine. The bass drum on that is a drum machine and Dave played on top of it. That was the first time we'd ever used any sample type sounds on the album. "Is She Weird," I sang backing vocals on that. "Rock Music" was one of the ones Charles was having problems just getting some lyrics up for, so he said "just put a mic up" so we put a mic up and that was the vocal, basically—he just went and yelled his head off. And we kept the guide vocal as a back vocal because it was such a great vibe, we all fell off our chairs, "That's one done!" It was definitely one of those periods where just finishing the lyrics off was a bit of a fun thing to do.

Thompson: Silver, cigar-shaped saucers. I don't know what they are, and I'm not saying they're from outer space. I think there's a very small percentage of people who actually have seen them, and I think there's a much greater percentage of people who really want to see them, so they see them. Therein lies the "Do they exist or not?" question. I think there is a small percentage of people who have seen them, and I'm one of them.

["Manta Ray"], that's my code word for UFO. It's about a UFO incident in 1965. I have it described to me in great detail by people who were there. My mother was there. This was in Nebraska. My cousin has a couple of UFO experiences, too. I've only had one and I don't even remember it; it's sort of undramatic. There were legit people who don't even follow that stuff. There was a flying saucer floating above the house for half an hour and everyone just stood there and watched it. . .It was just hovering. Then the state police came and chased it, but they couldn't catch up with it. A big red fucking saucer, a glowing, fucking, flying saucer. My mother's weird, but she's not that weird. She's got no reason to make this stuff up. I have a couple of memories as a young boy seeing things in the sky that did not look like airplanes. Once a rocket ship, but I thought it was a blimp because we lived right near the Goodyear blimp in L.A.[12]

Norton: There are spacemen [in the lyrics], and he was convinced he was abducted when he was a child. His mom was convinced he got abducted or something, and told him. I think he definitely has a bit of a fascination with space. Well, "Velouria" as well, he was trying to write about space, a superhero type person, and he had this material, velour, that he really liked the touch of, and that's where he got the "Velouria" from, what she would wear. We were trying to do things that excited Charles, so to have an instrument that he wasn't used to having was exciting to him. So we got a Theremin player [Robert F. Brunner]. I found him in a musician's union book under "Theremin." There were like, three of them in there, so I phoned him up and he turns up and he's got white trousers and a red top on, and he's the straightest guy you've ever seen in your life. Charles started to play "Velouria" on the guitar, and he said, "So it goes, C - G" and the guy goes, "No, that's D - A." I'm looking at Charles' fingers on this guitar, and it's a C to a G, and the guy's saying, "No, no, that's definitely D to an A." It turns out the guitar was tuned down. So the guy's got perfect pitch, but we were just freaking out thinking, "What's going on here? Are we losing the plot?" He was a real character, he was fantastic.

Lubin: "Velouria" was the first single. I love "Velouria," I think it's one of their best singles. What I remember about "Velouria" are two things. One is the New Music Seminar was a big thing at the time, and suddenly everything at that conference was for sale, wall space, floor space, tile space on the floor. We bought the rights to erect a pedestal in the middle of the lobby, and we had a window dresser make a Velouria doll out of mannequins that model baby clothes. They created this two and half foot, three-dimensional, living, breathing, really spooky Velouria girl, and mounted her on this pedestal in the lobby of the New Music Seminar. We didn't say what it was, she was wearing a face mask and a skull cap, and it had a V on it, and it was just supposed to be a conversation piece in the lobby. And years later, it went on tour of Tower Records stores around the country, and of course it never came back home. And a couple of years later this guy who worked at Elektra rang me up out of the blue and said, "I was at my friend's house, he's a buyer for Tower Records out here in San Francisco. The guy was cleaning out his closet, and guess who was in the back of his closet?" I said, "You're kidding!" He said, "I'm bringing her home." So he flew Velouria back from San Francisco and gave it back to me.

And the other thing is that they made a fantastic video for "Velouria" that was simply them running down a hill in slow motion. The Pixies had developed this severe aversion to making videos, so to get videos out of them was a major, major, major undertaking and it only got worse over time. Charles wouldn't lip-sync at all, so when they did "Velouria," it's just them, and when the record starts they're at the top of some hill—it looks like a typical side of the highway hill in L.A., off the 405 or something—and they just run down the hill in slow motion, and when they get to the bottom, the record's over.

That was another problem, well, at least it was perceived as a problem at the record label, which was their videos started to be considered non-events because they wouldn't put any effort into them and they weren't competitive at the time. And so they didn't hop onto MTV like people hoped they would, and when they didn't, that's when promotion departments start to lose enthusiasm and the direction of things can head south pretty quickly. So that's what happened with *Bossanova*. "Velouria" was the first single, and "Dig For Fire" was a single.

Angel: Right after they finished *Bossanova*, Charles and I went out to get burritos at this place he loved called Uptown Taco. They played oldies in that place all the time, and the song "Summer in the City" comes on, and he turns completely grey. I said, "What's wrong?" and he said, "Listen to it, 'in the summer, in the city, in the summer, in the city,' my God! That's in 'Velouria.' Oh, shit!" And I laughed and said, "So what? It was a subconscious thing. It's not the first time this happened to you anyway. What is 'Here Comes Your Man' but 'Never My Love' by the Association?" He said, "What?" I said, "Yeah, you can play one right over the other. It's no big deal. It's the same feel, the same key."

Watts-Russell: I think all the Pixies records are really good. The character that sucked you into them as a group was less evident on the last two albums. I'm not saying that Kim singing backup makes the Pixies, but it was a personality that was so endearing and it became less and less on those records. And I think the rest of the world would give five stars each if there had been more time between them. And the songs had been finished by the time they had come to record them. I still think they are all brilliant, though.

Lovering: We were always trying to be different on each album, just have a different sound, just make it unique, dynamic. I think it's a combination of different things, the evolution of the band, as well as just the situation that we were leading towards. It's that direction of surf songs and stuff.

Dolan: *Bossanova* has a kind of astral pastoral sound. It's their surfiest record and their warmest. Though it starts with a couple of vocal-shredding songs, the album kind of resolves on the second side into low-key driving music. It's a subdued record, with brushed drums at points, languid, dreamier guitars, which provided a nice context for Thompson's sci-fi whimsy.

Larbalestier: [The album cover] was a nightmare. I had no interest in it. I didn't want to do color, I wanted to do black and white. We had that model [of the globe] made and I think we had three hours to photograph that before it disintegrated or slid down the pole from the heat. It was a transparent globe, picture of the world, which we had to be careful about because the world map was copyrighted, so it had to be a representational thing. And it had this satin type ring. It was very pressured, and very funny—we were laughing about it afterwards. No great shakes as a shot for me. I got the lighting wrong and it had too strong a red gel on it, but we couldn't see the red gel because the eye isn't sensitive to red light. The cardboard single ("Dig For Fire") had the subtler version of the globe, it had a more blue/orange glow to it which is how we saw it to the naked eye. But most of the shots turned out totally red and they went with the red for the album cover. I also don't feel the portraits [shot by Kevin Westenberg] went with my images. They are completely different things.

NME review by Terry Staunton, August 1990: *Bossanova* is the Pixies in the Twilight Zone, Black Francis exploring the obscure and the unknown; Carl Sagan with a guitar cranked up to full volume. . .If there is some kind of theme to *Bossanova*, it is the most obtuse thing in the world, a voyage into the unknown with a tour guide who is obviously missing a couple of buttons on his overcoat.

Q magazine review by Mat Snow, September 1990: The Pixies are masters of the calculated incongruity. Where previous albums boasted perhaps one or two songs—"Gigantic" and "Debaser," for instance—where a heaven-sent chorus came delivered courtesy of a rock sound of offhand swagger, *Bossanova* is chock-full.

***Melody Maker* article by Ian Gittins, November 1990:** Pixies are the best band on the planet.

Above David Lovering, Kim Deal, Charles Thompson, and Joey Santiago in a photograph from the Pixies cover story in *The Noise*, 1987 (courtesy T Max)

Above Death to the Pixies poster from 1986 (courtesy T Max)

Right Joey Santiago, Charles Thompson, David Lovering, and Kim Deal onstage at the Rat in Boston, 1987 (courtesy Gary Smith)

Below The first Fort Apache studio in Roxbury, Massachusetts (courtesy Gary Smith)

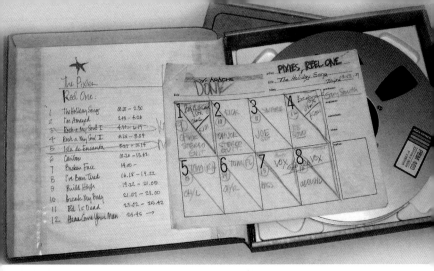

Above The original 16-track Fort Apache Pixies recordings and track sheets (which became known as *The Purple Tape*), produced by Gary Smith, 1987 (courtesy Gary Smith)

Left The cassette liner from *The Purple Tape*, the first time Pixies' names are listed in print, 1987 (courtesy Gary Smith)

Below Charles Thompson at the original Fort Apache, 1987 (courtesy Gary Smith)

PIXIES P.O. Box 381 Kenmore Station Boston, MA 02215

Caribou · Here Comes Your Man · Subbacultcha · Vamos · Broken Face ·
Nimrod's Son · Isla De Encanta · Ed Is Dead

side two

Levitate Me† · The Holiday Song · I've Been Tired · Break My Body · Down To The Well ·
Rock A My Soul · I'm Amazed · Build High · In Heaven (Lady In The Radiator Song)*

side one

PIXIES

side one

Levitate Me†	2:30
The Holiday Song	2:08
I've Been Tired	2:36
Break My Body	2:00
Down To The Well	2:36
Rock A My Soul	1:40
I'm Amazed	1:40
Build High	1:41
In Heaven (Lady In The Radiator Song)*	1:43

side two

Caribou	3:17
Here Comes Your Man	2:50
Subbacultcha	2:52
Vamos	3:10
Broken Face	1:23
Nimrod's Son	2:15
Isla De Encanta	1:42
Ed Is Dead	2:32

Black Francis: vocals, guitars
David Lovering: drums
Mrs. John Murphy: bass, vocals
Joey Santiago: lead guitars

Produced by Gary Smith.
Engineered with Paul Kolderie.

All songs ℗ © 1987 Black Francis except * © 1976 Ivers Song & O.K. Paul Music and † © 1987 Music by Black Francis. Lyrics by Black Francis, David Lovering, Mrs. John Murphy, Joey Santiago, Jean Walsh. All rights reserved. Recorded at Fort Apache, Roxbury, MA in March 1987. Package by Gary Smith.

Above left Kelley and Kim Deal in a Boston subway, 1987 (courtesy John Murphy)

Above right 4AD's Ivo Watts-Russell and Charles Thompson at England's Town and Country after a show, May 1988 (courtesy John Murphy)

Right Kim Deal and John Murphy, 1988 (courtesy John Murphy)

Right David Lovering, Charles Thompson, and Joey Santiago with their specially-rigged tour van during their U.S. tour, 1988 (courtesy John Murphy)

Above Nimrod 1: image appeared on the cover of *Come on Pilgrim* (Photograph by Simon Larbalestier/www.simon-larbalestier.co.uk)

Above Surfer Rosa #1: image appeared on the cover of *Surfer Rosa* (Photograph by Simon Larbalestier/www.simon-larbalestier.co.uk)

Left Alternative version of Surfer Rosa: image appeared in liner notes of *Surfer Rosa* (Photograph by Simon Larbalestier/www.simon-larbalestier.co.uk)

Right Spike 1: image appeared on the cover of the *Here Comes Your Man* single (Photograph by Simon Larbalestier/www.simon-larbalestier.co.uk)

Left Monkey Gone To Heaven: image appeared in liner notes for *Doolittle* (Photograph by Simon Larbalestier/www.simon-larbalestier.co.uk)

Right Gouge Away: image appeared in liner notes for *Doolittle* (Photograph by Simon Larbalestier/www.simon-larbalestier.co.uk)

Left Planet of Sound: image appeared on the cover of the *Planet of Sound* single (Photograph by Simon Larbalestier/www.simon-larbalestier.co.uk)

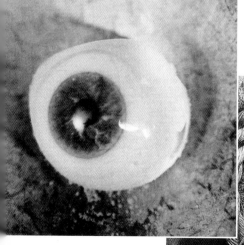

Right Neptuna: image appeared in liner notes for *Doolittle* (Photograph by Simon Larbalestier/www.simon-larbalestier.co.uk)

Above (sitting) Throwing Muses' Tanya Donelly and David Narcizo; (standing) Throwing Muses' Leslie Langston, Pixies' Joey Santiago and Charles Thompson, and Throwing Muses' Kristin Hersh in Europe, May 1988 (courtesy John Murphy)

Above Pixies Fun: A page of humor from Geoffrey Bell and Andy Barding's *Rock A My Soul* No. 2, 1991 (courtesy Andy Barding)

Right Cartoon starring Charles Thompson by Allen Salyer from *Rock A My Soul* No. 3, 1992 (courtesy Andy Barding)

Above (from left) Kim Deal, Kristin Hersh, David Lovering, and Charles Thompson during Pixies' first European tour, 1988 (courtesy John Murphy)

Below Charles Thompson and Kim Deal onstage in Europe, 1988 (courtesy John Murphy)

Left and above Pixies at London's Mean Fiddler, July 1991
(Photographs by Alison Hale)

Below Pixies publicity photo from 4AD (Kevin Westenberg)

Flansburgh: *Bossanova* is strangely kind of my favorite. I feel like it thematically holds together, and there's kind of a grab-bag quality to all their other records. I feel like that one is the only one that's really of a piece. It doesn't have as many singular breakout songs, but I remember being on a tour and getting an advance copy of that record, and I had a cassette walkman and the tape had no song titles on it, and I would listen to that on the tour bus over and over. It just seemed incredibly mature and complete and fully realized in a way that was very compelling.

Angel: When they moved to Elektra, I think at that point they started wising up as to what a big deal it was. You can tell the difference in the sound, too, it went from cutesy on *Doolittle*, to big and powerful. Mega sound, you know? It was weird, too, because in between those two records, I think Charles started to realize, like, wow, this really is a big deal and there's pressure on me to write more stuff now. I think that influenced that record somewhat. That's why it's really well put together. The rest of their stuff before that seemed much more haphazard.

Lubin: *Bossanova* did not do as well, it was not as well received as *Doolittle*, and I have a pet theory. My theory was that *Bossanova* was really not well sequenced, and that that colored people's perceptions of how good an album it was. And I remember having back and forth, and I assume that was with Ivo, about changing it or strengthening it, and losing. It didn't go gold. It ended up not being a powerhouse follow-up. One, I think the perception of the album as weaker than *Doolittle*, personally I think as a result of the sequence, two, they delivered videos that while I thought they were quite good, the promotion men and whatnot thought they were toss-offs and that the Pixies were sort of giving the finger to the effort involved in promoting their own careers.

Thompson: There are so many rules about making videos. Because it's just like so many bland guidelines for the people programming the videos like on MTV or charts shows they have in England and Europe. They basically want a nice simple thing or a lot of fast editing and you know, it's just like a commercial, which is fine. I understand the concept.[13]

Hurley: Following *Doolittle* it was obviously a much-anticipated record and it probably charted very high in the U.K. Looking back, people think *Doolittle* or *Surfer Rosa* are the real masterpieces, but *Bossanova* was a very commercial record that broadened their audience.

Watts-Russell: The record that got the most positive reviews at the time when it came out was actually *Bossanova*. In Europe that got the most positive reviews. They had not gotten too big for their boots or anything. I mean the English press is like, build you up and then slap you down. People wanted to like them, and people did.

Geiger: In 1990, I was at Reading Festival, and the Pixies headlined one of the days. I was onstage with them, and watched 45,000 people jump up and down and scream the lyrics to "Debaser," which I thought was interesting, coming from America, because Americans didn't even like the song, it was one of those noise songs. And here was 45,000 English kids screaming the lyrics in unison, dancing up and down. I had a tear in my eye at that festival.·

Craft: It was their biggest show that they'd done in the U.K. to date. My main recollection was that it was incredibly hot. They did a warm-up the night before in this little club near Reading, in Windsor. It was the Old Trout in Windsor. They had to stop the show because all the gear started melting. It was a very hot summer's night and the venue was like a small room at the back of a pub and it was incredible. There was only 400 people there 'cause it was a small room, but it was brilliant.

Lovering: And that was the hottest gig we ever did, as far as temperature. It was absolutely deadly. I played in my underwear. I wore a long shirt.

Banks: When we headlined the Reading Festival and we played on the Sunday night, you have to go to these production meetings. The Inspiral Carpets were playing on Saturday night and they had this whole thing where they were going to light all these fireworks off and let all these balloons off, and they're going to come down on these hoists—they had this big, spectacular finale planned. And the guys on Friday night were doing something else. And then they turned to me and said, "All right, Chas, what are you going to do, what have you got?" And I said, "Sixteen fucking brilliant songs. That's it man, some lights and 16 brilliant songs, we'll take care of the rest." That was it.

Lovering: We got paid whatever festival amount, but it was staggering to us and it was great. It was absolutely fantastic.

Banks: You know, they were actually nervous. I remember trying to make them laugh and stuff, they were quite intense because there was so much at stake. And then they loosened up and it was great. It's tough to play those big outdoor gigs, you don't get anything coming back, and you have to really learn to do those shows, you have to learn to speak slowly. For the Pixies it worked because they don't do a lot of stuff, talking to the audience or whatever. They would have had to have been very, very bad to disappoint that crowd. And they weren't. It was a really good, professional performance, and they were very elated at the end of it.

Rolling Stone **article by Michael Azerrad, November 1990:** The Pixies walk onstage amid a constellation of flashbulbs and butane lighters filtered through clouds of choking smoke. The opening surf instrumental, "Cecilia Ann," rocks, and the rest of the set, the band is ferocious: The guitars roar and whistle and buzz; Black Francis howls as if into some unseen hurricane; the rhythm section slams. Deal is beaming, and even the normally stationary Black Francis pulls a few rockist moves.

The rabid fans recognize virtually every song from the first couple of bars—even the new *Bossanova* material—and their voices are almost as loud as Black Francis' as they turn "Where Is My Mind?" into a soccer chant. There's a song whose lyrics is "It is time for stormy weather," repeated over and over again—hearing it during the Persian gulf crisis is eerie; hearing it played to 50,000 kids with no future is downright chilling. The sheer size of the crowd hints that the band has what it takes to reach the masses, and the Pixies prove it all night.

Banks: Beyond belief. They played at Roskilde which is a bigger festival, there's 120,000 at Roskilde, they played bigger festivals than Reading. It wasn't the number of people, it was about being the biggest festival in England. In terms of England, to close the festival on Sunday night, you've got to remember this was before Lollapalooza. . .

Geiger: That's where the idea for Lollapalooza came from, that show. The Pixies and Jane's Addiction, Living Color, Siouxie and the Banshees, a bunch of them were on that Reading Festival. I was a big Pixies fan, I was there with Jane's. Jane's was huge in

America, Pixies were not huge in America, Pixies were huge in Europe, Jane's was breaking in Europe. And basically, Jane's went over and did a club show, and *everybody* in London showed up, it was the hottest thing going, so hot in the room Perry actually lost his voice and they cancelled Reading.

Perkins: Jane's Addiction had to cancel, it was a fucking heartbreak for me. We were going to headline Reading and Perry had laryngitis, lost his voice, and he was upset, he was crying in the hotel lobby. He said, "I can't do it, man, I'm not going to be able to sing." He was at the point that he wanted us to get someone else to sing the songs. That's how freaked out we were. So everyone's like fuck it, we cancelled. I'm like, "I'm going, I gotta check this out, even though it might be heartbreaking," and me and Geiger walked around for hours and checked out all the bands and talked about how this could work great in America if it's done right and we picked the right bands.

Geiger: And so we hung out and we had such a good time at Reading that Perkins and I were discussing how do we do this in the States, it coincided with Perry's circus-type plan. So that festival really was the time we started to talk about it openly as a concept and started to recruit artists. I was on the bus with the Pixies in Germany going to one of the two big Bowie festivals the Pixies were opening for, and for some reason Charles didn't want to do it and turned it down, although they would have been in one of those spots.

Perkins: Marc Geiger and [agent/Lollapalooza cofounder] Don Muller introduced the Pixies to my world, and Geiger was always pretty hot on a bunch of up and coming bands, including Jane's Addiction, and his ear was open to this great stuff so I was always checking out his music collection. The big tour was Primus, Pixies, and Jane's, we did that for a month or two.

Geiger: Pixies had opened for Jane's Addiction in the States, several times, including with Primus, legendary shows.

Perkins: It ended up in Los Angeles, I know we did three or four nights at the Palladium which still stand as some of the best shows I think Jane's Addiction has ever played. It was West Coast, I remember playing Arizona and Seattle, and it was great because Jane's Addiction was at the point where we were decorating the stage and had a lot of flashiness going on. And then there are the Pixies: It's black-and-white, it's raw, dry, well-written music, and they don't cover it up with anything. It's as raw and dry as you can make it, especially with the production, the sound of the music. You can see that they were just in love with playing music and obviously being from a different part of the country—I'm from Los Angeles, Jane's was surrounded at the time by Ratt, Mötley Crüe, Poison, Guns N' Roses. We weren't part of that scene, we were with the Chili Peppers, X, and Fishbone, but all of that stuff was happening in L.A., so a lot of that stuff rubbed off everywhere. It's Hollywood, there's always glitter. So it was great to see people show up on stage with a pair of jeans and a T-shirt but play this music that visually could be very glamorous, but they didn't think of it that way. From the artwork to the sound to the lyrics, it was blunt, it was to the point, and it wasn't covered up with anything. I really respected that.

Santiago: We got rid of all the excess. The '80s were totally excessive, everything excessive. Long leads, drum solos. There might seem like more crap to rebel against in the late '80s, I guess.

DRIFTING...

ACT THREE

LE MONDE

MAP SHOWING THE LEY LINES
OF THE UNIVERSE (not to scale)

12. PLAYING THE FOOL—*TROMPE LE MONDE* (1991)

Back from Reading and in the studio once again with Gil Norton, Pixies were hardly the giddy, upbeat quartet that had recorded demos with Gary Smith four years prior. Charles Thompson, Joey Santiago, Kim Deal, and David Lovering rarely came to the studio at the same time during the *Trompe Le Monde* sessions.

Norton: There was one point where Charles had sacked Kim about a week before we were supposed to start the album. I remember a lot of phone calls went down. We had the studio bought, it was just ridiculous, it was like, "Charles, you can't do this, mate. This is mad." And he was like, "Oh, I'm not doing an album. I'm not recording." I think it was just them being together all the time, just getting on each other's nerves. I think Kim got drunk one night and did an interview, and I think she had said something detrimental about Charles and he just really freaked out, it was like final straw for him. I think they had a row and she called him selfish, I don't know what it was. I did try to talk him out of it, but he's pretty stubborn. I just said, "I don't think we can do an album without her, it would be ridiculous and we're going to start in a week." I think Ivo talked to him, everyone, I don't think anyone wanted Kim to be out of the band. It was all calmed down when we got into preproduction. It's like any family. It calms down.

We started it in L.A. in Burbank at Master Control where we did *Bossanova*, and we didn't finish actually. We finished quite a lot of it but Charles had to finish some lyrics up on some songs, there were some vocals to do, but they had to tour so I ended up having to follow them around Europe for a little while and then they had a couple of days off in Paris so we booked a studio there and then we were in London for a while, so we came back and finished a few things off in London.

Geiger: Charles stopped doing demos, so that was a problem.

Haigler: I engineered and mixed *Trompe Le Monde*. That's when things were getting more tense. It was obvious that things were quite different. Songs were being written on the spot, there was more experimentation. There was some confrontation between Charles and Gil because Gil was wanting the songs to be completed and they were not. And Gil and I were in the control room recording drum tracks and basic tracks to songs we didn't know what the melody was going to be, because lyrics were not finished, lead lines weren't finished, so we were kind of working very off the cuff, it was very spontaneous—kind of whatever happens, happens. It was left to Gil and me to sort it out, there were some tense moments. It was obvious there wasn't good communication among the band, it was more Charles doing what he wanted to do on the record, and doing it very spontaneously and writing songs in the studio. That's certainly not what a producer wants to see. He wants to see things a bit more together. When Charles was in there doing his guitar parts, Kim, Dave, they wouldn't be around. Charles was usually there, though, always.

Norton: "Subbacultcha" is a very old song, I think that was from one of the original batches from way back, even. We had a demo for that, I think it was a Gary Smith version. Most of the others were new besides "Head On," obviously, which is a cover. Nearly all the other songs we just got together in rehearsal room. We knew each other really well and on your third album [as a producer/band team] you're on a roll, so nobody was embarrassed about ideas, throwing things into the pot and getting them rejected. It was easy just to have Charles come in and go, "La la la, I've got this idea for an intro," or "This is going to be a verse, this is a chorus bit." We'd just play around with it for a day, and everyone throws a little bit of ideas in and try to come up with stuff. Again, the backing tracks, it wasn't hard really, it was just lyrically finishing them off. And sometimes you think your song's going to be about one thing and then it's about something else, and then you think, I would have done that differently had I known it was about whatever. It was always a bit difficult, it was a bit tense, really, because I think the more prepared you are and the more you've got ready when you go into the studio, the better.

Banks: *Trompe Le Monde* they hit a wall, you know, he was writing in the studio. As soon as they're writing in the studio, kiss it goodbye. Believe me, I've seen it happen with a thousand bands.

Angel: I think a lot of the stuff on *Trompe Le Monde* were old songs for Charles, anyway. He was kind of cleaning out his closet then. That was sort of to him what that Stones record *Tattoo You* was, like, "Well, I don't have that many new ideas. What do I got in the back?" Because "U-Mass" was real old. "Planet of Sound" was old, "Subbacultcha" was old. He might've said, "The well's dry, fuck it, I can't do this anymore."

Norton: [Kim's contributions] became less every time. Especially towards the end, when we did *Trompe Le Monde*, I wasn't very happy by the end of that. Because there was one song, "Bird Dream of the Olympus Mons," that I thought was perfect for her to sing. The whole backing track and all the way through it Kim was writing words and a melody and stuff, and she sang it to me, actually, and I thought it was fantastic, and then Charles changed his mind and he didn't want her to sing it. He definitely didn't want her to have a big imprint on the songs. She's hardly on this album singing, which I thought was such a sad waste of such a talented voice. He was still annoyed with her so he wouldn't let her sing. And when she did get a backing vocal it'd just be an *oooh* or an *ahhh* or something. She was getting really frustrated as well. You could feel there was animosity.

Donelly: Kim was always there to make the records, she was always at the shows. I just think everybody was so pissed off and not talking. Kim's a very communicative person, but I think maybe there was not so much communication going on in that camp, and when she got frozen out of that—if you can't talk, and no one's talking to you—I would go crazy.

Haigler: I remember Charles wanted to sing everything through this bullhorn he had gotten, I mean *everything*, and Gil was worried about the lyrics and next thing I know the bullhorn is getting crashed against the brick wall of the studio. Charles just threw it, I think he had just let it fly. And then of course, the mad dash was on to find another one so we could use it when we wanted to.

Eric Drew Feldman (former Pere Ubu keyboardist; former Captain Beefheart keyboardist/bassist; played keyboards and synths on *Trompe Le Monde*): The dynamic of the band at that point was like no dynamic, in terms of social interaction. People were pretty much recording separately and were not around when the others were. When I recorded my tracks it was with Gil and Charles only. I remember I had this one idea for a song, it was one of the only times everyone was there, it was a song called "Alec Eiffel" and I had come up with this sort of melody for the end, this repeating thing that went over and over. Charles liked it but Kim heard it and didn't really relate to it, wasn't into it. Charles said he wanted it, and he went and wrote words to the melody that I made up and she sang it.

Dave Thomas (former Pere Ubu singer): There was clearly tension by that time. I don't think it helped matters that Charles started incorporating Eric Drew Feldman into his band so quickly and completely. I think that caused problems. He was interested in doing something different with it.

Feldman: I hooked up with Charles in 1989. I was playing with Pere Ubu. We were touring in Europe and we were hearing about a band that was doing well on the circuit called the Pixies. We played a show with them and that night I met Charles. He just came up and introduced himself to me at sound check and he had a Los Angeles type accent, which I had and recognized. I didn't know he was a member of the Pixies, I thought he was just someone that was hanging around and had a friendly demeanor and we just started chatting. It was just a random meeting. Around that time Gil Norton started to produce a Pere Ubu album and he was working with the Pixies, so Charles came around to visit us a few times. A few months after that I was back at home in San Francisco and the Pixies came to town and I was thinking I'd like to see them, and I was trying to figure out how I would bust my way into a chance to speak with him when the phone rings and it's him and he asked me if I wanted to come see the show. I believe that's when Charles was starting to talk about wanting to do a record independent of the Pixies that was going to be covers that he liked. Since Gil had been producing his music, he approached

Gil about it and Gil said, "Well, I don't think I should do it" and he recommended me to work on it with Charles.

To Charles it was kind of an afterthought, having me play on the next Pixies record. Because he was having a hard time. We talked about some songs for his solo project, and I remember saying to him, "You know, the songs sound pretty good but I think it would be much more interesting if maybe you did a cover or two—but why don't you try doing your own music instead of all covers?" As I listened to the Pixies I became more interested in his writing and singing than the band per se. In a certain way I felt like they were doing what they had done for a couple of records and I got the impression that he was feeling a bit constrained. So we were not getting any real time to work on this project. He said he wanted to do it and I believed him, but the Pixies were (as they are again) a fulltime concern. And he kept apologizing, saying that he just couldn't do it yet, he had to work with his band right now. But around that time he also said something like, "Maybe you should come by and play sometime, if ya ever want to play with us," but to be honest, I don't know if at the time he meant it sort of like when someone says, "Oh, we should go out to dinner sometime."

So somehow I talked to Gil and he had heard about this and they had started working on *Trompe Le Monde*, and one day Gil and Joe Santiago drove up from L.A. to San Francisco to give me rough mixes of basic tracks. And I think it was more of a lark, I don't think they actually knew how long a drive it was. I think they thought it was three hours or something.

Norton: I'd done a Pere Ubu album with Eric [*Worlds In Collision*] and I really liked him, he's a very talented guy, and the whole thing about the Pixies is it always had to be portable, so besides the strings on "Monkey Gone to Heaven," I don't think we ever had any other musicians playing on it, so they could play it live, so it wasn't too embroidered. And I talked to Charles and I said, "I'd love to get some keyboards on some of this," and Charles said, "Oh, we can try it." So I said to Joey on Saturday, "Come on, Joe, I wanted to drive up Route 1." Being English, I've got no concept of distance, and Joey was like, "It's going to take us forever," and I said, "That's all right, it's half past ten in the morning." So we went out, we bought E.L.O.'s *Greatest Hits* and got in the car and started driving. Long story short, it took us over 11 hours to get up to San Francisco and we were absolutely exhausted. So we got there on a Saturday night, saw Eric on Sunday morning, and then drove back. It was a mad weekend. I took him up some songs so he could have a listen and see if it sparked him off, gave him a few ideas of songs I thought we could have some keyboards on. So then he came down and played.

Feldman: And they basically dropped the tape off, turned around and drove back. I listened to it and thought of some ideas. I knew they were in the studio, so I just sort of took a leap of faith, threw some gear in my car and drove down and showed up at the studio. And nobody knew who I was except for Gil and Charles, and Joe had just met me for a moment, and Charles said hi and was happy to see me and we were talking and at some point I was just hanging around and listening and I think he didn't know if I just happened to be in town. I remember him saying, "So are you just here to work on this?" and I said, "Yeah, is that okay?" He said yeah, but he seemed slightly puzzled. But then everything became okay. A few days later he approached me with I guess you'd say a business proposition, you know how much money I would be paid to be there. And that was it. So I showed up and we just started, I put down the stuff that I knew that I wanted to do and then started trying stuff and then Charles and I started working on B-sides.

Norton: And then we got Eric's brother in, as well. Jefrey, for "Space (I Believe In)." We didn't have any lyrics for some of the stuff, especially on this album, trying to get Charles to finish lyrics off could be quite hard sometimes. He'd be, "Oh, I nearly got it, nearly got it" and we were running out of time. On that one, I just thought it'd be nice for the groove to have some tabla, and Eric said, "My brother is a professor of tabla," and I was like, "Oh, fantastic!" So Jefrey came in and sat on the floor with Charles and he sang this thing, he went "Oom bang gong a bum dum dum," this 16-bar tabla phrase, he sang it and then played it exactly the way he'd sang it. Charles flipped out, he was just like, oh, I can't believe this, and then Joey came and he said, "Joey, Joey! You've got to see this," so he made Jefrey do it again. It was mind-boggling to Charles that someone could do that. And then we hadn't had any lyrics for the song, and that's when all of a sudden he wrote a song about him. I thought it was going to be a cool song about a space thing or something. "Jefrey with one *f*, Jefrey" it ended up being, which obviously is very cool now, but at the time I wasn't a happy producer.

Haigler: Jefrey was this strange guy who sat in the middle of the floor on his rug and played, and he made it clear to Charles that he was Jefrey with one *f*.

Norton: Very rarely were they all there at the same time. Charles would be there with Joe when he was doing guitars. So now, there was definitely tensions going down, especially after Kim didn't sing "Bird Dreams," that definitely changed the dynamic, especially her opinion of what was going on. I don't think she was as interested and didn't want to be around Charles that much.

Then we did the "Head On" cover [originally by the Jesus and Mary Chain], and I remember we mixed the album in London, and it was a Saturday and I'd just finished mixing that song, and Tanya Donelly was in town, so we all went out and came back to my house. There was a ring at the door and Jim [Reid] from Jesus and Mary Chain was standing on my doorstep, and it really weirded me out because I just finished "Head On" and then the guy was there on my doorstep and I'd never met him before. It was just one of those mad nights where everyone from 4AD ended up around, and Tanya's friends.

Watts-Russell: By the end of *Trompe Le Monde*, Charles was alone. It was a really sad evening. I think Gil had finished mixing the last thing he was going to mix. So the next day it was planned that 4AD was going to go up to the studio and take everyone out for a meal, and I went up to the studio and me and Gil and the engineer went out to dinner while Charles stayed in the studio doing a running order in alphabetical order. It was just really sad, nobody else at the label wanted to up to the studio, no other members of the band were in the studio. I always, apart from *Surfer Rosa*, used to do the running order for their albums. It's one thing I used to be quite good at doing. To just try doing a running order in alphabetical order just for the hell of it just seemed like part of the plot had been lost.

Larbalestier: Sand, desert, salt, this thing I had about salt. *Trompe l'oeil*. It was a glass eye we used. Although we did use cows eyes on the album. The Petri dish which was the same Petri dish we used with the doll in the early ones. They were all references. And they were very small sets; they were maybe four of five inches square. But I really liked all that stuff. I shot a load of other stuff that linked to that that was never used and never seen. But then again, that was me going off in my direction. But 4AD had to satisfy them, and they had become bigger and you know they split after that.

I like Steve Appleby's drawing a lot, I just didn't see the relevance of them put over mine. I didn't see why they had to be pushed together. It was just things going in a different direction. At the time there was no recognition of the work we were doing. I sell the prints now, but I don't know the importance or significance that people attach to it.

Appleby: I don't think I even knew they were doing *Trompe Le Monde*, I was just kind of doing my work, and at that time I was trying to get an animated TV series started with Captain Star, which was the cartoon I did with all the little rockets and stars. Captain Star was appearing in a German newspaper and in London, and Vaughan Oliver just rang up one day and said, "I'm working on the sleeve for the latest Pixies album," and I said, "How's it going?" and he said, "Nearly done, just needs some final touches, will you come over and draw me some little rockets?" And I thought, "Wow, that's really great," because if you are a big fan, it was really exciting to be asked to contribute something. So I just went over to his studio at 4AD and he asked me to do a whole sheet of little rockets and spaceships and stars and planets, that he could Xerox and cut up and use how he liked. And then he suggested how about one that sort of curves around, for the CD middle, that rocket that curves, and that Eiffel tower one, he suggested and I did that right there. And that was sort of it, it was an exciting day of seeing this sleeve come together. Vaughan talked to me about the album and the context of the album and things and was telling me that Charles had had a UFO experience and that he saw one hovering over his home and I thought that was brilliant.

And I went off sort of wondering whether the Pixies would like the drawing or whether they would hate them. Because it seemed to me that it was quite different from Simon's photographs and the way the graphics had worked previously. One day I was listening to John Peel, and he was playing the whole of *Trompe Le Monde* and talking to Frank Black about each song in between and then suddenly Peel said, "You have drawings by British cartoonist Steve Appleby on the cover, how did that come about?" and I remember this kind of complete chill of horror going through me because I thought Frank Black would sort of say, "Oh yeah that was a real mistake." But he said he liked them and that was a real relief.

Lovering: Yeah, that one [*Trompe Le Monde*] was definitely hard rock, that's the direction we were going. That one I'm happy with it, but I could have been happier with it, 'cause as I said, as each album went on and on we had less time to really work it out. Our whole thing was just pushing 'em out. We kept pumping 'em out. I think I would have been happier if I had a little more time to play the songs.

Norton: We were all pushing each other at the time. We didn't want to make the same record twice, so I don't think any band wants to do that, it was a natural evolution, really. Because the budgets got slightly bigger we could take a little bit longer recording them, I think just that end of it meant we could experiment a bit more, rather than having to just go in and do it, we could spend a day on a drum track and it wasn't the end of the world, we could try different snares and bass drums, or a whole different kit in a different room just to see what it sounded like. I think we had six or seven weeks to try to get it done, not counting pre-production, which is another two weeks. It goes quite fast, especially if you haven't got lyrics for stuff, there are days, working on lead lines, that can take a day to get a guitar part because you haven't got it there. It takes longer studio times if everything is not prepared.

Haigler: It seemed clear by the end that this had turned into more of a Charles project than a Pixies project.

Banks: When you get to a certain level, it was always very much Charles' band, and I think that was part of what came to the fore, certainly in Kim's case, where she was writing certainly more than David or Joey who were prepared to tow the line because they weren't writers. From Kim's point of view, she became very much aware that she was the bass player in Charles' band.

Feldman: *Trompe* felt disjointed to me, it felt looking back on it now like the people were at the time.

Norton: Yeah, it's funny. I had a bad time with it for a while just because it was the most frustrating album to do, even though I think some of the songs are fantastic. That was definitely an album you think could have been better if they were getting on better, I think.

Lubin: With *Trompe Le Monde* I think there was some difficulty in isolating a good track for a single. Marc Geiger, he never, ever stopped—

Geiger: *Trompe Le Monde* had their biggest hit on it that they never had, "U-Mass," which I thought would be an anthem. It was a cock-up that they didn't use it. It's not even a question, it would have been fucking huge! The record company just blew it, every step of the way, and they knew it. Pixies were poised to explode, they had the U2 tour, which can be argued as good, bad, or indifferent, but from a record company and a legitimacy standpoint, you had the most important band in Europe opening for U2 with a very, very good record that had a college anthem on it, and they chose not to put it out as the single, and nobody understands why. The single was "Letter to Memphis"—I was right. I thought that was a not very smart choice.

Lubin: I always know he says, "I can't believe it was 'Letter to Memphis,' it should have been—" and then by then I've stopped listening. I like it quite a bit, too, but even today I'm looking at the track list and I'm still perplexed, what could be a good single from this record.

Angel: When he would finish his records Charles and I would go riding up in the mountains and just play them from beginning to end to see what I thought of them. I remember one opinion I had of the last one, I said, "The hit is the 'Memphis' song." And he said yeah. And I said, "You should edit it so that 'tryin' to get to you' thing repeats over and over and over and over and over again. That would be genius." And he's like, "I'm not going to do that." That was the best song on the record.

Lubin: My promotion department was furious with me for not choosing "Alec Eiffel." "Head On" was my choice, and it flies in the face of conventional wisdom, because you're never supposed to lead with a cover song. That led to this big, big, big, big issue of they have to do a video for "Head On." Now that was a long, long, *long* running back and forth issue. Pixies didn't want to do any videos, then it was like, they'll only do a video if they do the song completely live, and by completely live that means full band, vocals, cameras roll, video's done at the end of two minutes and 13 seconds. One take, that's it. So those became the ground rules, that was the only way you were going to get a Pixies video for "Head On" or anything else.

I actually came up with a fantastic idea, which to this day I'm still proud of. I said okay, we set up the Pixies and we divide the Pixies into 12 blocks, so we get 12 cameras and we stack them three up and down and four across, and the Pixies start to play and all 12 cameras shoot the performance. Then we go into post-production and we create these cubes, this is the part that actually didn't quite happen, we create these cubes like a Rubik's Cube and the cubes keep rotating so that what camera nine shot could be on the left hand face of cube one in the upper left hand corner and things would keep rotating around and you'd get mix and match Pixies.

I remember I got dispatched to Orlando, Florida, to sell Charles on this idea. So I flew to Orlando because they were doing a show there, and we went out to a Chinese restaurant and I charmed, begged, pleaded, cajoled, argued, debated, and somehow Charles, God bless him, said, "Yeah, okay that sounds like a good idea." We hired Scott Litt to produce it, at great expense, I might add. Do you have any idea what the cost of hiring 12 cameras and shooting film relentlessly until they were happy with a take, as well as renting a mobile recording unit and hiring an engineer with sufficient technical ability to record the Pixies live? So we had to pull it off perfectly sonically as well as visually. We spent a fortune doing this. We loved the Pixies. Well...well. I would say there were certain quarters of the company that were getting less and less patient with the Pixies as time went on because the Pixies had definitive thoughts about what they should and shouldn't do, and what was right and wrong, and sometimes, oft-times, maybe, it was at odds with what the record label thought was right. And that includes Ken Goes, who in many ways is an extraordinarily good manager, he's also incredibly hard-headed and stubborn about what he believes is right and wrong. And I gotta tell you, I tend to agree with him 9.9 out of ten times, but his intractability certainly didn't endear him to people in the company who thought they needed the Pixies to do this in order to make their lives and their jobs easier. That probably started with *Bossanova* and things like the "Velouria" video. And yet, but believe me, they were beloved where and when it counted.

After the "Head On" video was shot, Elektra went to the extraordinary length of inviting the whole decision-making team from MTV over to our conference room (we certainly must have bribed them with offers of food and drink!) to view the thing. Bob Krasnow hosted the meeting and turned on his considerable charm and it worked because the video received the special distinction of Breakthrough Video, meaning that it had particular technical and artistic merit (of which I was particularly proud) and was added at the channel in meaningful rotation. This gave the label a certain renewed enthusiasm for the group and the new (at the time) album.

Norton: Charles wouldn't do any of the press for the album. I had to go out on a photo shoot with the band.

Dolan: *Trompe Le Monde* fuses all Pixies' sonic aspects in a pretty palatable package: the drums are heavy but not scary, the guitars hone the noise thing, the leads are pretty rock-hero precise. Black has pretty much turned into the obscurant rock theorist he later became on his solo records (and *Trompe* even kind of sounds like a solo record with a really good studio band). Santiago can rip out a surf solo at whim, but his heart isn't in it. Kim's personality is totally missing. The cover of "Head On" is so much more stream-lined and hooky than the Jesus and Mary Chain original, almost to say that they can refine any sound and it doesn't get them shit in terms of commercial success. "Letter to Memphis" is Black mixing heavy noise with a pomo take on Chuck Berry's "Memphis, Tennessee." It's also their most rock historical album, sort of Black saying, "Well, here all the things I can do that you people obvi-ously don't give a shit about." "Subbacultcha," (pretty much a remake of "Bone Machine") and "U-Mass" are where Black decided that if he couldn't dictate the terms of the alt-culture wars he'd stand outside them, poking fun. In a way it's the band's most intelligent album and at times it kicks ass ("Looking Into the Sun," is such a pacific, funny version of old Albini-era Pixies), and it's really sad because they're so smart and a really excellent "unit," but by this point they're all theory and no heart.

Melody Maker **review by the Stud Brothers, September 1991**: All this said, *Trompe Le Monde* is, if not Pixies' most inspired album, then certainly their most technically accomplished. And, though one third of its 15 tracks, like its cover, are damnably obvious and purposefully loopy, at least another third are excellent. This is par for the course. Pixies have always been flawed and, because they are the kind of people they are, always will be.

NME **review by James Brown, September 1991**: *Trompe Le Monde* is a greasy slab of noise, devoid of the variety of previous Pixies works, and strapped with a desire to sound harder, grungier, and more love-less than ever before. . . .*Trompe Le Monde* is a tedious beast, but climb inside it, rip it apart and explore the pock-ets of brilliance and you'll know the Pixies are still up there. . .It's dark and dirty, and some of it's downright unbearable, but it will grow on you.

Q magazine review by Mark Cooper, October 1991: Boston's Pixies have already ascended close to stadium status judging from their recent triumph at Crystal Palace. Yet their mounting success betrays no loss of tension in their angular guitar rock and no desire to tame Black Francis's willful muse. . . .God knows what Black Francis is on about but any man who can happily compare a girl to jellyroll and sculpture in the same breath is clearly alright. Daft but deadly.

Banks: Towards the end there was a lot of tension. Everywhere. Charles was traveling separately for all of the last tour, Jean was driving with him in the car. He would arrive at the venue for the last part of the tour, because we had such a good team of guys together and a good crew, we stopped doing sound checks. We used to start with "Cecilia Ann," which was a nice instrumental which doesn't sound too bad. So the PA would be off, and the monitors would be off, and the band would start playing and you'd hear them and gradually fade it all up and bring it all in, and by the time they finished "Cecilia Ann" [the sound man] was ready to go out front and he knew where the vocal was going to be and Charles would start singing and within three lines he had it. End of story. And the monitor thing was great. All Charles wanted to hear was himself and very little of the others and we taught them how to, instead of having bass guitar in your monitor, what you do is Kim's over on stage left, so you put one of her cabinets over on stage right, you put one of Joey's cabinets on stage left, and they hear it. It's an old trick the Who used to do. They were working with a lot of top quality crew, so a lot of times Charles used to arrive for his meal at like six-thirty, seven o'clock in the evening, and then go on stage. Reduces the tension, everyone was nice and relaxed. We got through a lot of stuff that way.

Marts: It's obvious that Charles knows how to get around. He can read a map. He's a smart guy. He does it in Europe, too, and frankly if you can do it in Europe you can do it in the States. He was never late for a show. It was fine. The only thing that happened was Charles tends to drive fast and he got a couple of speeding tickets, but he never missed a gig.

Dolan: The first time I saw them I really did kinda stand there with my mouth open. My best friend in high school and I went down to First Avenue in Minneapolis where Prince shot *Purple Rain*. I snuck a tape recorder in my pants. They just came out with this real mercenary fervor. It was like they were condescending to blow the roof off. My idea of that kind of music was a jumping around beery Replacements thing. They were refined, stoic. They just knocked out these songs. Maybe they didn't really have much chemistry as people anymore (this was 1991), because in earlier show footage they'd smile and look psyched, but in this case they seemed pretty detached. No banter. No smiles. We really couldn't believe an actual human was making the vocal sounds on those records, it was like if you bumped into Dennis Hopper on the street and he was the *Blue Velvet* guy. We just assumed if you made those sounds more than once you'd have to destroy your voice or end up in Bellevue. And the appearance was a big thing too. I had a friend say, "Kim Deal is the sexiest greasy, shorts-wearing, chainsmoking woman on earth." By getting onstage and singing "Gigantic" she seemed like this weird sex symbol even though she looked like she went to Smith and hadn't left the dorm room since 1986.

Barding: The night of one of those two Brixton gigs, I was just walking around the venue and I saw Kim kind of waddling towards us, smoking a cigarette and looking really shifty, and so I just thought, "Oh fuck, there's Kim Deal," so I went up to her and said, "Hey Kim, there's this fanzine I've been doing, how about an interview, then?" And she said, "Wait while I make this phone call, and then we'll do it." She went in a phone box, I waited outside, then she came out and said, "Okay, let's do it, where should we do it?" We ended up going to this pub around the corner and just sat in there for about an hour, basically. She got really into it. She was drinking my beer, smoking all my cigarettes, and she was having a great time. She kept saying, "You guys are listening to everything I say, it's great!" She really liked the attention. She mentioned this secret gig that was coming up on the 14th, a couple of weeks later, and that turned out to be one of their last gigs in Europe, and it was a really bizarre gig. It was like a request show, and you could request songs and the Pixies would play them for you. You were just yelling them out. Someone would shout out "Monkey Gone to Heaven!" and they'd go, okay, then play it. At one point Kim would say "Okay, let's do a song in F, the choice of songs in F are... 'Manta Ray,'" she'd list all these songs and you'd give your vocal support to whatever tune you wanted. That was a hell of a gig. It was in this little venue that's not there anymore, the Mean Fiddler, it held I think about 150, 200, it's very tiny.

When they came onstage the sound guy was playing "I Wanna Be Your Dog" by the Stooges, and he faded out the song so the Pixies could start playing, and Black Francis grabbed the mic and said, "Let the song finish, please, out of respect for Iggy. Let the fucking song finish!" and then he started to get really angry with the sound guy, they had to start the song again and stuff. The whole band just basically stood there while the bloody song was playing. My friend Alison was down in the front taking photos of the band as they were playing, she got some great shots of Kim drinking white wine from a thin neck glass, real un-rock'n'roll stuff, and then Joey was looking for a bottle to play a bit of slide with in the middle, and he saw Alison snapping away so he grabbed her camera and started rubbing it up and down the neck of his guitar, and while he was making this racket it was firing off pictures from the stage, so he took some pictures of the audience, and took some pictures of the rest of the band from his perspective onstage, took some pictures of the sound guy and stuff, and at the end of the song just gave the camera back. Alison got it processed as soon as was humanly possible and got these fantastic pictures.

Banks: They played this big show at Crystal Palace, this big open-air show, which was okay, but it didn't do quite what it should have done. The promoters were kind of pissed with Charles because he was offered the cover of *Time Out* and he refused to do it. I don't know why, he was fed up with doing press at that point, but that didn't help.

Barding: There was a souvenir program made for the gig they did at Crystal Palace, big open air show they did in London in 1991. That was a really good gig, actually, because the stage is separated from the audience by moat, a lake, it's about 100 yards between the audience and the stage. It was outrageous, really—how there wasn't a riot, I don't know. You couldn't get anywhere near the stage and there weren't any video screens or anything like that, so the Pixies were these dots on the horizon, and they were huge at that point over here, the place sold out, I think it's 20, 25,000, and one idiot swam across the lake to get to the band during "Where Is My Mind?" It took him the whole song to get over to the other end, and then they pulled him out and got rid of him, poor bugger.

Thomas: They asked us out of the blue [to tour with them]. Just at that time we had finished doing an album, *Worlds In Collision* produced by Gil Norton. Charles took to me and I took to him. It was a very charming time. We were quick friends. We were just an opening act, but they treated us great. Charles as I remember always went out of his way to make sure we were being treated well and comfortable.

Feldman: A situation came where I kind of lobbied, because I had played on that stuff [*Trompe Le Monde*] to play live and Charles had said, "You ever want to play with us you should," but I was in Pere Ubu, and I said, "Why don't you have Pere Ubu open for the Pixies?" and he said, "Well, I think that would be interesting. I'll propose it." I don't think anyone was really thrilled about it. I think there were two or three other bands at the time that were probably more timely, one of which was Nirvana, and that didn't happen, at some point they thought that was a really bad idea, and three months later they went from some cool underground thing to this massive band. So Pere Ubu got to do it by default. And I got to play with both bands. I don't remember much about the Pere Ubu sets, opening is never a totally satisfying place to be, especially when the audience is dying to see the main event.

Lovering: I was the one who said no [to Nirvana supporting]. I'd heard the album. I knew Nirvana were going to be the next big thing. It would have been lopsided.[14]

On February 6, 1992, the band played *Late Show with David Letterman* for the first and only time.

Deal: Paul Shafer is the only person we actually talked to there, and he's a really nice guy. I think it was just *Trompe Le Monde*, just one time, the song "Trompe Le Monde." It was fun, we just played it live, like we set up and played the song. We did a little sound check earlier in the day, and then you wait until they kind of run the program from beginning to end. And they call your name out, because it's taping and the audience is there, you know, it's like, five o'clock now, and you do the same thing, and then you leave, and then you go to a bar in New York City and watch yourself on TV that night. It's just a little room they put you in, your gear is already there, you don't even see it loaded in. It's just like, wow, there's my amp! Weird.

13. THE SAD PUNK—TOURING WITH U2 (1991)

By the time Pixies made their fourth and final album, they had more than a few famous admirers. Two of the most prominent were Bono and the Edge, U2's singer and guitarist, who pressed for Pixies to come along for their Zoo TV tour in 1991. But what seemed like the opportunity of a lifetime became a sad disappointment for a band that needed something to get excited about.

Lubin: *Trompe Le Monde* comes out and U2 decides they're going to go on tour, and I guess that was a fairly big bit of news because I think they hadn't been on tour for quite a long time. The opening slot on that tour was the object of desire of every up-and-coming band and every label and every band's manager... everyone wanted the slot as opener on the U2 tour, and then it turned out U2 wanted the Pixies. So that was a fantastic bit of news.

Marts: It didn't seem to be a secret that U2 had asked Nine Inch Nails and Nirvana to open up for them, and I guess those bands passed and Pixies said yes.[15]

Banks: When we played in Dublin, I remember U2 coming to the gig and they sent a note back, I've still got it, actually, framed: "To the Pixies, keep digging for fire." U2 and Bono, the Edge, they were massively impressed with the Pixies.

Bono (U2 singer): I just saw the Pixies again recently. They have a fanatical following here in Ireland. It's really beyond comprehension. They had to do an hour-long encore. But they always bring me to tears. When Kim Deal sings that one song about "heaven" I just want to scream. It goes right through me. The Pixies are really an original species. They invented something. You have to put groups in certain categories, and they are in the category of having actually *invented* something that didn't exist before they came along. And it's not just the hard cut—you know, the cut from savagery to sobbing in a split second—but also their subject matter. As a lyricist, Charles can find playfulness on the way to big questions. He's like [artist] Damien Hirst: there's surreality, but there's also something oddly touching. It's subject matter, it's structure, and it's the craft of those chord progressions. They are off the map.

Lovering: It was great, that was probably the biggest tour we opened up for. It was funny, it was also the only tour that no one knew who we were. Many U2 fans, I don't think they were aware of the Pixies in some way.

Banks: I personally thought it was a mistake, the tour supporting U2. It's very rare that doing support does you any good as a band—it's good for the main band but not so good for you.

Watts-Russell: Oh, God. Why does it always happen? I remember before that Throwing Muses were opening for R.E.M. and being in the audience with the Throwing Muses coming onstage, so excited that they were touring with R.E.M.—they both like each other, audience is gonna gobble it—the place was a third full. I felt so strongly that this never works, you always get so excited, the idea that this is going to do them so much good, that this is gonna expose them to a much bigger audience, and it just never fucking works. No one had learnt their lesson.

Hurley: It was on paper a great opportunity to play in front of that sort of crowd. The reality of it is you're playing in a basketball arena that's three-quarters empty because most of the fans are still buying their U2 T-shirts. The acoustics in those venues are poor and you get a small proportion of the crowd who'd come to see the Pixies or at least appreciate them. It wasn't the right arena or environment for that band.

Kolderie: They were the critics' darlings, sure, but you're playing pretty much to an empty hall, people who don't really care about you. Even if you're cool and you're the Pixies, it's really sort of soul destroying. It's like you're out there and you think it's the biggest gig of your life, but you're playing at a half-empty arena where no one cares.

Lubin: Now, the bad part about it was even though U2 claimed that they thought the Pixies were the greatest thing in rock'n'roll to come down the pike in ten years, and they wanted to help the Pixies, when it came to paying them to go on tour they were about as ungracious and ungenerous and unsupportive as an act could have been. Which is to say, I think they agreed to cough up 750 bucks per date. Now, they're selling out arenas and they want the Pixies and it's 33 dates and they're willing to pay $750 per show. To this day I still think that's just disgusting. And certainly we asked nicely if that number could be, oh, say twice that. The answer was no, and therefore when all the calculations were made and all the totals were totaled, it came down to Elektra had to spend, I think the number was $95,000, to underwrite the cost of this tour. And that is just part of doing business, it's not like it was unheard of that labels paid tour support, it's just that this was the biggest tour in the country with the biggest grosses and probably the highest ticket prices at the time, and for them to treat the Pixies like they were some local pick-up band, to me and I think everyone else involved, was fairly insulting and disgraceful. I went to maybe five or six of those U2 shows, and it was the same every night. Which was the house lights were on full blast, maybe one-twelfth had people in the seats at the time, you get to play for 35 minutes under these circumstances to people who are not paying any attention whatsoever, sometimes they didn't announce who you are and what you're doing there, and then you're done. And that's exactly what it was like for the Pixies, and it was horrible on many levels, not the least of which was they weren't having so much fun being a band to begin with, and that just was brutal in that context, as well.

Marts: That was disappointing. When there's a row of eight kids, six sections back in the hockey rink going berserk surrounded by either empty seats or non-caring fans, it's hard to do it. But the Pixies played just as hard in those circumstances as they did when they headlined. The biggest disappointment was playing Boston Garden in their hometown on St. Patrick's Day and yet nobody cared that we were on the bill.

Lovering: What's kind of sad for me is that we played cur hometown in Boston, the Boston Garden, which is where I saw my first show, all my sporting events, everything, so it was the most amazing thing to be playing in Boston Garden, not only opening for U2, but on St. Patrick's Day in Boston. So oh man, I thought it was gonna be a huge show. First of all, I didn't get a dressing room. My dressing room was the regular men's room, I swear to God. We did the show, and no one acknowledged or knew who we were. It was amazing. Of all the shows we did with U2, all over North America, that one was the worst where no one had a clue who we were. I mean I can understand, you know that Irish Catholic, Bostonian U2 crowd had no idea, but still, we got to play Boston Garden. It was nice. The tour was very easy, you were back out of the venue by eight o'clock, 'cause we did an early show, we were the opening act. It was so wonderful, by eight o'clock, you're done, back to the hotel, whatever.

Marts: It was also somewhat depressing that there was no interaction between U2, the band members, and the Pixies. We played Nassau Coliseum and Larry Mullen came in that day to talk to the band and it's ironic because it was the day before Boston and they were all doing interviews for the Boston show and he said, "Oh, I'm interrupting you. I'll come back later." And I went to grab him and say, "*Please* come talk to us cause we've been dying to meet the band." And he said, "No, no, I'm gonna leave you guys alone," and took off. And I was just depressed. We want him to hang out for a minute and say hi.

St. Thomas: They were opening for U2, even though the gig was not the best Pixies gig I ever saw, it was still like, "Holy crap! The Pixies are opening for U2 at the Garden!" We were like, whoa, fuck yeah! There were people there to see the Pixies and fucking loving it. You're talking 30,000 people and 1,000 people know who the Pixies are, even in Boston. Everybody wants to fucking go to U2.

First of all, U2 in Boston is a whole thing in and of itself. It was on St. Patrick's Day, and every Irish Catholic kid in 50 miles was there. There was this little section in the front that were like ten rows deep, who were probably hardcore FNX listeners who were freaking out that the Pixies were on, and everybody else in the stadium was getting hotdogs and beer and they didn't give a shit about the Pixies. The fact of the matter is that U2 is one of those bands where people don't really care about the opening act. There was no backdrop, nothing. Their equipment was just in front of U2's equipment. It was really stripped down

Deal: We opened up for U2. Yeah, but when we opened up for U2 we opened up to an empty hall, people finding their seats. People came to see U2, we were just the dumb opening band. Which was fine, I was fine with that. It was just like the Velvet Underground, being popular never corresponded with whether you were a good band or not. It absolutely had nothing to do with anything.

Iha: I saw them open for U2 in Chicago, they were playing a big arena, obviously. I went backstage and I met Charles for a second, he was with his girlfriend and he was leaving and he had one of these slim, I think it was a classical guitar that he brought along so he could write songs in hotel rooms, or something, and he was showing me it. It was really small and he was playing it, and he goes, "There's a song, right there."

Thompson: I remember my first opportunity to meet Larry Norman came through U2 of all people. A lot of people in the U2 organization are Christians, basically. Back in England in the early '70s there was this so-called Jesus movement, you know, hippies, and Larry Norman had a bit of a career in the early '70s. He wasn't on Bible Thumper records, he was on Verve, MGM-Verve. Somehow I heard that he was going to be at a U2 show I was opening up at, their lighting guy or something said, "Hey, I heard you like Larry Norman. He's going to be here tonight." This was in Sacramento.

Lubin: I think backstage there was an extremely severe line of security between the two camps which was not to be crossed for any reason. They were not welcome, they had to watch where they went and which door they went in and where they stood in the corridor. Just horrible stuff. The whole thing was joyless, I have to say, which was too bad.

Marts: It was depressing, sort of for the first week. There was a point in Atlanta, like the fifth show, and U2 had so many dressing rooms we were made to use our tour bus as our dressing room. And we were really depressed about that. It became a joke. There were all these signs backstage—this way for food, this way to stage, stuff like that. And I put up a sign: "Pixies. Don't even go in. We're using our bus as the dressing room." And, apparently U2's manager and band members saw it and were like, "What's this sign all about?" and we said, "Well, there is no room for the Pixies." And after that we got a dressing room every night in the arena. And that made a difference in how everyone felt.

Iha: There was a *Spin* article [Jim Greer's U2 tour diary "Animal Farm," published in July 1992], I remember when that came out and it was like, the U2 camp is pissed about it because there were pictures that said "Support band" that were plastered on the Pixies' dressing room door. I don't really blame U2, they brought them on tour, I'm sure they liked the band. If they didn't do the U2 tour they would have done their own club, headlining tour, and they would have still broken up. I'm sure it was part of it, but whatever, it was nothing but circumstances all culminating together.

Feldman: There was this drama about how a boyfriend of Kim's at the time [Greer] wrote an article about what it was like to open for U2 and it was not a nice article. It was funny, I thought, and largely accurate but kind of painted a nasty picture of corporate rock, and Charles was fumed about that and embarrassed, it made them into being spies and it came out in the middle of the tour. So that didn't help.

Spin **article by Jim Greer, July 1992:** Here's the real zoo: laminate-bearing henchmen and women, walkie-talkies strapped to their sides, power-walking with tight, urgent faces down endless corridors; phones constantly gurgling; tattooed strongmen barking incomprehensible Irish orders; wheeled crates full of unidentifiable but doubtless phenomenally costly equipment hurtling down corridors; strange wispy men in capes... Resulting perhaps partly from the behind-the-scenes anarchy, certain weird hierarchical inconsistencies crop up backstage. Little things, mainly, most of which aren't probably even under the purview of the band members, themselves, but they look to me likes clues. For instance: Even though the Pixies have been handpicked as opening band for the first leg of the North American tour (the Edge and Bono are reportedly big fans), U2, which has gone to the trouble of printing up signs for just about every conceivable subset of its own organization, can't manage better than to slap "Support Act" signage on the Pixies' dressing room.[16]

Marts: But ultimately what happened was there was such mania where they would put the shows on sale, and Pixies never got advertised. Our name was only on a ticket or poster in Vancouver, the last day of the sale. Everywhere else it didn't really matter. Sure the Pixies could sell 2,000 tickets, but they were opening up for U2 and the ticket prices were the absolute highest at the time.

Lubin: The tour sold out everywhere instantaneously. So the general manger of Elektra, Brad Hunt, had this plan to do fly postering all over each of the cities that would say, for example, "Pixies at MSG" and have a big soldout sign slapped across it. Ken and Charles heard about that and said absolutely not. No fucking way. And I think Charles even said, "If I have to roll into town and see Pixies at the Omni: Sold Out I won't even be able to take the stage, okay?" So it fell to me to call Brad Hunt and tell him that there's just no way he could do this poster campaign. And he was having trouble selling enough Pixies records and we had just spent 100 grand to put them on tour, and that's on top of I guess making a "Head On" video with 12 cameras. The Pixies, because they were beloved amongst the A&R side of the company, there was no luxury they weren't afforded, and so it fell to Brad to sell enough records to justify the expenditures, so this is one of the things he came up with. So I had to call Brad and say, "Look, Charles called to say we can't do this," and Brad Hunt flew into a massive rage. It could have just been the pressure to make the Pixies thing work, but he flew into a huge rage over how the Pixies were so precious that he couldn't do his job, and how was he supposed to sell a goddamn record under these circumstances with his hands tied. And that escalated into me saying, "Look, Brad, we don't treat our artists this way, we don't defy them and do exactly what they call up and beg us not to, that is not how we behave," and I think he said, "Well, it bloody fucking well is," and I remember it got into "Yes, I'm going to" and I said, "No, you won't!" and we slammed down the phone and I picked up the chair in my office and I threw it against the door. Howard Thompson, another A&R guy came running down the hall because he heard screaming and this chair, he ran into my office and said, "Pete! I thought you killed somebody!" Brad ended up not doing it.

Banks: I think Charles let himself be talked into the tour. I don't think Geiger thought it was a great idea. I just think that one was a bad call. I don't think it brought the band to an end, but if you're touring and you're touring hard and you're working hard, then that hour that you get onstage, if that isn't a good experience, it can soon become very depressing. Because you're going through all the shit that you go through and all the misery and the boredom, it's not particularly romantic, if you're not getting the hit from the show, there's nothing more depressing, and I've been there. And the people who benefit are the main acts. So when these big acts like U2 or David Bowie see a band like the Pixies, David Bowie wanted to get in there so he could produce them, they're like leeches. They want the association, they want to be seen as cool, they want to be associated with a cool band. They get what they want out of it. What's the support band get? It works all in the favor of the big guys. I think they would have been better off not doing it, but what do I know about America.

Geiger: The band worked their ass off. If there was a mistake, it was doing the U2 tour. You know what, you couldn't know, they were fucking huge. Now I say no all the time because I've been through it twice. I've watched everybody fail on it.

Craft: I don't book the band in America and let's put it this way, there's no way they would've ever have done a U2 tour in any of the markets that I represent because I would've just told them not to do it. Basically I think it helped speed up the process of breaking up the band because they obviously weren't enjoying it at all. And they realized it was a pointless exercise.

Marts: We were on different tours. We were on a bus. They had a private chartered jet and it's a different thing. At one point, we took a break for a week between the legs of the tour, and Charles jumped on the U2 plane and flew to New Orleans and he got to hang out with them a little bit. But for the rest, it didn't happen, I don't think until the last night of the tour in Vancouver. U2 had an end of tour party, but we did a headline show in Seattle or something and we didn't get there in time because they did it on a chartered boat. And we didn't make it in time to get on the boat, so we missed that party. But we hung out in the dressing room the last night. And Bon Jovi was there.

Feldman: They kept trying in this sort of official way to say [U2 and Pixies] should all get together and have a drink and the Pixies were more resistant to participate in it, just because Charles and Kim were not really speaking at that point.

Feldman: During that tour, when they had off days on the U2 bit, they did their own shows and the very last one was a show in

Vancouver when Charles told the band he wanted a year off. It was a normal night, it was okay, but I pretty much knew he was going to say the stuff that he did and people just seemed a bit stunned. And the idea was that we were going to go afterward to try to record a solo record.

I was often on the whole U2 episode much more then. Half the time I drove around with Charles in his car, not on the tour bus. Kim was traveling in an RV with her family and there was a tour bus that just had Joe and Dave Lovering. But sometimes Charles was traveling with his Jean, sometimes it was the three of us, but sometimes they would prefer to be on their own so I was on the bus. There were no outward animosities at the time, but it seemed like there was a lot of tension between Charles and Kim. They had gotten to a point where they could afford financially not to have to be sitting around each other all day. They could manage to play shows and not hang around together. There was really no communication between the musicians at that point. Seemed like everyone came to the gigs separately and were only together onstage. I started to get the vibe that this was coming to an end. I don't think anyone else did, except for Charles.

Craft: They finished the U2 tour in Vancouver and then they played their own headlining show just to finish off the tour. I don't recall thinking at the time that this was the last show that I was ever gonna see them do, to be honest. My main thing was that I was just disappointed that they wasted so much time supporting U2 when they could've been spending their time touring in one of my markets and making a bit more money and doing better. Because they've always enjoyed Europe far more than America, anyway. They get different audience reaction in Europe. In America it's more about curiosity whereas here it's like the Church of the Pixies. It's total adulation and adoration. It's a completely different type of thing really.

Deal: We had just done this series of shows opening up for U2. But the last show we did was our own show, in Vancouver. We played it, called the Commodore. That was in '92.

On April 25, 1992, Pixies played their final show at the Commodore Ballroom in Vancouver. With plans to record a solo album in mind, Thompson suggested the band take a one-year break.

14. DEATH—IN HEAVEN EVERYTHING IS FINE (1992–1993)

Pixies broke up in the summer of 1992 when, as legend has it, Thompson sent a fax to Ken Goes informing him that the temporary break was now permanent. The split became public knowledge during a January 13, 1993 radio interview on "Hit The North," a show on Radio 5. Host Mark Radcliffe asked Thompson point-blank whether Pixies had called it quits. Thompson replied, "In one word—yes."

Deal: In January of '93 I was in San Francisco recording [the Breeders'] *Last Splash* and Kelley comes up to me and says, "Pixies broke up."[17]

Watts-Russell: It's something that we certainly carried for a long time without making it public. Ken Goes probably called.

Santiago: Breaking up? Well, Charles just did it. Just broke it off without anyone knowing, actually. I don't know, it stopped being fun at one point, too. You know, the backstage started getting more weird. Nobody would talk to each other. And it's not like we were going down, we were going up. I don't know, it was just weird.

Thompson: But every band breaks up! There's two kinds of bands in the world: bands that break up and bands that don't break up. You know what I mean? Everybody breaks up, or they don't. People made such a big deal about cold-hearted Black Francis sending a fax. I realize people may be mad at me because I kind of broke up the band ungraciously. I don't know if that's the right word, but I just wrote a fax and sent it and just skipped out without so much as an explanation as I recall. And so I think people, maybe rightly so, were insulted by that, but hey, what can I say? That was years ago, I was in a different place emotionally or psychologically and whatever. And I didn't want to have any kind of confrontation with the rest of the band, I didn't want to have a band meeting and discuss it. I wasn't happy, and I left.

Iha: I think it's like any other kind of dysfunction, things just get so murky and weird that sometimes people can't even bother dealing with the whole face-to-face, look me in the eye and have this whole big emotional confrontation. So it doesn't surprise me.

Lovering: It was disappointing, definitely. It was an interesting time, I remember that. So then I started looking for things, studio work and stuff like that until finally I just gave up on drums, and then magic took over.

Santiago: The first thing that came to my mind was, I guess things happen for a reason. Another side of me said, shoot, we have two more records on our contract. And we came off a pretty successful, high-profile tour. We definitely had a trampoline set up for us, I thought. When he did that I was about to get married. So I had other things to look forward to. Maybe I was a little bit numb from it. I felt a little bit of relief, too. I felt all things, you know? Bands have to break up in the end. After every tour, it's like, "This is it?" I'd been feeling that for two years, after every tour with the Pixies. "Okay, when are we gonna break up?"

Geiger: That was the famous fax story, I just heard about it. Nobody consulted anyone, he was pissed off. He didn't go, "Hey, do you think this is a good idea?" That's not Charles, he didn't give a fuck.

Feldman: He had said that he wanted a year off to make this Frank Black solo record. In the meanwhile, booking agents and managers and things were approaching him and saying things like, "We have a great opportunity to play these three gigs on Mars," or whatever, and he would say no, and they kept bringing up things, like would he do a gig in nine months? Basically the vibe was people were trying to wait out this year, like okay, you can do your stupid thing, but nobody was going to take it seriously. They were just going to wait [for Pixies' return], so one day he showed up at the studio and said, "I ended it, I quit the Pixies, so now if they want to do anything with me they will have to deal with Frank Black, not the Pixies." This was in the middle of recording the solo album. The record was nearly done and he said, "Guess what I'm going to call myself now: Frank Black."

Banks: And then we heard that they'd split. It was no big surprise. It was in the cards. Sad, but you know, you move onto the next thing. Charles was going to continue with his solo career, we stayed friends.

Geiger: In history, a band is a magical combination of individuals and oftentimes when the combination breaks up you find it's not the same with the individual members, or even when you substitute a member. The truth is that Kim Deal started to get a disproportionate amount of love, so to speak—fan love, whatever love—and it pissed Charles off. Probably wrongly. But, they're young, and I think that was the underlying fuse for all of it. And Charles, I believe, was ultimately unhappy that whether it was Kim's songs, or the applause she got, or whatever, they didn't realize, "Hey, hey, I made the records, I wrote all the records, I fucking wrote all the songs, except for one or two, I'm working my ass off, and what, what the fuck is this?" And Charles was very diligent, as was Joey and David, a very hard worker, and Kim was physically addictive to various things, and now that impacts the work ethic. The disease is already there, here comes the symptoms. Kim frankly could get ornery and hard and tough. She hit me a couple of times, I mean, punched, physically, and she did it to the band, it wasn't just me. That was what happened, and that created the rift, those two things. You have to have zero ego in this and a lot of tolerance, it's a lot like being married and bands don't have to be married. I think it was more or less a benevolent dictatorship and that Kim started to rise. She was cute, female, great smile, quotable, the whole bit, great bass player, great singer, the whole thing. That's really it.

Charles is a hard-working in every way, writing, recording, touring, no-bullshit guy. And as much as he got a lot of glory and I think ultimately people knew the brilliance, I think that those two things combined, I'm not sure if either one of them by itself would have done the trick, but the two of 'em combined, was I think what did it.

Walsh: I think out of all the people, it's obvious from the career paths, the other two [Joey and David] are satisfied to be a sideman, they were content with their roles, and Kim obviously wanted to be the star of her own thing. I think it was a band, but as Charles said many times, it wasn't really a democracy. I think it was just too much of a tug of war. It was like a competition. Out of the band, yes, those two got along the worst. I think it's obvious why. Because if someone wants to be the leader of something and they're not, it creates a lot of friction. Also she has an antagonistic personality. It wasn't like somebody silently wishing that they could somehow take control. It was more antagonistic and weird. It seemed like that was the main personality conflict that was going on.

Deal: Charles called me a cunt once. That was after I called him an asshole. But I thought cunt was a little overboard. That was before it was in a song. Maybe in England they use cunt a lot. But he didn't use it in his vocabulary.

Banks: John Lennon and Paul McCartney fell out. The Eagles fell out. People fall out. The basis of it, I believe, was that there were people who didn't like Charles and liked Kim more. Kim was very, very, very, very popular in England and Europe. People really liked her. And a lot of people said, "You know, you could be successful on your own, you could do more, Charles treats you badly because he doesn't give you enough songs." There were people who whispered in her ear that she should get more songs on the album just as there were people who whispered in George Harrison's ear. Plus she was drinking and she was smoking a lot of dope. And then Kim became dissatisfied. But the reality was it was Charles' band and always was Charles' band. He formed the band. He advertised. She answered the advert. The tension was more artistic. You know that there was friction between them, and it all just exploded. Yes, there was a sexual tension. Some nights when he used to sing "Tame" I used to think that anyone under the age of 18 shouldn't be allowed to watch him perform that song.

Craft: There were lots of things that they didn't do that they should've done because Charles didn't want to spend any more time with Kim than he needed to. They never toured Japan. They never toured Australia. There's lots of places they didn't go to that they could've done, but my feeling was that he didn't want the responsibility of having to worry about how she was gonna be in these places. And I think it just became too much.

Donelly: [I saw tension] but it didn't seem like anything insurmountable at the time. When we were touring together it was fine.

There are very, very, very few bands that can withstand constant work. Not because of the work itself, but because when you throw people into a microcosmic situation things get way too intense. It's like holding a magnifying glass over a colony of ants. Because it's different than just working with somebody—you're making something together, which is already intense, and then on top of that you're in the studio for 16 hours a day together, or you're on the road for 24 hours a day together. I know it's important to milk a situation that's ongoing, but people need to get away from each other, too, they need to have downtime and they need to relax, and it does get to be way too much. And when you're in this environment, small problems. . .it's like a familial environment without the family ties.

Gilbert: There weren't that many major incidences. They weren't one of those kinds of bands to hang around with where it was just mischief and trouble. When I hung out with those people, I never got the sense that it was like a powder keg. It just never had that atmosphere.

Murphy: People don't really understand it. You're in a four-person company, and you're all kind of in charge—or it's like *Survivor*, somebody comes out of the woodwork and they say, let's follow him, and obviously the singer or the guy writing the songs is the one you're going to follow, more than likely—but you're still in a little teeny, tiny company. And if you're pissed, who do you go to? You can't go to HR or an entity like that. You have to talk it out. And if you don't talk it out, you end up getting things build up and you go home and you vent to your parents or boyfriend or husband or whatever, but eventually, it's going to come out right in front of them. And that's what happened, I think. Different things bugged different people and then they finally just let it all out.

Angel: I always thought that what really got to Charles is the same thing that gets to so many bands. I know when they were touring on *Trompe Le Monde* that a lot of the places that they were playing they'd played a lot of times before and it was the same people there. That starts to get to you as a musician, when you don't feel like you're moving. When they did the U2 tour and their sales didn't improve and it was an enormous tour in front of shitloads of people and they got zilch reaction, I think Charles is like, well, we did this with the Cure, same thing, now U2, same thing, I'm stuck. I think maybe he figured, "What the hell? I don't need this. As long as I'm going to be at a certain level, I might as well just do it under my own name." And they were tired of each other. I don't know Kim very well, though she seems to be extraordinarily friendly. Joe is very high strung and Dave is unbelievably high strung. It's trying to travel with people who are uptight. They're a lot different now. We're talking about 14 years ago. Now, Joe's a dad. You're a dad, everything changes. Now that Dave's been a frontperson, he's so much looser. It's hard to believe it's the same guy. He was very tightly wound back then.

Murphy: I think Kim learned a lot, she didn't want to be difficult, but at the same time, she could see that the band may be struggling a little bit, the new material was getting thinner and thinner as time wore on. And a lot of it was really good, but some of the songs on *Bossanova* and *Trompe Le Monde*, you could throw them away and nobody would ever care, they're never going to play them again. And I think what happened was she was like, "Well, this song's not that bad," at least in her head, and it sort of got dismissed. I'm not really sure if it was that they weren't getting along was the reason why, but there were issues with this is a lot of work, and when the work became big they just had different opinions on how it's going to go. You're in this tight, small unit and you want to grow but the other people in the band think it's in the best interest to keep going the way you're going, you're going to get frustrated.

Watts-Russell: Everybody knew it was over for a long time before it was over, and the infamous fax I have no recollection of. Nobody was sad about it, it's like any relationship, when something is bad, it's a sigh of relief to end it. Charles was not an easy person to deal with, his manager was. . .no joy. The whole situation had gone from something that had been a shared celebration to a real struggle. Quite possibly any future records they might have made would have not been good, they had already tried to fire Kim at that point, I'm happy when people stop. Creatively, with music, you do your best music over a certain period of time, then you stop. I think that Joey and David were the least happy because Kim had already started the possibility of the Breeders and Charles jumped to do solo stuff really quickly, so it seemed to be a positive thing [for them].

Donelly: I can't remember how I found out. Things became very blown apart in a lot of ways because Throwing Muses split with

Ken. That happened right after we made *Pod* and right before we went in for *The Real Ramona*. Everybody sort of went off on their own, because we weren't really speaking to him anymore. I quit the Muses, and then everybody just drifted for a while. I don't think people should stay together forever unless they're. . .there are very rare examples where it works, like R.E.M. and U2. I think those are the only two examples. But you know, the Rolling Stones probably should have called it a day a long time ago. I'm not the kind of person who thinks bands should stay together forever.

Iha: I remember when the Pumpkins broke up I had a lot of people who would congratulate me on, man, you did it, you played in that band, you did everything. Not congratulations the band is done, but you accomplished something because it's really hard to be in a band for that long.

Flansburgh: Honestly, Charles seemed kind of happy all the way through. Not to interfere with people's *Behind the Music*, third act, preconceived notions of how bands break up, but it was actually relatively organic. I wasn't there, but again, the Pixies were a comet, they just blazed across the scene, and when they broke up I don't think anyone was surprised. Obviously there was probably more animosity at the end because that's the way things end. I don't think they necessarily were drawn out of the most organic circumstances in the first place. Some bands form very organically, and some bands don't, and you'd have to be painting in broad strokes to say this band had to come together. I think it was as random as any band, and the fact that all the players really complemented each other's skill sets so well was just a lucky circumstance. But it's not like they were brothers or grew up together, or some incredibly organic thing happened. It just wasn't that way.

Thompson: No one died, there was no big brawl on stage. We didn't fight, that's the thing that people misunderstand about the Pixies.

Craft: I don't think there's any one reason other than that basically they just grew apart because they are totally different people. I mean, my recollection is there was one tour that they didn't speak to each other at all on the entire tour, Charles and Kim. So, again, they would get onstage and play and they would fulfill their obligations, but there was no pleasure in it.

Mascis: I guess you can stay together forever like the Ramones and then all die of cancer.

Murphy: For a band that never really made it big, they still had a lot of the same kind of VH1 story. For their genre—the college music genre, which is basically what they were back then—they became too big, too fast, and then imploded. They were number one on Rock Pool out of the box, every record, number one, for weeks. To the people who were interviewing them at the time, radio stations, fawning all over them! Again, they weren't getting sprayed with money, but people literally thought they were the second coming of something big, and that's a lot of pressure. They got famous too fast and then they died quickly.

Iha: I guess the single-mindedness about being in a band that's going somewhere, it pulls you all together and you're just like this machine. And only later you realize, oh yeah, we're not really alike at all, and we don't have anything to say to each other. It can happen.

Perkins: Of course they were together in '86, '87 making their music just like us. Before your release, you're working like a dog up there. Writing a bunch of great songs in a short period of time and touring the hell out of them, you get a little burnt. If Jane's had a great manager someone should have said, "Hey, take a year off and then maybe talk about breaking up, don't just break up." We just said, "Fuck, we're not taking a year off, we're breaking up." That doesn't mean it was time for the Pixies to break up, it was time for them to take a break, but no one wants to take a break and stop working completely so you start other things. And sometimes you have legal problems or drug problems, those are just life problems that could happen to anybody, but to keep a band together and be creative with four people, it is tough after spending five, seven years on the same songs and now the world knows the songs. Boy, we need a break from each other, but really no one wants you to stop. You got to get back in the studio, get back on tour, so hey, just break up. They can't force us to be creative.

Murphy: They're not rules-followers to start with, and then you put them in a situation where you have rules, and record companies are expecting this, and there's a lot of pressure. Let's say you're Charles, and they're saying, "Okay, well you just signed a five-record deal, where's the next one?" And he feels the pressure to crank these things out. Now, he could have said, "You guys are gonna help me," or he could have said, "Oh my God, it's all on me"—and that's the choice he made. It's all on me, I got to deliver. And in the meantime Kim's like—in a maybe not so helpful way—

I'm ready to help, I'm smart, I can do this, and I think it got proven over time that she's a pretty good songwriter. I think that Charles was getting interested in some different styles and I think it's pretty evident in the music. I mean "Allison" doesn't sound like "Isla de Encanta." Kim liked the older sound and the crunchier sound and wanted to be a little bit lo-fi and whatever, and so I think they kind of grew apart more than anything. And I don't really know if there was any really huge animosity. Anyway, they broke up.

Angel: I think Charles was just glad to be free of the burden of trying to placate three people that were still his equals and peers. I mean, when it's your band you just tell the other people what to play and if they don't like it, fuck 'em. I don't think he could do that in the Pixies.

Thompson: It isn't about every song being some genius home run. Music is more eclectic than that. Records are more eclectic than that. That's why "Wild Honey Pie" is on the "White Album." It's not "Hey Jude," it's not "Revolution," it's just some weird thing they did one day with a tape recorder. So there's a lot of room for that kind of expression, but it's just you're doing it all the time and you're spending more and more money to get it done. And the record company keeps trying to like "get to the mixed level of success," or whatever, and you start to get grouchy and burned out and tired and you just don't have good perspective. So that's my biggest regret about the Pixies records—we made five records, and had we been given some really good creative advice, and maybe I got it but wasn't in a place where I could hear it at that time, but if I had been open to the right advice from the right person at that time, and those five records could have been shrunken down to three records paced a little further apart, that would have been a good thing. We would have had three killer records. But then again, that's not really what the Pixies are about. The Pixies are way more about, "Here's a song that a lot of people like, here's a song that only a few of you like, here's something that a lot of you hate." It's more schizophrenic and all over the place. Every single Pixies record is like that. It's like, "Here's a slow one, here's a fast one, here's a sort of country cowpunk one, here's a moody one, here's one where they're screaming, here's one where they're singing like a couple of little elves."

Barding: As Kim said in the interview I did, they had like two-thirds of a follow-up to *Trompe Le Monde* recorded and in the can, ready to go, and in bootlegs from the U2 dates there were these funny little instrumentals being played that you could tell were from another work in progress.

Lubin: Well, you can't get records out of a group that's broken up. I had to actually fight to sign the Breeders because [Sire president] Seymour Stein wanted them, too, and whether or not Ivo had had a bad experience with Throwing Muses, Seymour thought he had a contractual right to them because Tanya Donelly had been on Sire, and of course my position was I have a contractual right to them, Kim Deal is on Elektra. So, we had to tussle back and forth over who was going to get the Breeders. It actually got uncomfortable from time to time during the talks, but I did win, which I was happy about. First there was *Pod*, that was out on some dodgy indie label that went under owing people money, so the court put the master tapes, which were the label's only assets, up for bid at auction. I wanted their whole catalog, so I went to the auction and bid for the master tapes for *Pod*. I submitted a bid of $500 or somesuch thing for the rights to *Pod*, and got them. Then we did a four-song EP, *Safari*, and nobody even paid any attention to that record whatsoever.

Larbalestier: It was sad for me when the Pixies broke up and Kim and Charles went solo, neither of them wanted me to have anything to do with the covers of the albums because they didn't want to be associated with the Pixies stuff.

Harvard: But if they had stuck it out another fucking year, they would have cracked that ceiling that Nirvana cracked. America was waiting for that. It was taking off and it broke my heart because for every Boston band you've heard of there were three more that would have got sucked along in the wake just like what happened with Seattle. And you can't blame the Pixies, but that for me was a regret. I don't think like many people do that it stopped them at a point in their progression, musically, that they would have been so much better, I don't feel that. I thought in fact it was the best thing they ever did for themselves, because they seemed to me like it wasn't there. Even when I saw 'em in Ohio in '90 I was like, something's wrong here, their hearts aren't really in this. Where before they would light a room on fire, now it was a good, pro set—at least to me, the chemistry had altered in a fundamental way. It's like you can still go fuck your ex-wife, but it's not magic, it's not prayer, it's just fucking. So I think it probably was the best thing that happened for them and the worst thing that happened for the Boston music scene, but you can't lay that at their doorstep. It's just history and the way things work.

15. A.P. (AFTER PIXIES) (1993–2004)

Between 1992 and 2004 Thompson, Deal, Santiago, and Lovering traveled down very different roads. Half of the band members' work during that period is better known (Thompson as Frank Black and later Frank Black and the Catholics, Deal with the Breeders and the Amps). Lovering and Santiago's careers grew in different directions. Contact between the four former bandmates was mostly nonexistent. Though fans cried out for more Pixies, there wasn't much hope for ever getting the quartet back in the same room at the same time, let alone ready to play together again.

Lovering: I had done a number of drumming gigs, and nothing was panning out. I did a bunch of tours with other bands, also studio work. I auditioned for a bunch of bands and different things. And then I was in a local band, I was with Joe in the Martinis. And then it just kept trickling and trickling until I just gave up drums. I actually just put my drums away. Then when I moved into a house that I was renting, they knew I was a musician so right on my lease it says, "No drum playing" handwritten across it. So I couldn't play drums anymore. And the Pixies has been sustaining me for a number of years, it was nice. And I have a friend, Grant Lee Phillips, from Grant Lee Buffalo, we're both magicians. We went to an international magicians conference that was happening in Los Angeles, and there we saw some magic that just blew me away. So I just rediscovered magic and I went full into it. It's been about six, seven years now that I constantly have a deck of cards in my hand if I'm not either in the shower or sleeping.

I love magic. I think what lured me to it was just that disbelief, just seeing something that's just impossible. And the performance is the same—I think magic and music offer the same things. It's almost an emotional kind of thing that you get from it, seeing something that moves you in some way. But magic offers one other thing which I don't think music does, which is a sense of wonder. You may get it in a band, but with magic it may make you feel that the impossible is possible. And it's entertaining, people really like it, and people walk away with something from it. It saved my life, it really did. I can honestly say that magic saved my life the last six years, 'cause I don't know where I'd be, honestly. I was kind of going in death's fan, and this got me out of it.

I belong to a place called Magic Castle in Hollywood, and I've been a member there four or five years now, and I perform there every Friday night. I do a show there. I'm in with the guys now at Magic Castle, and we all critique each other. I'm not gonna leave Los Angeles because of the Magic Castle. I'm gonna stay there, just because I love that place.

I do things that are more nontraditional. I don't do cups and balls, ropes tricks, bunnies, things that you see all the time. I like things that are more mental, using mental powers, or sleight-of-hand. It's not only cards, I can use rubber bands, I use other objects, I make things move and stuff like that.

I've done four tours for Charles. I call myself a scientific phenomenalist. And basically, I come out in a lab coat and do science and physics experiments. It's all kind of upbeat, really weird physics experiments that you never see. Then I bring out a meteorite that gives me special powers. And that's where the physics gets a little weird and the magic starts. But that line's kinda fuzzy. I'd rather have them leave going "Is it or isn't it?" rather than "It's all science" or "It's all magic." So I do kinda weird things that most magicians don't do. Very nontraditional. If you were to see me, you wouldn't think it was even a magic show, you'd think it's more entertainment in a way, which I like better. I can just say I'm an entertainer. It's actually a stage show that I've done all over L.A. in clubs and I've taken on the road, toured all over with different rock bands, as well as taken it overseas. For a rock band, I think it's a nice alternative form for a support act. The crowd's seeing something that's completely different, your ears aren't blown.

I remember when Foo Fighters were forming, I think it was Mark Kates over at Geffen, he had once asked me if I wanted to play with Foo Fighters. I didn't know who they were, I really wasn't up on it. It's just something that, you know, passed by. And then I ran into Dave [Grohl] for the first time in over 11, 12 years, at the Troubadour about a year ago and we were talking about how the Pixies meant so much to him and he asked if I'd want to come down and just jam with them and play drums. And I was like, "Oh, yeah, that'd be great." But it's been tough. I've been really busy. There was talk about it, but it didn't come to fruition.

There was always talk about a reunion, and we were quietly talking to ourselves, Joe and I. But from day one, I knew it was never gonna happen, impossible. Everyone asked a million times, no way, no, forget it. And it was interesting, 'cause honestly my life this past year had gone down the shitter, wasn't very good, relationship was absolutely horrible, involving police and prison, and also financially, and I was drinking a lot, everything. It was looking pretty bad. Couldn't stay in my house, I was kicked out of my own house. I was going to the bank, and it must have been the most depressing day I'd ever had. And just as I got to the door, my cell phone rings. It was Joe. "Guess what?" "What?" "The Pixies are getting back together!" Nothing in my life could have been more—it was amazing.[18]

Hersh: Billy [O'Connell, her husband and manager] just took a couple of the kids to this great club here, Largo, and saw David, he was doing magic tricks for the kids. It was so adorable. The last time I saw Joey was at the Muses show here, last year (our reunion was before theirs). I don't think [he had any clue about the reunion] because I think he was looking for a job. Joey was emailing me all the time about getting the kids together for a play date, and I'm thinking, "You've got too much time on your hands, dude!" I liked the Martinis, I thought they were great, but that didn't keep him busy enough, I guess.

Santiago: The Martinis are very sugary. Give you cavities. It is what it is: light pop. A lot of songs about Linda's dad. It's just Linda and me. We got the record out, finally, but the first couple years I pretty much went into this little depression. Maybe not little—my wife would say huge. You know, I stayed in my room. But then I woke up from it, took some antidepressants, and started going, "Hey, look at this! There are trees!" I started learning these computer programs and was like, "You can record in a computer? How the fuck do you do that?" I did it, and I did a film, I co-scored a film, and I did a TV show. It was easy to do that.

I'm a rookie. I've been composing for film and TV. I did a season of *Undeclared*, it's by the people who made *Freaks and Geeks*. It was actually pretty good, which is part of the reason why it got cancelled. It's tough meeting with those people. I got an agent and she's trying to get me into this meeting vibe.

Judd Apatow (screenwriter; creator of the television series *Freaks and Geeks* and *Undeclared*)): I was looking for a composer, and you always get a stack of CDs of different people who compose music for movies and television, and one of the CDs was from Joey Santiago. It was some scores he did for some independent films, I believe. And it just sounded great, it was perfect for what we were doing because we needed it to sound like the feeling of going to college, and at least for me, as a 37-year-old, college sounds like the Pixies. And so Joey came on and did an amazing job, he was so easy to work with and so funny. He's just an incredibly creative, easygoing guy. Sometimes when you work with a composer you give them notes and they look like they want to kill you, and Joey was so easy to collaborate with. But he was supremely overqualified for the job. We would laugh about how much better Joey was at what he does than we are at what we do.

He probably mentioned his association with the Pixies which immediately sparked my interest. It was really fun, and every once in a while he would be scoring an episode and he would say, "Yeah, Frank came over last night and I was finishing up the score so he helped me out on a couple of cues." And we would laugh and say we've got the Pixies reunion backing up our crappy *Undeclared*. There was actually one cue Joey brought in and it was him and Frank playing guitars and you could very faintly hear Frank Black sing like "La la la la la" and we got so excited. Everybody on the show was a big fan of the Pixies.

I didn't find Joey quiet, I thought he was really nice and warm and seemed happier than most people I know. He did seem like one of the most well-adjusted rock stars I've ever come across. There's nothing more awkward than having a rock legend be your composer and having to give him notes. You're so happy when it's actually as good as you hoped it would be because it saves you from that weird moment when you have to tell a guitar god how to fix something.

He had a room in his home and he played all the instruments, for the most part. You would give him a rough cut of the show and tell him where you thought the music should go, and then he would start roughing out ideas, and then he would start sending in cues. It's a difficult job because you have to score the entire show in a week or two. You always have a few people in a production that I call no-brainers, who just nail everything and surprise you and make everything better than you ever thought it could be. I always used to think that about Ben Stiller when I was working on *The Ben Stiller Show* in the early '90s. Everytime Ben directed everything was so much better than we thought it could be, and that's the way I always felt about Joey's music.

Then Frank Black came to the premiere party for *Undeclared*. It was at a pool hall called the Yankee Doodle on the Third Street Promenade in Santa Monica. It certainly made our party a much more interesting event than it would have been with only us there. *Teenager of the Year* is one of my favorite records. I can't tell you how many scripts I've written to *Teenager of the Year*. It's a great album to write to. When I was rewriting *The Cable Guy* I was listening to that all the time. I'm really drawn to artists who don't care whether or not anybody likes them. The Pixies certainly go their own way and are more concerned with originality than pandering to their audience, and so that's why when I'm writing I tend to listen to the Pixies or Warren Zevon, people I think write from the heart and do what they feel and let the chips fall where they may commercially.

Watts-Russell: I don't know what other people thought of Charles' solo albums at 4AD. It wasn't a surprise that regardless of what they sounded like, that they didn't sell like the Pixies. You become a solo artist after having led a band and I don't know what the equation is, but I think the industry has an expectation of something like a third of the sales. He had Eric Drew Feldman there, he was just shedding the other members perhaps, but they don't sound like Pixies records. I think his writing had changed. I like the two records we put out, but I didn't want to work with Charles. It just seemed like by the time of the second record, *Teenager of the Year*, it really wasn't a very good relationship. Charles can get in your face and I've seen him do it to other people, and that's when he started doing it to me. I just really felt that he and Ken wanted to get off 4AD and Rick Rubin was in the wings at the time. They put something out on American [*Cult of Ray* in 1996].

Banks: What Charles didn't do, what he refused to do was play the game. And the game would have been that he would have played Pixies songs, then introduced his new stuff and the audience would have gone with him. But the Pixies audience went to see him and it was all new songs and no Pixies songs. They were kind of disappointed. That's why they were successful in the first place. That's what great artists do. They are relentless. They don't do what the public want, they do what they want and the public either love them or hate them, but they don't care.

Geiger: The first solo album that had "Los Angeles" on it [1993's *Frank Black*] came up pretty strong. I think that the decrease in popularity was expected given every great band that broke up, when I worked with the solo members, the drop-off was the same. I think that's just standard when a band breaks up and one of the members goes solo. Very few actually equal or surpass the success of his or her band.

Feldman: I had a big hand in how *Frank Black* was made and how it was going to sound. I was producing it. I wrote the drum parts, played the bass, keyboards, and left space for guitars. Joe came in and played, Charles did his part and sang. It was pretty thought-out and structured in a certain way. Charles wrote them, I laid 'em out with MIDI templates and it was just sort of like now, you just have to sing and play. And that's in a way completely different than how the Pixies did it. Charles seemed pretty at ease with it at the time. I heard later on from Gil or someone else that people perceived it as Charles being lazy, but maybe I just bamboozled him by doing it this way. I think he was okay with it but for whatever reason a year later when we started working on *Teenager of the Year*, he said, "Let's not do it like before, let's just play it." That was fine with me.

Flansburgh: I directed the first couple of Frank Black videos off the *Frank Black* album, notably the "Los Angeles" video, which was in Buzz Bin and on *Beavis and Butt-Head*. A lot of people noticed it. Charles enjoyed They Might Be Giants' videos in that they weren't so self-serious, and while I certainly was not inside his head, there is a tedium to being a contrarian and I think the Pixies had made enough anti-videos that Charles was ready to do things that were just more visually hopped-up. The "Los Angeles" video that we did, the last minute and a half of the song is this open field of grey over which hovercrafts are floating. It's about as tripped-out as any video I've ever been involved in, and it was also realizing a dream of Charles', getting him in a hovercraft.

Feldman: On *Teenager of the Year*, I didn't lay them all out in advance. We just kind of did it like a bunch of musicians. He showed me the songs and we played. It was the three of us and [guitarist] Lyle Workman was around. He just sort of showed up at the last minute, and we stuck him in a room and he played along. It was a lot more spontaneous, and Charles was just writing a shitload of songs. That was really him sort of coming out, becoming who he was. It's a little closer to things to come. The first Frank Black record is this kind of thing that connects *Trompe Le Monde*, and at the same time it is an island, like nothing else he did.

We would spend hours together driving in a car to a gig, so you just talk about stuff. We were driving around once and talked about our love of the Three Stooges and that became a song called "Two Reelers" on *Teenager of the Year*.

Blake: Charles was in London to do a John Peel session. The band had broken up and he got in touch with us and asked if we would like to back him up on it and we were thrilled because we were such big fans. So we went to London and booked a rehearsal studio for a couple of days. Getting to see how Charles writes was really interesting. At one point I had been telling him a story about how I'd gone to see Jonathan Richman and that halfway through the show he turned down his amplifier and you know, you normally see people turning their amplifiers up, and Charles thought that was an amusing story. So we get into the studio a few days later and Charles had written a song about it, "The Man Who Was Too Loud." So it was interesting to see that little story would just spark off a set of lyrics. It was really fun recording the session because Charles likes to record things live and most people don't like to do that. But Charles sees it as being liberating—you go for the take, capture it, it's done, you go home. We did all the songs live with a few vocal overdubs. Charles likes to use quite complex time signatures and have several in one song, too. We also covered "Sister Isabel," the Del Shannon song. We did four songs with him. We worked through the arrangements the day before. We did "The Man Who Was Too Loud," "The Jacques Tati," "Sister Isabel," and "Handyman."

Gilbert: Charles put out the first Catholics album, *Frank Black and the Catholics*, so that one has Lyle Workman on it, but Lyle was doing so well with studio work and was maybe a little burned out from touring that he just didn't want to keep going on the road. So I got the call and played on the next Catholics record, *Pistolero*. Charles is incredibly prolific. He's a very hardworking gentleman. Charles and I will lock horns, historically, in fact it's tradition, we will lock horns once during every recording session for an album. We're both really determined and passionate and a little strong-minded. We'll have one huge fight during the recording session. It has no residual effect, whatsoever, like a half-hour after it everything is fine, the air is cleared, we just get back to work.

Feldman: We were just sitting around, I told him a story about Don Van Vliet (Captain Beefheart) and his lack of sleeping at one point in his life. And that became a Frank Black song, "85 Weeks" [on *Pistolero*]. And it starts with him singing, "Once Eric said / come gather round / I'll tell a tale / That is sure to astound," and he just sort of bent it to be poetic to his needs.

Harvard: I think the Catholics got critically short-shrifted. I think the stuff that Frank was writing, it didn't ever have that immediate, whoa, Pixies impact, but there was some very thoughtful, well-constructed rock music on those records.

I think Frank was competing with Pixies songs, but he wasn't playing Pixies songs, he was playing Frank Black and the Catholics songs, and it seems impossible for people to look at something as itself. The sad thing is I think Frank had, and may still probably have a great Frank Black album waiting, but there was too much bullshit shoveled in the way that he had to get through before he could even start the tremendous job of making that record. Because people wouldn't just judge it by itself, they had to always go back to well, it's not the Pixies. Well, no shit.

Walsh: I feel his songwriting has improved. I know he used to refer to his songs in the early days as being automatic writing, as if he wasn't really that conscious of what he was writing. I don't think there's that much automatic writing that goes on now. Because now he has whatever skills or chops it takes to do it more fully consciously. Just his little games that he likes to play in the lyrics, it seems like that's a whole new level that wasn't present before. How long can this kind of "This is all just spewing out of my brain" go on? I think there's a certain point where you get a lot of stuff out that needed to come out, and then you have to actually do some work.

Feldman: I think his musicianship has just gotten stronger and stronger and he has an ability to sing in more different ways. Definitely not a guy who has plateaued. I think his solo work has had varied results, but for a lot of musicians he is quite an inspiration. He doesn't get stuck in certain concepts, he always seems to be moving forward.

Watts-Russell: What a difference MTV makes. [The Breeders] made a good video and so it didn't surprise me at all about "Cannonball." MTV was interested in that kind of stuff at the time. That was the only video we were ever involved in that did that, just through the roof.

Deal: We were on the MTV video the whole time. It was really odd. To be on 4AD and to be used to going under the radar all the time. And the fact that then people think you're mainstream, and I'm gonna fail miserably if you think I'm mainstream 'cause I'm not, but the song got played a hell of a lot. It's vocal feedback from a microphone plugged in through a Marshall amp. I mean it's not intentional. My mother's sewing machine is on the record, on "S.O.S." It's so fucking strange. And you know what, I just was watching a piece of *Charlie's Angels: Full Throttle*, and "Firestarter" is on there, and Prodigy sampled the "S.O.S." thing. It's so weird. It's everywhere. It's so strange.

Geiger: I think you had a couple of great songwriters in that band. Maybe some of these were types of songs that Kim wasn't able to get done with the Pixies.

Mascis: [After the breakup] I talked to Kim Deal the most, probably. I produced some Breeders stuff at one point. Some B-sides for *Last Splash*, some other stuff. She's pretty intense. We had different schedules. I'd want to record from 11 in the morning to maybe seven, and she'd get up at four, so we didn't see too much of each other. I didn't really feel like staying up all night.

St. Thomas: I remember the Breeders sent us a ten-inch vinyl with "Do You Love Me Now?" on it, and on the B-side was "Do You Love Me Now Jr." with J Mascis on it. But to get a ten-inch single? That was just cool. They would also do very elaborate postcards.

Iha: Lollapalooza with the Breeders was great, they were really nice. The Deal sisters knew how to party. I wasn't really close to the partying, but Kim was either drinking or smoking or doing both, but she was really nice. I actually played on stage with them once. They invited me to play "Divine Hammer" with them. I figured out a harmony to the main guitar line, and when we got offstage they were like, "That was like the Allman Brothers or something!"

Donelly: Kim and Kelley are distinctly different. I've never confused them. They're very different people, they have a different way of carrying themselves. They have a great relationship, they do have that twin dependency, which I like. It's like that dream you have when you're a kid: somebody just like me but different. [Kelley takes care of Kim], and Kim sort of takes care of her in different ways.

Norton: Kim did want me to do *Last Splash*, actually. She sent me the demos for it and I really liked it, and I said, "Great!" and then I didn't hear anything from her for six weeks or something, so I assumed she'd decided to do something else. And then I took on another band, and the day I said yes to do something else she rang up and wanted me to do it. And I couldn't do anything about it, because once you say you're going to do what you're going to do you can't say, "Oh, I can't do you now because I'm doing this." And to be honest with you I never really wanted to get involved in any of the solo projects years ago, just in case they got back together.

16. LIFE TO THE PIXIES—THE REUNION (2004)

The list of '80s and '90s bands who tossed aside their differences for a reunion cash-in includes Gang of Four, Slint, Dinosaur Jr., Bauhaus, and Mötley Crüe, but—like so many facets of their career—Pixies did it first and Pixies did it best. In February 2004 the band announced plans for an international tour, their first in over a decade. The news spread from traditional news outlets like CNN to music newswires like Pitchfork media.com and tickets began to sell out just as quickly. While some critics wondered how they'd sound and others pondered how they'd get along, Pixies quietly prepared to reintroduce themselves to fans from the old days and a new generation of devoted listeners.

Banks: Charles carried on working and there was a demand for him to play Pixies songs, which he refused at first, but then he started to play an occasional one here and there, and the crowd went apeshit. When I went to see him in Liverpool in September (2004) I would say the average age of the audience was 19. There was a lot of young kids down there going crazy. These young kids could never have seen the Pixies, so they've obviously grown up listening to their brothers' records and accepted them as a ground-breaking act, an act that opened the doors for so much that came afterwards. And so people went along just to see Charles, to get any tiny little piece of it that they could.

Craft: I've been Kim and Charles' agent all through the 12-year period between the Pixies splitting and reforming. So I booked all the Frank Black and the Catholics tours and I've booked all the Breeders tours. The subject of Pixies was never on the agenda until very recently. Obviously I have had plenty of offers in that time but it's always just been well, there is no chance of the band ever reforming so don't even bother. As far as I was concerned, the band split and that was the end of it. I was never expecting them to reform.

It was always going to come from Charles. Obviously, it had to be all four members if they were going to reform, but he was gonna be the catalyst for it. Over a very gradual period of time, from not even being able to even mention the word *Pixies* in his company at all for years, gradually it would pop up in conversation. And then each time that Frank Black came to Europe, he always got asked. And usually he would just dismiss the question or ignore it and then gradually he would maybe actually reply. He would always say no, but he'd at least give some slightly more measured response. And then the breakthrough, I think, is Frank Black and the Catholics started playing Pixies songs. I think it was a gradual acceptance of the fact that he'd written some great songs and people wanted to hear them again. A certain amount of time had to pass for this to become a reality. If you'd said five years ago, here's $10 million to reform the Pixies, it would not have happened. It wasn't about money. I could've gone to Charles at any time in the last 12 years with a heap of money and he wouldn't have done it.

Geiger: I think Charles put it out there pretty strongly that it was a non-issue, so it's not like you could say, "Hey, Charles, let's talk about the Pixies reunion." He was completely, vehemently against it in every way. He told me he'd never play a Pixies song. There's an expression "Time heals." I think people got older, they have families, there was a number of forces that came together. The last two Frank Black tours Charles played Pixies material live. I can tell you this: his solo touring started to get better, attendance-wise. His attendance started to get better, and you can say it was *Dog in the Sand* and the other records, or you can say it was because he was doing Pixies songs, but something up-ticked the attendance both here and abroad. I saw him a couple of times, and hearing the great Frank Black solo stuff alongside Pixies songs made for a pretty impressive show. Joey played with him, David would open up with the magic act, so you're kind of half there. And the Catholics were a great band, they were tight, so when they played a Pixies song it wasn't that disparaging.

Gilbert: In terms of us playing Pixies songs, at that point I felt that Charles had already established himself as a solo artist. The Pixies are a band that had chemistry and created the sound of those songs. But at the same time, I felt it was totally valid for him to want to perform songs that he wrote. I felt that when we were playing Pixies songs I was playing another band's material. You can never recreate another band's sound, so in a way I would never really try to totally recreate the sound of the songs as the Pixies performed them. For instance, I would never try to play the way Joey played, just because you can't. I used to feel a funny sense of regret and empathy when we would take Dave Lovering on tour with us as the opening act. He would sometimes do tours with us with his magic show, his scientific illusionist show. And so, you'd hang out with Dave, and it was always fun to be around him, and I would always feel so weird and wonder how he felt being in the room whenever we were playing these songs. Because at that point we'd maybe do a half-dozen Pixies songs, and we're playing "Wave of Mutilation" or "Gouge Away" or "Velouria" or "Where Is My Mind?" or "Caribou" and I'm looking across the band at the side of the stage, and there's Dave. And no disrespect to Scott [Boutier], the Catholics drummer, but I'd just be thinking, "Oh man, it's just got to sting a little bit every time for him." Later, when Scott was sick and Dave was doing the opening act, he filled in on a couple of shows.

Angel: I used to ask Charles every year, "When are you going to do it?" He'd always hem and haw, and I'd say, "You know you're going to do it eventually." He'd say, "No. No." At one point a few years ago, he said, "Everybody thinks there's all this money to be made. The offers aren't that good."

Deal: I had heard that the Pixies had offers. Ken Goes, the old manager, sent a letter once to each of the band members that if we were ever interested this is the type of money they're looking at for summer tours, that was like in 2000 or something. It was a lot of money. 'Cause for some reason over the decade we got popular. People would be interested in seeing us. So then Joe said when he was visiting family in Massachusetts Charles had left a message on his machine pretending to be an English journalist and talking about, "So, the Pixies are gonna do a tour." But then when Joe called him back and thought it was funny Charles said, "Well what do you think, seriously?" And Joe goes, "Really?" 'Cause Joe had wanted to. It never occurred to me. Never wanted to. Never thought about it. So I go, "I don't know, Joe." But he goes, "Kim, this is not just a lot of money for me, this is a change of school district for me." See, I knew he had just had a baby and he could actually go someplace where there's nice schools. He had a kid now and he had to start thinking about money. And he goes, "Well, Charles wants you to call him." And Charles and I hadn't talked in 12 years. April '92, and I remember because that was the last Pixies show, the last time we talked was backstage at the last Pixies show.

Craft: Since the Pixies split until last fall Charles and Kim had not spoken for 12 years. But Charles and Joey and David had been in constant contact because obviously Charles and Joey had worked together quite a lot and David's been doing his magic. So it's only really been Kim that's been the one that hasn't been involved with the others.

Geiger: It was up to Charles and Kim. Like I described, Charles is the leader. If the leader says no, it ain't happening. What happened with me was, I booked Frank Black, I've been with him forever and I love him. The last solo tour before the Pixies he played eight Pixies songs, the attendances went back up, and I kind of could feel it softening a bit. And then one day Ken called me and said, "Hey, Marc, Charles is kind of thinking da da da da da, and would you go out with him?" and Charles and I went out and had a couple of very long business meetings about it, pros, cons, how to do it, what to do. And then I came back and laid out the whole plan and we basically executed it exactly to plan.

Thompson: The only reason I considered getting the band back together this time was I sarcastically, humorously, contemplated a reunion in a radio interview in England. And I thought it was so obvious that I was being tongue-in-cheek because they're always asking about that. I forget what I said but it was like, "Yeah, we get together all the time and jam." And somehow that got interpreted as "They're doing it, they're getting back together!" and suddenly it was on the CNN ticker the next day, it was in the *New York Post*. Somehow I created this monster by just like, fucking around on this radio show. And then everyone was calling me like, "Charles, what's up? Is there a reunion finally?" And I was like, "No, I was just joking around." And then I was like, "Well yeah, what the hell." It seemed like a good time and I had kind of let down my guard a bit, I wasn't so uptight about it.

Steven Cantor (cofounder, Stick Figure Productions): The second [Stick Figure producer] Matthew [Galkin] and I heard the Pixies were reuniting we looked at each other and said, "Holy shit, the Pixies are getting back together, we have to buy tickets," and in the same conversation we were like, "Wait a minute, we should make a movie about this," and we started talking with Ken. Ken said there were 17 people who wanted to do a film, and we just started pestering him, sending him tapes, notes and emails, and love letters, and it actually whittled down to us.

The agreement was we could film anything we want. We had total, 100 percent access to do whatever we wanted, exclusive. We started with rehearsals in L.A. before they started the tour, which was really interesting because I think they were very different people in the beginning than they were in the end. They kind of had been living for a long time not being stars and towards the end they really had become stars. They dressed differently, they had different confidence levels, there was a whole different aura about each of them.

Santiago: It felt good. Dave, Kim, and I met up first, because we knew Charles knew the songs, so we met up in L.A. to get our shit together before he comes over. I was nervous with Dave because he hadn't been at a set in a while.

Deal: I went out to L.A. and I moved to the Oakwood apartments on Barham Blvd. in November. And I stayed out there and me, David, and Joe rehearsed. And then Charles came in from Portland. I went to my sister's wedding in January, so he came in February, I guess. So we had about four separate rehearsals, four days each. Then we rehearsed in Minneapolis before the tour.

Watts-Russell: I spoke to Kim before all this happened, and I didn't think she was going to do it. Last year the three of them were rehearsing, Kim, David, and Joey—she hadn't spoken to Charles, she was still thinking about doing it, Charles was in Portland. She was testing it out. And even then I didn't think she was going to do it, but I think she was really enjoying it. I remember saying to her, "Aren't you terrified of the day that Charles does walk into the studio?" because it's been sort of stretched out to the last moment, but apparently they kind of walked in, smiled, shook hands, shrugged a few shoulders, and after a few moments said, "Well, let's play", and then they did what they do well together—played.

Cantor: At the rehearsal in L.A., Kim and Charles were trying to work through songs, and they got to "Where Is My Mind?" and they totally messed it up, they were like, "God, I can't remember how this song goes at all. How does it end? I don't know," and then Charles said, "You know what, I'll just have to bring in my iPod tomorrow and we'll listen to it." Matt had his iPod and obviously had that song, so he was like, "Um, guys, I have my iPod, and you can listen to it," and they said, "Okay, great." So Matt came and took his headphones and first Charles listened to it then Kim listened to it and they were like, "Oh, yeah," and Matt was looking at me like, is this really happening?

Thompson: It is a band, but it isn't exactly like a democracy. At least in terms of the creative stuff, you know, they've got a frontman named Black Francis who writes basically all the material and kind of started the band. It was my ad that they answered in the paper, you know what I mean? And I'm not saying they're not an integral part of it. Hey, I'm not going to go out there and hire three other people and call it the Pixies. I understand the marketability of the original lineup and how people hold that to be precious and dear, so that has value. Every single one of the Pixies has ultimate veto power, they can say I don't wanna participate in it. At the end of the day, it's my band and I can't really have all kinds of terms, business included, dictated to me from other people, even if it's other people in the band. At some point, I have my own ego, and it's like, "Eh, fuck off, man, it's my band. You don't dig it, whatever. Sorry." I can't just totally make it the way that they want it to be exactly. And now I've been gone for 12 years, the whole time I've been swearing I would never do it, I would never get the band back together, and what can I say? Because I got a divorce, I've had a lot of psychotherapy in my life the last year, and I'm older, so I don't have as much attitude about the whole thing. I'm not as uptight about it. Things that I was uptight about before seem a bit childish and silly to me. I'm kind of more like, what the fuck? Every year these guys are offering us tons of money to play a few shows. Let's go do it. I'm fine with it now.

Nobody got ripped off. We all made lots of money. I know everyone's made a lot of money because I'm privy to how much the checks are for. Everyone did good. For a little indie rock band, we did really good, and I kind of feel we're having the breakup we never properly had. There was not really much of a breakup the first time we broke up. I just left via fax. The reunion, it was off. And it was only then that we were able to go, "All right, we're not doing it. So let's do it." Maybe we had to go through this whole squabbling thing and everyone yelling at each other on the phone. For me, it's kind of a healing thing. I've been able to put aside whatever bad attitude I've had about it and kind of just say "Hey, you know, I'm sorry about the way things were before and now we're older, we're more adult-like, and let's go do this and get back to this good place that we were at one point early on in our career." I'm just talking about the atmosphere between the personalities.

It was just like, "Let's go play some gigs." Why can't we just go play some gigs? That's what everyone keeps saying, but you have to understand, it ain't that easy. I knew it was gonna be a can of worms as soon as this thing started out, as soon as someone says, "Hey let's talk about renegotiating some stuff from the past," I was like, "Here we go." There's an old saying, "A partnership is a sinking ship," and right now that has become true. So creatively, aesthetically, it's a fine ship, but in terms of negotiating business now, too many cooks in the kitchen.

They rehearsed, they've rehearsed because I was on tour, and they said, "Hey, we're gonna do some practicing to see if we can do this." Because Dave hadn't played drums in a long time, and Kim, she has her band, but she plays guitar—even before she joined the Pixies she was a guitar player, not a bass player—so she wanted to brush up on her bass chops. So the three of them got together and they said it sounded great, they felt good, they were just missing the singer.

Lovering: It felt the same, like I hadn't left. And I think to all of us it was the same feeling, our abilities were there, musically. Nothing changed, there was no time off, it was just the progression contin-ued, we just started off again. It was amazing. It was really nice and everything but we were still walking on eggshells around each other to make sure everything was just nice and easy, going out to eat and everything, it was interesting. But it was fun.

Cantor: David was probably the one who had the biggest change. He was kind of losing his hair up top and had long scraggly hair and a beard. He's the drummer for the Pixies and 40 years old and single and hot girls all over the place are screaming and dying to meet him and go out for a drink with him. It's kind of a no-brainer.

Norton: If you would've asked me if they were ever going to get together, I would've said, "Definitely not." The day before, I think Joey rang me and said, "You're not going to believe this." But I was surprised. I'm really pleased for Joey and Dave as well, because obviously Charles has his solo career and Kim's got the Breeders, but those two, Joey was doing the Martinis and Dave, his magic stuff is amazing, but he wasn't really playing and it was a bit of a shame.

Murphy: I thought it was done. I thought Charles was just unhappy with the rest of them, Kim in particular. And last December (2003) I was talking to Jean, we had a little mini-reunion in my neighborhood, and she said, "Yeah, it looks like they're going to get back together," and I said, "You've got to be kidding me!" And she said, "Nope, they're practicing, and they are really serious about it." I think they looked at it from a per-spective of, I mean Charles already said it, it was a good time to cash in on the notoriety. The second thing is I think they looked at it like, we're all grown up now, we don't have to pretend anything anymore about who's this and who's that. Plus, if there's no drink-ing going on in the back, the emotions aren't going to go through the roof, and f-you and f-that. Because sometimes backstage that's what it would be like.

Cantor: They said it very openly, with the possible exception of Kim (because of the Breeders Kim had to be talked into it the most), Dave, Joey, and Charles floundered since the Pixies broke up. They created this legendary thing, they were too young to even appreciate what they had, they made four albums, broke up before they were 23, boom, they were over, 1992. And for 12 years they floundered. Dave gave up drums and became a magician. He says in the film that for a while he was sleeping in ten-dollar flea-bag prostitute motels, Joey was about to have his second baby, living in a very small apartment, Charles as Frank Black and the Catholics *really* not making it, and just the mention of a Pixies reunion had such good buzz about it, it seemed like such an obvious way for them to make money: I think that was a huge motivating factor. Kim didn't need to, financially, she made more money from "Cannonball" than she did from the entire Pixies catalog. She had to get talked into it. Joey and Dave had to say to Kim, "Please do this for us, it would really change our lives." I think she did it primarily for them. And I think she started to have a great time with it. After that first show in Minnesota she came back down to the dressing room and was like, "Oh my God! Wasn't that incredible? They were so happy to see us! There was so much love there," just glowing and exploding and couldn't believe it.

Matthew Galkin (producer, Stick Figure Productions): Kim's whole thing was she didn't want to go out there and suck. Charles at least projects this take-it-in-stride attitude. Very few things actually ruffle him. We have a couple of moments in our footage right before they go on in Minneapolis for the first time where he actually says, "I'm going to puke I'm so nervous," but beyond that he shows very little emotion. In London they were very nervous because they were so well-received there back in the '80s, and their tour manager let us know that this was a very special show, the first night at Brixton Academy. Minneapolis and Brixton were the two shows they were the most nervous for, but beyond that, they could be in Iowa or New York City, it didn't matter.

Geiger: Coachella was part of a plan. Part of the recommended strategy was to launch it with a big festival, and Coachella made a lot of sense. The promoter of Coachella was also a massive Pixies fan, and it was his dream to get the Pixies to play Coachella. The plan was to tour the world in the year 2004.

I think Coachella was the first anchor. And the reason Coachella played a big role was because if you're talking about one of the reasons to do it is hey, I have a real life, I need to realize the money from it—not every reason, just part of the reason—I need some validation, I wanted to and had to show them that the market potential was much bigger than what they remembered, and that it could be significant and worth everybody's time. Coachella was the first one to say in the U.S., where you weren't ever mega, you guys are mega.

Tollett: Standing on the stage at Coachella looking through the Pixies onto the crowd, that might have been my career highlight. Just the feeling of a band playing to this many people is kind of. . .obviously they're not *American Idol*. Good music prevailed. What was great about it was looking out at the crowd, it was a bunch of 20-year-olds singing along and I'm thinking, "They haven't played since these kids were in kindergarten."

Geiger: It was one of the most dominant performances I have ever seen by any rock band on any festival ever. Maybe a little sweeter because it was America, and watching 55,000 kids leave all the other stages and come and worship every single song the Pixies did, it was incredible. Especially next to bands like Radiohead and Kraftwerk, and others that were brilliant bands, and to see the Pixies be that dominant is amazing.

Beck (musician): Oh yeah, that was the highlight, definitely. Oh, God. It was just. . .you know, it just schooled all the bands in the last ten years. Just 'cause they've been gone for a long stretch to just get a shock of those songs in a row for 45 minutes, it was kind of stunning. They were one of the few things that was poking its head up above the surface back in the mid-'80s that was decent, that was a respite from all the crap.

Mico: When I saw them at Coachella last year, it really did not sound dated. And the reason for that is they were so out of joint with what was going on at that time, anyway, also with what they were wearing at the time, everything else, everything that they had performed in from their look to the way they spoke was so out of joint with everything around them that it sort of ends up being timeless because it never had a time to tether it. So they can come back ten years later and it sounded as powerful, in some respects more powerful, than when they left. All I kept thinking was, "Oh, Lord, the poor band that's going on after them." I guess the strange thing is when I saw them at Coachella people were so impressed that a band like Pixies could dominate a festival of that size, but I'd seen them at so many festivals in Europe, headline and supporting the Cure, various other things...they're used to it. It was only here, the American audience didn't connect with them the same way. Slow on the uptake, maybe. Americans are not dumb, I think some of the media gatekeepers were asleep, and I certainly think that radio was never their format. And I'm not sure that would change now. I mean, going back to the out-of-jointness of it all, if they were to release stuff now I don't think it would make it on the radio, either. The closest radio ever came to playing the Pixies was Nirvana. "Here Comes Your Man" was their salute to pop.

Albini: I was at that Coachella performance and it was amazing to see 50,000 people who'd never seen this band before but for whom this band was really important having that experience. But I couldn't tell you what about their music appeals to so many people. I think they're one of those bands where they make an impact on their immediate audience and then those people leave their records to their kid brothers when they go away to college and then those people get into the band and then they get all their friends into them and then when they go off to college they leave that bigger pile of records to their kid brothers.

MacKaye: I saw them at Coachella and it sounded good. What was interesting to me was that, I mean they played for 50,000 people—I was really struck by the songs. I don't even own a Pixies record but I knew so many of those songs, and I don't listen to the radio, so it made me realize that they really crafted music that got through the filters, they wrote songs that worked. People were emotional, people were crying when they were playing and I was touched by that.

Watts-Russell: It's extraordinary isn't it? Everyone talks about these songs as if it's a greatest hits performance now, but it was then, so why has it taken so long? Again I blame this disgusting industry. If anyone had a brain in their heads at MTV they would have been playing the music then, supporting the band, because they are as important as the Beatles. Elektra as a label could have been more committed at the time, as well. I will freely say, when has a band ever reformed and it's been nearly as good or as important as it was before, let alone better? I can't think of any examples. The brilliant thing that appears to have come from this is first and foremost that they have healed some wounds. Whereas the Pixies within the four of them must have felt some uncomfortable scab, they truly must be able to celebrate the past as well as what is going on now because they have kind of put it behind them.

Thompson: The financial stuff is great, but I really feel like there's kind of a peaceful, joyous thing about just playing music with people. It's something that we had when we first started and somehow it got messed up as all of our friendships or peaceful productivity changed into something that was still productive but that wasn't friendly and not as joyous, and so, I hope that this time around I can make that up. Kind of, "Okay, sorry I used to be such a grouch. I'm not so grouchy now." It doesn't feel like it's about the money, it's about this kind of healing or something. It's nice. I didn't expect it be so spiritual. Nothing's changed. It's very anticlimactic. It's all like, "What do you want from Starbucks?" That's the main thing we've been catching up on. Everything else is the same. I forgot how much I like the sense of humor that we have that we probably had a lot of when we first started and then we had less of that as the band went on for five or six years.

Cantor: Actually, the entire tour they were very professional and they were together for the music, there wasn't that much interpersonal communication between them. Once the tour got going they almost never saw each other. The only time they're a band is when they're onstage. Onstage, you're like wow, they are so in sync, they seem like they love each other, they smile at each other and there seems like there's so much love in the music, they must be best friends. And then they go home and don't talk to each other until the next show.

Galkin: There's no real band there, there were four people that got back together to play music. They're consummate professionals in that sense. They're there to do a job. There wasn't that much drama because there wasn't that much emotional immediacy to what they were doing. Charles and Kim aren't going to get into an argument onstage because they're past that. All of that stuff seems to have been buried, all the anger from the past. They're doing their job, and they did a really good job on the tour. By the end of the tour they were saying "goodnights" to each other onstage.

More of a wink, wink, like look, we're all hugging and getting along and we talk to each other, see?

Craft: They sound better than ever because Kim's playing well and she's singing well. She didn't always do herself justice. I'm sure she'd be the first to admit that.

Deal: Me and Charles were talking after the Minnesota show and then we did another show in Winnipeg, and after the Winnipeg show we were like, man it feels like we've been out for a month already. It was so weird at first. Playing bass is weird. Standing on that side of the stage, usually I stand on the right side of the stage for the Breeders. Weird things like that are weird. The green pick and not an orange pick is weird. But then it was like, oh yeah, okay. So we've been doing shows ever since. The End.

The first tour was so successful, Pixies announced another round of dates that included a July 2005 performance at the Lollapalooza festival—the event they declined to play in 1991.

Minneapolis Star Tribune article by Chris Riemenschneider, April 2004: The T-shirts on sale called it the "Pixies Sellout" tour, but the truth is the Boston band that helped give birth to the early-'90s alternative rock boom could have done a lot more to milk its first public gig in 11 years. Tickets originally sold for $30 were going for as much as $400 on eBay. The crowd howled along to obscure oldies such as "Broken Face" and "Levitate Me" as readily as it did to latter staples such as "Here Comes Your Man" and "U-Mass".

Chicago Sun-Times article by Jeff Vrabel, November 2004: One strange after-effect with a band of the Pixies' vast legacy is how their sound holds up; after a decade-plus of bands that have stolen from the Pixies, there's a quaintness to hearing the genuine article, like finally watching *Casablanca* after hearing its most famous lines referenced for years. But one gets the sense that legacy preservation is the last of the Pixies' concerns. There's a refreshing simplicity to their comeback, an almost wistfully nostalgic glimpse of a former age, and it's good to them have back.

Dolan: The reunion was weird because the room was full of people who'd never given a shit about them at the time or even knew who they were—people who'd heard Nirvana and went back and retroactively become these college rock people. The sort of black fingernail/army surplus/Goth element that I remember standing in line with waiting to see them back in 1991 was gone, or they'd become accountants, which was entirely possible. Their performance was more a vindication than an act of rediscovery. Though I expected something more cynical. They made eye contact, which surprised me, and even went for the group bow, which was fumbling and sweet. Kim missed a note or two but Santiago and Lovering were still really agile. One thing about Pixies people don't remember is how tight they were. Lovering was really a spot-on drummer, heavy yet concise and tricky. And they were pros during the reunion, which they could have blown off quality-wise and treated like a *120 Minutes* version of the Four Tops play Atlantic City.

Murphy: Kim and I were married in Ohio, '85, and '89 it came to an end. I had seen David running around the auditorium in Lowell, so I ran up and he said, "How are you doing!?" When they were onstage, probably two-thirds of the way through the show Kim walked up to the mic and said, "I'd like to say hello to Mr. John Murphy," so she knew I was there. And since she was traveling with Kelley, when people were invited backstage Kelley was down there looking for me. I was a little nervous, actually, my wife was with me, and my sister and her husband, so it was like the first people who went to the first show, that was kind of cool. I saw Charles and David first and gave them big hugs, and then Kelley said, "Do you want to go see Kim? She's in the back, she doesn't like to hang around in the meet and greet area,'" so we went back and there she was. I gave her a big hug and everything was great, sort of like picking up where we left off in a kind of cousins way. So it was a lot of big hugs and how you doings, but it was so anti-rock show because a) there's no booze in the back, b) we're talking about each other's parents and kids. It was pretty funny. And then the rest of the Pixies ended up coming in when the meet and greet was over, and that was the first time I got to see Joey. It was really cool to see everybody.

Galkin: Kim looked so great by the end of the tour, it was remarkable. Compared to six months later, she's glowing, she cut her hair off, she looks beautiful. She turned the clock back ten years by the end, as if this was something that was really good for her, physically. She looks great onstage, she's got this great energy about her. She's a cool rock chick. The fact that she smiles through the shows really helps a lot. It's a great thing to watch. To my knowledge, Kim was completely sober the entire tour, and seemed to get healthier and healthier as the tour went on. I witnessed her working out a couple of times, she seemed really good.

Cantor: She has got fans that absolutely worship her. She would sign people's arms and people would fall over themselves to meet her, get to the show early to stand in the section where she playing, particularly female guitarists and bassists, and young, 16, 18-year-olds, just worship her.

Lovering: What was funny, when we put out the word we were getting back together, we thought it would be a legitimate reunion tour, but I don't think any of us realized how big it's been going, how well it's been received. The adulation that we've been getting, it's been unbelievable. And what's amazing is every show, they're all kids in it. They're kids that were nine, eight years old [during our career], that never saw us in the day. In every venue I'll have a beer, I'll walk out front where everyone's coming in, I've never had anyone stop me. Because no one knows who I am, they're all kids. The Pixies only had maybe one picture on an album, plus I shaved my head. All the pictures [from the albums], I had long hair. So I think that's part of it, but still, nobody knows who we are. They know the music, they know all the words and everything. But it's amazing, I'll see maybe two people my age at the whole show. Just the amount of love, it's insane.

Donelly: I love the fact that they're doing this tour and they're back together for this mainly because from a sociological standpoint, I think they're really important and I think that people need to see them, especially young people, because they don't have a hell of a lot right now. And I think that nothing but good will come of this, to see this band that started so much, and never really got the props they deserved on a widespread level. The world cites them, but that never really translated into the historical place they deserve. So I think it's great that they're back together, but I also think that when they broke up it was the right thing.

Banks: After Kurt died I think everybody realized what an incredible influence they'd been, and then all these bands that had been 17, 18, 19 when the Pixies became successful started being successful themselves, and started listing Pixies as an influence. And everyone started talking about them in the same way as the Velvet Underground, a band that never sold that many records, but almost everybody involved in their records formed a band, or joined somebody else who formed a band, you know, so very influential.

Deal: Sometimes people come up and say, "Oh, I started playing bass because of you." It's like, oh, cool. I don't think Velvet Underground charted, you know what I mean. It again, goes back to people finding people by doing their own research because they're so passionate about music.

Thompson: The records are still in print, people like them. It's the snobby rock kids who have developed snobbish tastes in rock music. Kids like me, kids like you, over the years bought those records. And they were too young to see the band when the band was around. "But of course! They're back for a reunion? We'll go out to see them!" There's at least two generations of rock kids coming out to see us because they heard we were good and they like our records. That's what it's all about—or that's what I think, anyway.

For me, that whole repertoire of Pixies records, especially the first three records, it's partially about the songs. It's one-third about the songs, another big chunk of it is about the band and how they play it, and another part of it is where we were at that time. No game plan as far as what the art was supposed to be like. It's kind of got this naivety to it, it's got this charm. The band has some kind of charm. That's what people react to. They like the band, and even our lesser songs, people still like it. They like the band. That's why we could never have a reunion without the original members. That would not go down. It has to be these four people. I realize it now in a reunion situation, I suppose. I had sort of ignored that aspect or put it out of my mind that there was this band sense of humor or band chemistry, and I maybe had focused on negative memories in my mind, of being in the band in the early '90s.

Gilbert: When the Pixies were going to start getting together, there was even talk back then that it would only go on for a few months, but I kind of always suspected that that wasn't going to be the reality because I just knew that the audience demand was probably going to be at a fever pitch, and that if they could get along, that they would be getting a great reception. You know, age and maturity and years away from each other, it goes a long way to easing any of that tension that you have when you're in a band and you're all, like 25. I know that the Pixies are booked until New Years, and I know that Charles is about to become a father [his son, named Jack Errol Thompson, was born to Charles' wife Violet on January 7, 2005], and I know that he's really very excited about this, this is something that he's been looking forward to, so I know he's going to want to take some time off for that.

Angel: I just did a band reunion myself (The Blackjacks). You think they're going to be really traumatic and miserable, but they're simple. On the phone, we're fighting about the set list, naturally, because we have to fight about something. I'm just like, "God, I fucking hate these people. Why am I doing this?" So I'm talking to Steve Jones about it and he laughed and he said, "The same thing happened with the [Sex] Pistols. The moment you get into the room with those guys, everything will fade away. You won't care anymore. You'll just start rockin' and everything will be gone." And he was right. We love each other now. We didn't love each other 20 years ago, but we love each other now.

Geiger: They're definitely much, much bigger now than they were at their peak.

The world caught up to them. They were always that good. I think they're grownups, in general. I think they're happy. They're getting huge positive reinforcement every night.

Mascis: The Breeders seemed bigger than the Pixies, and now the Pixies are way bigger than the Breeders.

Cantor: Kim goes into this hardware store in the Midwest somewhere, and she's talking with the guy, orders the things she needs. The guy handed it over to her, she gave him her credit card and the guy said, "Oh, Kimberly Deal, like the Breeders." She said, "Yeah." He said, "Do you like the Breeders?" And she was looking at him like he was kind of kidding, and he was like, "Well, do you listen to the Breeders?" and she said, "No." He said, "Oh, you really should check them out, they're pretty good." And he kind of walked off and she looked at the camera and she was like, "Is he fucking with me?" She just doesn't look like a rock star, I think that's a big part of it.

Craft: Any major guitar band in the last ten years that's come here has always cited them as one of their major influences and the reason why each year that goes by there's more people that want to see them is because each year that goes by there's more kids who become old enough to be interested in that genre of music, and that's as simple as that. Every kid who's bought any indie guitar band record in the last ten years will know that Pixies are somewhere behind it. And that's it, I think.

Geiger: Clearly Nirvana and Radiohead and Bowie and Bono saying how it's the most important band, that's one [reason for the newfound popularity]. And over time, especially thanks to Nirvana, they accrued a benefit. The timing's good because underground music is coming back now. Four years ago nobody cared, right now it's all good, the Bravery, Louis XIV, the Killers, everything. Let's call it Nirvana 2.0, even though it's much smaller in its own way, it was good timing like Nirvana 1.0 was good timing and Pixies 1.0 was *not* as good timing. It was influential and groundbreaking but it didn't ride the wave, this one kind of rode a wave. The other thing is the songs aged *unbelievably* well and in my arguments with my friends and coworkers, they think that's the big one. I can't tell because I'm too close to it, but I'll tell you that when I went to Minneapolis for the first show I was just stunned that every song sounds like a pop hit, when this is a band that everybody thought was abrasive, screaming, nutty, crazy, whatever. So that may be the big one, and it may just be the credibility was always there. I also think the world wanted something like this at the time, too. The world wanted a Pixies reunion for a while, the world wanted a story that year.

Smith: And you know what, when they broke up I started thinking, "I guess that was just kind of a funny moment, just like a lot of the stuff that I liked in the '90s has now evaporated and nobody knows who Belly is and Throwing Muses don't sell any records, and it's like it never happened, that moment in time before the consolidation of radio when music was actually good and Nirvana made a huge hit, that moment's almost gone right now," and then all of a sudden the Pixies are the biggest fucking thing since sliced bread! They played to like, 12,000 people or more in Northampton! It's insane!

Thompson: I'm not anti-record company, I'm not like, "They're so evil." Whatever. It's just a business. And there are a lot of people out there out to fuck you over, and it's kind of satisfying in this day and age to be on a successful reunion tour and suddenly have people offering us money to record music, and they're not even record companies! They're like, "Oh, we just want some song." They don't even care about what the music is—all they know is you're marketable. That's all they know and that's all they care about. They're so slicker and so much more evil than some old timey record company. They're like, "Yeah, whatever, we don't care who you are, but we heard that you're hot, and give us some of your mojo, because we're trying to sell some shit." We're dealing with people who are even more corporate, and it's satisfying because there's not really any strings attached, or there are very few strings attached. It's not like saying, "We're gonna own your soul now." They're just like, "Give us your thing for a second." And we're like, "Great, sure, here you go." So it's nice to have that kind of feel. When the Pixies first started, there were a couple of Boston bands like the Del Fuegos who did commercials, and it was over for them. They had become so uncool. The poor guy was trying to make ends meet, and someone gave him 50 grand to be in a TV ad, and everyone was like, "Oh, have you heard?" Now everyone does it. I'm into it. Sure, corporate still sucks, it always has, it always will. But I don't give a shit. I don't care if ClearChannel wants to buy everything. Let them buy everything. I don't give a shit.

Deal: So we were rehearsing for these shows. And then Charles was at the airport leaving, so he calls me from the airport: The *Shrek* people just called the manager. They wanted to see if we want to do the song from the title sequence for *Shrek 2*. I go, "Oh, that sounds like fun." You know, Joey has a kid now and stuff. So Charles said, "I'll try and work up something in Portland, you guys try to work up something." And Joe has a Pro Tools studio in his basement, and he lives really close by, and me and him were getting Starbucks together. So I would just pick up the Starbucks and go to his house, to his basement. And he got the videotape of the title sequence that they wanted us to do. And Joe had done soundtracks, so he had a whole system. So I was playing Joe a couple things, licks, that I had. And there was one that we worked up, and when Charles had come down for something he listened to that. He had something, it was cute, I liked his, too. But David and Joe and Charles were all there and they thought mine was a poppier, more kid-friendly thing so we kinda worked it up a little bit in Joe's Pro Tools thing. And then the *Shrek 2* people gave us some money to go into a demo place to demo it. So we did. And that demo is what's coming out [the iTunes-only single "Bam Thwok"]. And they didn't take it.

In the late '90s in New York City I had found this discarded book on the floor, and I'm always looking for paper. There was a lot of it that was not written on. It was almost like a black book, like a graph person's book but it was from a child. That's how it first began. I was using it to write—Kelley was sitting at the apartment and they told me they wanted to use that piece of music and I thought, "Oh, crap, now I have to write lyrics—oh, well here's some paper," and I kind of looked through some rows and found some of these old words sitting there that I thought were kind of funny and *Bam Thwok* was one of them. It was a story about a party with the monsters or something. On other pages there are some old drawings of a ladybug and stuff like that. But that's how it started. And then I just wanted to keep it kind of clean, not too condescendingly stupid and clean. But they didn't want it.

Lovering: That was our first studio effort in a while, it was good. And again, I was in the same boat, hearing a song that I had just heard the day before, and it gets frustrating for me, because I like things to be right, and it just grinds on me when I'm put under—I mean that's just the way it is, I just have to adapt to it, and I have. But it would just be convenient for me if I really knew the song, it makes me feel better that I know what I'm gonna play and I know I'll put down what is my best. Not that it wasn't good, but. . .it's very unlike us. I mean, it's a Pixies song but it's still unlike a Pixies song.

Geiger: On the second leg of the U.S. tour Charles pulled me aside, it was kind of cute. Everybody was taking it easy, "Let's see what happens, see how it works." Obviously the success was more than even bullish people thought, myself included—it was overwhelming. So, we're all hopeful, but Charles kind of pulled me into the dressing room one day, nobody else was there, and he goes, "Look, I don't really want to tell anybody, but we are back together." And I go, "Yeah, and?" And he goes, "No, really back together." And I go, "Yeah, no shit." And he said, "Well, you know," he was all sheepish, "I just wanted you to know." I was like, great, it's fucking rocking. And we're booking a summer (2005) tour for them. And there's a lot of good stuff and we'll see what happens with making a record. And I'm thrilled they're playing again because I want them to take their time before they make more music. Do things seem different? Yeah, they were happy and sober. Everybody was sober including Kim, which is the big differentiator, and they're happy because, again, things happened fast. Well, now you're away from it, people are either not successful, or in ill health, or financially not successful, or solo career is struggling, and then comes overwhelming success and you're 40 and you have your loved ones and your family's set. You're not being rushed and you have perspective on, oh my God, I missed it all as a kid because of all this shit, I'm going to enjoy it and revel in it this time. So the answer is fuck yes.

Feldman: It's a great idea in terms of the fact that none of them are ever going to have to work again. It's like seeing them play exactly as they were 12 years ago. The audience doesn't seem interested in anything they have been doing separately for the last 12 years. When I said to Charles, "Are you going to make a new record?" his initial thing was, "Everyone wants to hear the old songs, why should we record, they don't want to hear anything new." I think if they continue to do it he would reconsider. It's a story that is still being written and he's just very prolific. Everything that he has done since the Pixies has kind of shown that he has been able to grow up, there is so much growth and intelligence. That's the part that bothers me the most about the reunion. There have been so many things that people have been so dismissive about that he has done since they broke up the first time.

Deal: Oh it's so good, it's so nice. So much good will comin' out.

Thompson: I forgot how much I like this band, how much I like being in this band.[19]

In the end, 185,000 people came out to see the Pixies' reunion in 2004. The 50-plus date tour grossed $6.5 million.[20]

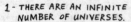

1 – THERE ARE AN INFINITE NUMBER OF UNIVERSES.

2 – PARALLEL, YES, BUT NOT IN THE WAY WE USUALLY THINK.

3 – IN FACT, EACH OF US LIVES IN OUR OWN UNIVERSE...

4 – OUR OWN VERSION OF REALITY, WHICH VANISHES WHEN WE DIE.

AAAK...

5 – THESE REALITIES OVERLAP, OF COURSE. WE ALL AGREE THAT THE SKY IS BLUE, FOR EXAMPLE.

CHAIR

CAT

6 – OCCASIONALLY SOMEONE CAN EXIST IN MORE WORLDS THAN JUST THEIR OWN. THIS IS RARE.

ENCORE

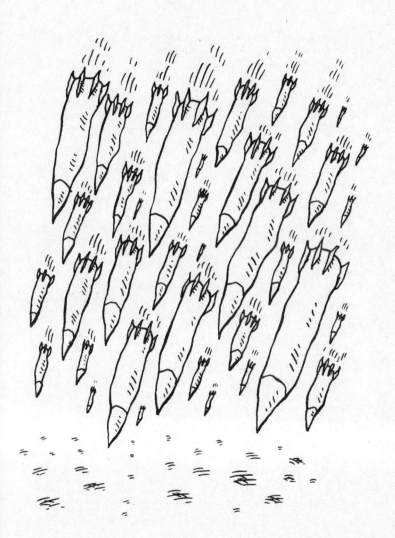

17. PLANET OF SOUND—PIXIES' LASTING IMPACT (2005+)

It's not often bands as groundbreaking as Pixies get a second act, but perhaps such a bizarre twist of fate isn't out of the question for a band whose seemingly last album was called *Fool the World*. It's also not common for bands to become as influential as Pixies. Everyone from Courtney Love to PJ Harvey, from Kurt Cobain to Rivers Cuomo, from David Bowie to Bono has found a way to profess their admiration for the group. Pixies' sound is not easily imitated, but elements of the band's formula—the screamed vocals, the abstract lyrics, the quiet/loud punch, the surf guitar lines, the delicately plunking basslines, the crushing snare drums—have found their way into the work of too many artists to catalog.

It's hard to resist explaining Pixies without the rubric of time. The band's unusual, forward (and backward) looking melodies and sounds were often described as out of step with their time. Examining their significance today, it's easy to call Pixies the quintessential artist of our time: Their efforts were largely responsible for pulling the underground up to meet the mainstream, but on their own terms. But Pixies were not an MTV band, they predated Internet bands, and they certainly weren't a radio band, either. Before their reunion, Pixies also seemed to have existed as a stitch in time—a fabulously exciting, invigorating, raucous act who passed in and out of our lives in one elegant motion. And now Pixies have extended their own timeline past our expectations, from 2005 to beyond.

Lovering: I think the whole run of the Pixies we were always critically acclaimed, and when you're that, that means there's no success. Everybody will love you—and that's the way it was always, from day one. Everybody loved us, except the buying public. So that's the way in our heads, we were. Sure I was really a little jealous that other bands had made it off of things that we did, but no, that was the way it was, that's the way it was for the Pixies.

Banks: This is a band that became big very, very quickly, it's not like they had a long history of playing in clubs behind them. They formed, they did some tapes, I mean it was like they stepped onto a moving walkway and it never stopped. Their career was always moving forwards all the time, relentlessly. They were a natural phenomenon, they were like a volcano exploding or an earthquake, it was something that really was a genuine phenomenon. I'd never seen anything like it in my entire career. It was as close to being with the Beatles that you could get in that period of time. I suppose the rise of Nirvana was similar.

Mico: I know the Pixies were pretty much every other band's favorite band for a long while. Everybody from Robert Smith to Nirvana just loved the Pixies. The ripple effect that that band had was so much more significant than the band, itself. Nirvana would never have existed without the Pixies, I do think that's the truth.

Suptic: They're one of those bands, kind of like the original college rock or indie rock band, pretty much all music in the '90s was influenced by them whether they know it or not. They took pop music and destroyed it with craziness and noise, but it still had a hook.

One of the hardest things I've ever had to play on guitar was the ending to "Alec Eiffel" [for the 1999 covers record *Where Is My Mind?: A Tribute to the Pixies*]. It's like, insane, it's this weird, strange pattern. The song's in four/four but the guitar's doing something totally different. The boy can play. I think sometimes when you don't know exactly what you're doing on an instrument, like when you're young, you do things that aren't usually expected. They seemed like a bunch of kids making music when they started, just tried weird things which turned out really good music.

Perry Farrell (Jane's Addiction singer): The Pixies were very underground, sophisticated in the funkiest, punk rock way, if you know what I mean. The music intelligentsia understood the Pixies, but maybe some other people did not, and they were not able to reach the mainstream consciously, but got in the subconscious universal mind. They were able to flaunt their disregard for the money, to have a great time with life and music and bring great music to us that if they weren't on the earth, the earth wouldn't be as great as it was.

Liz Phair (musician): I love the Pixies. I used to paint and draw to them, they were my CDs of choice to listen to when I was working. I think it's rare that you get a male and female who play off each other—you know that classic Keith and Mick thing, you need two people with tension to be the two leaders and that's what makes a great band, the Lennon/McCartney thing. But it's rare when it's a male and a female, and I feel like Pixies are a perfect example of a band that had a tension inherent in it because they had two drivers, and yet that was what made it beautiful. I could feel the two points of pull, I could feel the two hooks going at once, and I always felt their pop was stronger than a lot of pop of that time because they had a really unique band structure. I almost felt like instrumentally, they'd be one-upping each other, there was a competition within the band to some extent. If you think about the Pixies' songs, they were always aggressive, but totally pop. And how do you combine that? That was kind of the style of the time, but theirs seemed less "We are now going to be aggressive pop" and more "This is how it came out." And I really liked that. I liked how organic it felt, that sound.

They had a polyrhythmic vocal style. It's really hot that way. They're a band where even though it's not all about rhythms in terms of what we traditionally think of as percussion, it's all very rhythmic—how they say what they say, when they say it, when the instruments do that. I always think of the Pixies as reaching out and thunking you on the head all the time. "Monkey Gone to Heaven," that's a great song! It ramps up in intensity, he starts getting even more intense about it and ahhhh! "Then God is seven!" I love it. They're very theatrical. I've always admired people who are really good performers and they're clearly working the medium of performance. Within the song, each time they say the word it's not just gonna be the word, it has a spin on it, there's emotion. They're not going to just talk about emotion in the lyrics they're going to demonstrate the emotion in the performance.

I saw them so many times. At least five or six. They were a huge draw for me in Chicago, in Cleveland when I was at Oberlin, in New York. It was one of those things where I knew all the songs, so I'd troll around feeling superior.

Banks: Every generation has its innovators and imitators. For every Elvis there was a dozen Dions and Fabians, kind of homogenized, fit for human version of the real, raw meat thing. The Pixies had so many imitators, inspired so many people, but they were the real deal and you could see it immediately. And the great innovators—you don't really understand them, you only feel them. The reason that it's so interesting is you don't really understand what it's about. You can try to analyze it forever but you'll go crazy with it because it's about a feeling. It's much easier to analyze Radiohead or all the other stuff, like Thom Yorke saying I went to see the Pixies and it made me want to be in a band, and that all makes a lot more sense and you can see where it derives from. But the Pixies stuff was so incredibly original in so many ways that it was of the man, you know. He was a genius really, that's the only word to describe him. I still feel that way about him. Those songs will live forever. He's gone on to do other things now and I still love all his work. But it was a moment in time. The Pixies were like a natural phenomenon, they were like a volcano exploding and it was going to last for so long and then it was going to subside. Nothing with that level of intensity could keep going that way. That's what the Who were like. At the end they had to come off the road and it killed one of them, but they were that intense.

Walsh: It had staying power maybe more than what I realized at the time. Maybe more than what they realized at the time. They were hoping something good would happen but I don't think they had that, "Yes, this will be remembered for years to come," at all.

Hurley: They were one of those bands that were way more influential than their record sales ever dictated. Same with a band like Sonic Youth who is in that same position, who influenced a lot of bands but a lot of bands who they influenced went on to sell a lot more records than they did.

Kolderie: It's so strange how things like Culture Club that were recording at the same time sounds so dated now but those first few Pixies albums are still completely fresh.

Angel: They're good songs. They're timeless. Little Richard songs are timeless 50 years after the fact. Mozart is timeless. Good shit is timeless. I think they move people of a certain age. They're a palatable version of the Violent Femmes. A kid will always identify with "Blister in the Sun" and will always identify with something like "Wave of Mutilation" or "Debaser." Fuck, man, I saw *Un Chien Andalou* when I was like, 19, watching that razorblade go through the eyeballs, it was one of the most repelling things I'd seen in my life. When he's singing this happy song about it, I'm like, "Oh, I get it." You get it. The Pixies are going to appeal to you during your first year of college. You'll crack up when you hear "U-Mass." It's the same reason that the Doors will always appeal to a 16-year-old. They get it.

Thompson: A couple of people have said to me, "Your records or your songs are kind of timeless, they fit in to whatever calendar year." That's nice. I don't know what to say about it.

Geiger: I think the Pixies were a band who were way ahead of their time, and they made timeless music that was not appreciated. But I have to tell you that I think just about every fine artist and classical composer in the world suffered from the very same thing. So I'm not sure it's any different than a lot of people. I think they were misunderstood, and they were way ahead of their time musically and critically in a marketplace in the late '80s where 4AD was not a label that was a commercial force, but they were an artistic force. When Elektra picked them up in this country, it was largely about show. But you never know what would have happened if they had pimped them and they had gone on MTV.

Iha: It was just on the cusp of all those bands that were about to happen. They really seemed to be ground zero for that whole alternative movement in the '90s. It was right in a revolutionary sense, but wrong commercially. I think Nirvana was more commercial, if you could call it commercial, but I don't know, I guess they have the same sensibilities, just like demented pop. Obviously so committed, lyric-wise, and the sound of it is like, you hear it and it doesn't sound like anything else you've heard, but there's pop, and the lyrics are. . .well, I don't know what his lyrics are about. They're all sex and death and some of it sung in Spanish. I don't know what any of it means, but it sounds important.

When we first started the Pumpkins were kind of alternative, we were a little bit heavy, a little bit gothic, a little bit psychedelic, but I think bands like the Pixies and Jane's Addiction and Dinosaur Jr. were leading the way to heaviness, and I'd say they were definitely an influence with their attitude and fearless sound. They closed the chapter on everything in the '80s and totally made this brave new sound, to be pretentious about it. Of course nobody knew at that time—"Oh my God, this is the beginning of a movement!" Like Jane's Addiction took heavy metal and just got rid of all the bullshit and made it cool, heavy riffs, the Pixies took the cool parts of old punk rock and pop music and the heavy sound that heavy metal has, and they melded it. That's what it sounded like they did.

Perkins: I can say it for the Pixies as well as us, we were the manure, we were the dirt and soil that the flowers of Nirvana and the Pumpkins and Pearl Jam grew out of. When you look at the beautiful flower, you don't look at the dirt underneath it. But you need good dirt. Without good soil, you're not going to have a good crop. So I think the soil was the work that we did on the West Coast, the work they did on the East Coast, and all these other bands, God bless them, got the benefits from it. So did we, I had a great career and a great life, but neither Pixies nor Jane's sold eight million records. But most of the bands after us, Alice in Chains, I can name 15 bands that are alternative, supposedly, Rage Against the Machine, millions and millions and millions of records. So I'm proud of it. I'm proud to be the manure of modern music. Everybody had a category and understood how to market it, by that point. When we came out it was art, it wasn't a product. So that time, when things flipped over, the scene changed for the better, I guess for a while. Everything keeps morphing. Who knows what it is now. But there was a time when alternative and hard rock and mosh pitting and all that shit was the norm. And I gotta say to the Minutemen and Fear and X, they did it for us. They didn't get half the shit we got. We sold a million, but X sold 100,000. And the Pumpkins sold 15 million.

It's not all record sales, but you can see how things rub off each other and move forward and the Pixies were one of those bands that set the standard for sound, and integrity with the artwork, and the songwriting. And then you break up and other people take that and go to the bank.

Banks: The Pixies created the environment that enabled bands like Nirvana to bloom. And to be fair to Europe and the European press, the Pixies weren't that hot in America. It took a long time for them to get off the ground in America, and it wasn't really until the tide changed in America, and the tide did change, that people reexamined it and that kind of music became more acceptable. America had to change. It wasn't like the Pixies changed America, America did change, and they suddenly realized what they had in their own backyard.

Watts-Russell: I don't really buy into that very much because, well Kurt Cobain was very good at giving credit, but Charles very early on would give credit to Iggy. I just see it as a line one after the other. Maybe it is true, Kurt was truly inspired and given confidence by hearing the Pixies' music. Their success seemed to change the map of music in America overnight, the whole Seattle thing skyrocketed, first for Nirvana then every fucking record label was shooting up to Seattle to sign anything that moved. So MTV and everything changed to that, it changed the face of music for a while, but I just think it's kind of coincidence in a lot of ways.

Geiger: I think the Pixies was the same thing, the substance was there, it was the timing. I think Nirvana's substance was there, but they hit the right timing, that's my view of it.

Kolderie: Kurt Cobain was basically on a mission to reward everyone who ever worked with the Pixies. We did Hole, we did *Live Through This*. When he was still alive, and he was very instrumental 'cause Courtney went to Butch Vig and was like, "You produced *Nevermind*, I want you to produce my album and make it big, make me big like Kurt." And Butch couldn't handle it. He said, "I couldn't do it." So Courtney was like, "Well if not you, then who?" and Butch said, "Well how about these guys?" and Kurt said, "Oh yeah, they worked with the Pixies. I like them."

Kurt was very influenced by the Pixies, Courtney not so much. She was more of a garage rocker. Even Kurt once asked me, "Hey man, what was it like working with the Pixies, wow, tell me about it?" and this is in '93, the guy's the biggest rock star in the world.

Love: There's a song called "U-Mass" that I stole completely—you know, "I went to school in Olympia" [from the song "Rock Star"]? "U-Mass," totally ripped note for note.

St. Thomas: The second time I met Kurt, we talked about the Pixies. It wasn't just Kurt, it was Krist [Novoselic] and Dave, because they were in Boston, and they were like, "Whoa, you know the Pixies?" I didn't know at the time that they were so influenced by them. They were blown away. Later, when I interviewed Kurt, he basically said, "We ripped off the Pixies, and 'Smells Like Teen Spirit' is a total Pixies ripoff, and we completely copied the whole heavy to light dynamic from them." It's weird, because "Smells Like Teen Spirit" to me doesn't sound like a Pixies song, but there's a lot of other songs on *Nevermind* that have those heavy basslines and those dynamics.

Harvard: I was far more pissed maybe seven or eight months after they broke up because I watched what happened with Nirvana in Seattle and I had only met Kurt once and I said something about Fort Apache and we had done this and that, and he said, "Pixies? You did the Pixies record?" and he was like, "You know what man, we're just a Pixies cover band," and I was like, "Get the fuck out of here," he was half-fucking around and he's copped to the fact that "Smells Like Teen Spirit" is basically his Pixies rip, but I still feel conscious that of the bands that made it out of Boston, if you look at what happened with Seattle, no knock on the Seattle scene, but Boston had it all over. Besides New York City circa '76, London circa '77, there's never been a fucking better scene in terms of quality of bands, actual sceneliness, camaraderie, fucking cohesiveness and the quality of writing and performing. I'm from Boston and I'm a hardcore Bostonian. Nirvana was a fantastic band and unique in their own way, but in terms of what they were doing, the crowd they were going after, the mechanisms, the devices, the explosive chords, the dynamics, there is a great similarity. And I think it could—what Nirvana was and what Nirvana did, taking nothing away from Nirvana, the Pixies could have owned a much bigger chunk of that real estate, had they stuck together. So I have always lamented that the Pixies crapped out when they did.

Norton: Definitely, I remember the first time I heard *Nevermind*. I just laughed. It was great, I loved it, but I definitely heard the way hi-hats were getting used and guitars pulled out, basslines, it was definitely a lot of stuff that we'd done. I didn't really think about it at the time, I didn't know it was going to be massive. I enjoyed it. I really loved his voice. That was the big difference in a way.

St. Thomas: I remember before *Nevermind* came out [Nirvana and I] went to dinner and I was telling them that I'd seen the Pixies a whole bunch of times and they were way into that. Kurt openly admitted that was the whole reason they did *In Utero* with Steve Albini. He was really good about plugging tons of bands. They would always talk about the Pixies, there are so many quotes of them talking about the Pixies. I mean, the Pixies kind of have this formula, and in many ways the Pixies really invented before anybody else, this formula of like, you break it down to the bass and the drums on the verse, and then when the chorus comes in, the guitars come in really loud with the fuzz and the drums get louder. And like, you scream, and then you go back to the verse and it breaks back down to bass and drums. On every song, Nirvana does basically that thing. Kurt would talk about how they have a song, "Verse Chorus Verse," that's basically what he's doing, making fun of the formula. But he said, "Yeah, I stole the formula from the Pixies." It's more of the essence and not the chords.

Banks: I mean I remember being in the Embassy Hotel in London, and Kurt Cobain was sitting in the lobby and I went over to him and said, "Are you all right?" and he said, "Yeah, I'm just waiting to see Ken," because he wanted Ken to manage the band.

Lubin: The Pixies couldn't have been Nirvana and Nirvana couldn't have been the Pixies. I think Elektra was exceedingly proud to have been the sponsors of the Pixies and we did it for precisely the right reason, which was they represented something nobody could comprehend until it had fully realized itself possibly in the person of Nirvana, but that's what we prided ourselves on, being on the cutting edge of talent and popular art. We were right and it turned out well, and okay, it was only one-fiftieth as profitable as Nirvana, but it was just as meaningful. So all's well that ends well. Or not.

Banks: I think that people saw them as this anarchic force, as real anarchists, crazed rock and rollers, when in actual fact they were incredibly disciplined professionals. The joke about the Pixies that nobody saw, everybody thought all this craziness with Charles screaming and all of that was anarchic. And it wasn't. It was thought-out, it was rehearsed, it was by design. They used to go on stage on time every night, they used to be in tune, the lighting was correct, everything was done just so.

EPILOGUE: WHERE THEY ARE NOW

Watts-Russell: Now my project is my life, just finding ways to be, to enjoy each day. I was never ambitious and I don't have any career ambitions. If you told me when I was a kid at 23, 24 who just loved music that I would have the experience that I did at 4AD and reach and touch as many people as I did, I would have thought it was impossible. It terms of achievements, I've achieved all that I could have ever dreamed. I live a very quiet life in the desert in New Mexico with my wife and my six dogs and that's really what makes me happy.

You can tell I don't like the music business. The Pixies were the first artist we signed longterm, and the reason I did that was because of what I said about Sire and Throwing Muses, how badly they worked with them—atrociously in Europe and pretty bad in the States. We sold more copies of their first album, *House Tornado* on import to America than they sold over here. I was stunned to see how atrocious this mega, mega corporation was at dealing with a band like the Muses and I was so proud that we, with our little indie network around the world, had handled the Pixies' *Come on Pilgrim* and *Surfer Rosa*. It was Throwing Muses' failure at Sire that gave me the confidence at 4AD, that made me feel I had the right to say to somebody, "Sign a five-album deal with us, you'll get X advances." In other words, a commitment to each other. I had learned about longterm contracts in the early days by Mark Martin, my partner, and I thought they were dishonest and corrupt so I hadn't done them. I felt like, fuck, we can do this for the right reasons! But funny enough, in taking those steps to commit to each other, you got to do the best for them, and as things started to change in the indie industry, college radio was enormous, everybody was considering how high into the top ten on the proper charts our albums were gonna go—that just hadn't been there before. So irony of ironies, in making that commitment you got to try and play the game, release singles off of albums.

Larbalestier: I just want to get back to Cambodia. As a photographer, you're telling ten or 15 different stories at one time, snapping shots for each story here and there, it's not linear. Power, simplicity, and longevity is what I am interested in. Things that have a lasting impact. I'm hunting for things that will last as a photographer. It takes a long time for a picture to develop a sense of power. You have to become involved in your environment to get that power, that truth. Forty percent of the Cambodia population is under 14 years old, my son is 14. I'll stay there for a long time, there is so much to do.

Appleby: I'm still working with Captain Star and putting out books, and working out of my studio. Star is still waiting for his orders that will never come.

Murphy: I'm living in the suburbs in Massachusetts. I've been married for 13 years to my wife, Linda, and have two kids, a 12-year old girl and a ten-year-old boy. I'm driving an SUV and a minivan—how mundane—and listening to Kings of Leon, Liz Phair, and Gorillaz. But Pixies are still my favorite band. Mente plays an annual Christmas show and this year we've been invited to New Orleans to play a charity show in September. After a ten-year hiatus, I'm now keeping in touch with Kim, Kelley, and David. We all remain close friends and plan to see each other whenever they are in Boston.

Widmer: I became a respectable person to everyone's amazement. But each phase was just as unexpected as the next. At age 25 I never thought I'd be in a rock band, and then for seven or eight years I'm playing every night. And then I'm not playing at all and I'm writing speeches for the President of the United States [Bill Clinton]. There were a lot of articles calling attention to me and to how shocking it was that the White House had hired me. That was embarrassing for everyone to get through, especially me. I don't think Clinton cared. He is a cool guy.

Mente never actually broke up. We just stopped playing together for about seven years. So in 2001 or 2002 I put the call out to see if everyone wanted to do a Christmas show and everyone was like, yeah. It was great. So we do that every few Christmases.

Now I'm middle-aged, kind of boring but respectable. I teach at a tiny college on the eastern shore of Maryland, which I like but I miss all my friends in Boston. I have a lot of freedom at my little college to be myself all day long. I'm still trying to figure out how to combine that fun of rocking with Mente with my political history writing. I'd like to figure it out and do that for the next 20 years.

Haigler: I've mostly been producing, still working with alternative bands. Now I work with Fuel, Brand New, Oleander. I live in Charlotte, North Carolina. The industry has changed for the worst! It all started with all the corporate takeovers. The merging of labels. With that came the corporate mentality of the bottom line is making money, it's not about artist development anymore. It's about do you have a hit single for me today? And if you do, then maybe we will sign you, but if your record doesn't do well you will be dropped. And that's pretty much the way things are now. The corporate takeovers have been the demise of development. Even the bands back in the day that maybe were not the best musicians, they still played together as a band, they still had a vibe, had a sound, had a direction. So many of the young bands out there today have grown up with [computer recording program] Pro Tools, they don't know what it is to be an accomplished musician, they simply rely on the technology to make them sound good. Nobody sits around in their bedroom and rehearses their guitar parts anymore, they just count on the computer to make it work. Growing up with this technology, the new crop is not being pushed to be better musicians and better at their craft. Back in the day you had to be good, you had to be able to perform it, you couldn't count on protocols to fix the pitch, correct the timing. Not everyone sucks, there are still bands that can sing and play really well, just not as many.

Iha: I've been a member of A Perfect Circle since their second record, *Thirteenth Step*. I also run a label called Scratchie records with Adam Schlesinger of Fountains of Wayne. Three of our current bands are the Sounds, Robbers on High Street, and the Sights. I also co-own a recording studio in New York City called Stratosphere Sound with Schlesinger and Andy Chase of Ivy, and I scored an independent Canadian movie called *Luck* starring Sarah Polley, and an independent Japanese movie *Linda Linda Linda*. Recently, I collaborated with Cat Power and Michael Stipe for two tracks on an upcoming Serge Gainsbourg tribute record.

Lubin: I took shelter from the music industry in 1998 by helping to found and develop an encryption software technology company called Digital Media On Demand, Inc. Five years later I returned to the fold as a manager, music publisher, and record producer. One recent production entered the *Billboard* Internet sales chart at number one, and I continue to consult to various artists and record labels.

Mico: I still work in what's left of the music business. At present, I'm carbon-dating artist index fingers, whistling in D minor, and occasionally yodeling in all the colors of Jesus.

Gilbert: I have moved to Nashville and am liking it there. I'm playing with a bunch of different artists and have been playing around town a lot. I'm currently on tour with Caitlin Cary and Thad Cockrell and I'm also working on my first official solo CD. I've put the Blackstone Valley Sinners on the back burner for now, but will probably be doing more recording and shows in the near future.

Hersh: Every year or so we tell the fans on our website what city we're going to play in and they all kind of show up. So for a weekend, we call it Gut Pageant, people fly in from all over the world to go to these Gut Pageants, and we play and do Throwing Muses karaoke, and we spend a weekend with them doing interviews and

I do acoustic sets and Tanya comes back to play with us. I have a new band called 50 Foot Wave which has taken some of the pressure off Throwing Muses to be a working band. 50 Foot Wave played 150 dates this year, so I don't have a lot of time to think about the Muses.

Kolderie: I took over the studio a couple of years ago. Gary had run it as an office and kinda didn't have a studio here. When he moved up to Bellows Falls, Vermont, it kind of opened up this opportunity here. We recently recorded Toots and Bonnie Raitt. Basically, because the world has changed so much, we are back to doing what we were doing about the time we did the Pixies. People are not handing out major label budgets anymore. We are back to being very proactive, anything that's good and coming out of Boston I try to get my hands on. One wonders if the glory days of alternative rock are behind us. There aren't breakout hits like there were. You have these kind of arcs in your career and from '92 to '97 Sean and I had a gold or platinum record every year, and in some cases two or three. So that enables me to continue as I am. In 1997, with the Bosstones, we had the number one video on MTV, number one modern rock record. So we reached a peak, and the last few years we have taken it easy. Slade had some kids and now we're kind of making our comeback, I guess. This is always the most fun, when you're sort of clawing your way back up the hill. June 21, 1997, we had the number one modern rock song, and I remember thinking, "Wow, there's nowhere to go now but down." Sean and I have been friends for 25 years, we always will be.

Slade: I was 28 when this all started. The early 20s was the rock band. I had enough brains to do it but still had the youthful energy. Paul says it well, he says we were out there playing for a while and then we went into coaching.

Smith: I moved and I never looked back. The recording studio Fort Apache now has taken up residence temporarily in the lobby of an old hotel, the rest of which is abandoned, it's in this town Bellows Falls, Vermont. And the hotel was called the Hotel Windham, and it closed after a five or six year stint as a crazy gay hotel in the '80s, and it wasn't really open for anything. The space was vacant and we moved in and opened a little nightclub and recording studio. It's nice and it's got white linen table clothes, and it's like the Rainbow Room, it's a beautiful, old hotel lobby, and we put a bar in there, and it's cool. It's tiny, it holds 50 people. And the studio's right there, and the goal is to have people make live records in front of real people, because I think that's what the music business needs. Everyone's gone so far up their own ass they don't even know what music is anymore.

Banks: I'm medically retired now. I cannot work. I carried on working for a bit, I was managing Teenage Fanclub. I had an insurance that I'd been paying called Permanent Health Insurance which is basically an income replacement thing, if you fall ill and it stops you from working, it carries on carrying your salary for a period of time. In the end it paid. So that pays me until I'm 60. We're just onlookers now.

Harvard: At that time my fundamental role was as owner of Fort Apache and producer, whatever. Now I'm an author and I'm still a producer. Jack of all trades, master of fucking. . .

Feldman: I would assume that at some point Charles and I would do something together again some time, whether it has to do with the Pixies I have no idea. I mean, they got together this time and the phone didn't ring. It would have been interesting to do something. Now I'm working with my own group now called Knife and Fork. We put out a record late last year, and we did some support for PJ Harvey and recently played three shows with the Pixies in Berkeley.

Thomas: I'm hoping to make it out to the end of my life without having to retool or retrain, because it's a bit late for that. I've got a good chance of it. I think I've got a good ten more years. I probably can slip through the rest of it. We are running up against *Star Trek* time now: Five P.M., every day, it's one of my vices, so I'm gonna have to go.

As of the summer of 2002:

David Lovering was performing at the Magic Castle in Los Angeles and opening with his scientific phenomenalist act for Frank Black and the Catholics.

Kim Deal was performing with the revamped Breeders composed of members of Fear and her sister Kelley.

Joey Santiago was recording music for TV shows and movie soundtracks, occasionally sitting in on a Frank Black recording.

Charles Thompson was still recording albums with the Catholics and touring in a van around the country.

As of 2004 they are officially Pixies once again.

FALLING...

THINKING...

HOPING...

SELECTED DISCOGRAPHY

Pixies (songs taken from *The Purple Tape*)
Recorded 1987, (Cooking Vinyl [U.K.]/SpinART [U.S.], 2002)
Broken Face, Build High, Rock A My Soul, Down To The Well,
Break My Body, I'm Amazed, Here Comes Your Man,
Subbacultcha, In Heaven
Produced by Gary Smith. Engineered with Paul Kolderie.
Original cassette design by Gary Smith/2002 design by
Andrew Swainson at Cactus.

Come on Pilgrim (EP)
(4AD, 1987)
Caribou, Vamos, Isla de Encanta, Ed Is Dead, The Holiday Song,
Nimrod's Son, I've Been Tired, Levitate Me
Produced by Gary Smith. Engineered by Paul Kolderie.
Sleeve by Vaughan Oliver/v23 and Simon Larbalestier.

Surfer Rosa (LP)
(4AD, 1988)
Bone Machine, Break My Body, Something Against You, Broken
Face, Gigantic, River Euphrates, Where Is My Mind?, Cactus,
Tony's Theme, Oh My Golly!, Vamos, I'm Amazed, Brick Is Red
Engineered by Steve Albini. Sleeve by Vaughan Oliver/v23
Envelope and Simon Larbalestier.

Gigantic/River Euphrates
(4AD, 1988)
Gigantic, River Euphrates, Vamos, In Heaven (Lady In The Radiator Song)
Produced by Gil Norton. "In Heaven (Lady In The Radiator Song)" by P. Ivers and D. Lynch/Paul Music.

Monkey Gone To Heaven
(4AD/Elektra, 1989)
Monkey Gone To Heaven, Manta Ray, Weird At My School, Dancing The Manta Ray

Doolittle (LP)
(4AD/Elektra, 1989)
Debaser, Tame, Wave Of Mutilation, I Bleed, Here Comes Your Man, Dead, Monkey Gone To Heaven, Mr. Grieves, Crackity Jones, La La Love You, No. 13 Baby, There Goes My Gun, Hey Silver, Gouge Away
Produced and engineered by Gil Norton. Assistant engineers Dave Snider and Matt Lane. Mixing engineer Steve Haigler. Additional musicians on "Monkey Gone To Heaven" Karen Karlsrud, Corine Metter, Arthur Fiacco, and Ann Rorich. Sleeve by Vaughan Oliver/v23 and Simon Larbalestier.

Here Comes Your Man
(4AD/Elektra, 1989)
Here Comes Your Man, Into The White, Wave Of Mutilation (UK Surf), Bailey's Walk

Velouria
(4AD/Elektra, 1990)
Velouria, I've Been Waiting For You, Make Believe, The Thing
Produced by Gil Norton. "I've Been Waiting For You" by Neil Young/ Warner Chappell Music Ltd.

Bossanova (LP)
(4AD/Elektra, 1990)
Cecilia Ann, Rock Music, Velouria, Allison, Is She Weird, Ana, All Over The World, Dig For Fire, Down To The Well, The Happening, Blown Away, Hang Wire, Stormy Weather, Havalina

Produced by Gil Norton. Sleeve by Vaughan Oliver/v23,
Simon Larbalestier, Kevin Westenberg, Chris Bigg, Pirate
Design, and Anne Garrigues. Engineer Alistair Clay.
Mixing engineer Steve Haigler. Additional musician
Robert F. Brunner.

Dig For Fire
(4AD/Elektra, 1990)
Dig For Fire, Winterlong, Velvety Instrumental Version, Santo

Planet Of Sound
(4AD/Elektra, 1991)
Planet Of Sound, Theme From *Narc*, Build High, Evil Hearted
You
"Evil Hearted You" by G. Gouldman.

Trompe Le Monde (LP)
(4AD/Elektra, 1991)
Trompe Le Monde, Planet Of Sound, Alec Eiffel, The Sad Punk,
Head On, U-Mass, Palace Of The Brine, Letter To Memphis,
Bird Dream Of The Olympus Mons, Space (I Believe In),
Subbacultcha, Distance Equals Rate Times Time, Lovely Day,
Motorway To Roswell, The Navajo Know
Produced by Gil Norton. Engineered by Steve Haigler. Assistant
engineers Andrew Ballard, Scott Blockland, John McDonnell,
Ken Gardner, and Philippe Tousche. Sleeve by Vaughan
Oliver/v23, Chris Bigg, Paul McMenamin, Simon Larbalestier,
Steve Appleby, and TPP LTD, London. Additional musicians
Eric Drew Feldman and Jef Feldman.
"Head On" by William Reid and Jim Reid (The Jesus And
Mary Chain).

Death To The Pixies, 1987–1991 (Compilation LP)
(4AD/Elektra, 1997)
Disc One: Cecilia Ann, Planet Of Sound, Tame, Here Comes
Your Man, Debaser, Wave Of Mutilation, Dig For Fire,
Caribou, Holiday Song, Nimrod's Son, U-Mass, Bone Machine,
Gigantic, Where Is My Mind?, Velouria, Gouge Away,
Monkey Gone To Heaven
Disc Two (Live): Debaser, Rock Music, Broken Face, Isla de

Encanta, Hangwire, Dead, Into The White, Monkey Gone To
Heaven, Gouge Away, Here Comes Your Man, Allison, Hey,
Gigantic, Crackity Jones, Something Against You, Tame,
Wave Of Mutilation, Where Is My Mind?, Ed Is Dead, Vamos,
Tony's Theme
Compiled by Chris Staley. Mastered by Don Tyler at Precision.
Sleeve by Vaughan Oliver/v23, Nicola Schwartz, and Kevin
Westenberg. "Cecilia Ann" by the Surftones.

Pixies at the BBC
(4AD/Elektra, 1998)
Wild Honey Pie (May 3, 1988), There Goes My Gun
(October 9, 1988), Dead (October 9, 1988), Subbacultcha
(June 23, 1991), Manta Ray (October 9, 1988), Is She Weird
(June 11, 1990), Ana (August 18, 1990), Down To The Well
(April 16, 1989), Wave Of Mutilation (April 16, 1989),
Letter To Memphis (June 23, 1991), Levitate Me (May 3, 1988),
Caribou (May 3, 1988), Monkey Gone To Heaven (August 18,
1990), Hey (May 3, 1988), (In Heaven) Lady In The Radiator
Song (May 3, 1988)
Mastered by Chris Staley.
"Wild Honey Pie" by J. Lennon & P. McCartney/Northern
Songs.
"(In Heaven) Lady in the Radiator Song" by P. Ivers and D.
Lynch/Paul Music.
Sleeve by Vaughan Oliver and Tim Vary at v23, Kevin
Westenberg, Chris Bigg, and Simon Larbalestier.

Complete 'B' Sides
(4AD, 2001)
River Euphrates, Vamos (live), In Heaven (Lady In The
Radiator Song) (live), Manta Ray, Weird At My School,
Dancing The Manta Ray, Wave Of Mutilation (UK Surf),
Into The White, Bailey's Walk, Make Believe, I've Been
Waiting For You, The Thing, Velvety Instrumental Version,
Winterlong, Santo, Theme From *Narc*, Build High,
Evil Hearted You, Letter To Memphis (instrumental)
Remastered by John Dent at Loud.
Sleeve by v23, Martin Andersen at v23, and Andrew Caitlin.
"In Heaven (Lady In The Radiator Song)" by P. Ivers and

B-SIDES: FUN FACTS

The following list was compiled by Christophe Gourraud and Jean Michel Biel from aleceiffel.net with additions by Josh Frank.

REFERENCES IN POP CULTURE

Movie Soundtracks
Married to the Mob (Jonathan Demme, 1988): "Isla de Encanta" plays during the closing credits
A Matter of Degrees (USA, 1990): "Where Is My Mind?"
Pump Up the Volume (USA, 1990): "Wave of Mutilation (UK Surf)"
Rolling Thunder (USA, 1991): "Cecilia Ann," "Blown Away," "Rock Music," "No. 13 Baby"
Singles (USA, 1992): "Dig For Fire"
Albert Souffre / Albert Suffers (France, 1992): 100 percent Pixies soundtrack
Hold Me, Thrill Me, Kiss Me (USA, 1992): "La La Love You"
Kicking and Screaming (USA, 1995): "Cecilia Ann"
Grosse Point Blank (USA, 1997): "Monkey Gone To Heaven"
The Adventures of Sebastian Cole (USA, 1998): "Where Is My Mind?"
Fight Club (USA, 1999): "Where Is My Mind?"
Unbreakable (USA, 2000): "I've Been Tired"

Janis et John (France, 2003): "Where Is My Mind?"
The United States of Leland (USA, 2003): "Gigantic,"
"River Euphrates," "Hang Wire"
Stuck on You (USA, 2003): "Here Comes Your Man,"
"La La Love You"

Missed opportunities
"Ana" should have been part of the *Lost Highway* soundtrack (licensing problems)
"Bam Thwok" was turned down for *Shrek 2*

Other references
The movie *Empire Records* (USA, 1995) features a discussion about Pixies
The trailer for Woody Allen's movie *Deconstructing Harry* (USA, 1997) features "La La Love You"
Chris Carter named *Millennium*'s main character Frank Black after Pixies' Frank Black
An episode of the TV show *Blossom* features a dialogue about Pixies and "Here Comes Your Man"
An episode of the TV show *Kids in the Hall* features a dialogue about Pixies
The book *Complicity* by Iain Banks mentions *Trompe Le Monde* twice
Bruce Sterling's novel *Holy Fire* features the line, "You know when you grope for Luna. . ." from the Pixies song "Subbacultcha"
The *Nephilim* roleplaying game rulebook has a Nephilim wearing a Pixies T-Shirt (flying *P*) in one picture
On Sol 98, which ended at 10.36 p.m. PST on April 12, Mars exploration rover Spirit woke up to the song "Where Is My Mind?" by Pixies in honor of its software transplant. The good news is that Spirit's "mind" is updated and operating as expected. (As per an official notice issued by NASA on April 12, 2004).

10 rare Pixies songs or versions to look for
1. "Boom Chick A Boom" (full band version): unreleased

2. "Born In Chicago" (Paul Butterfield Blues Band cover): Rubaiyiat (Elektra's 50th Anniversary)
3. "Brackish Boy" (later released on *Frank Black*): unreleased
4. "Brick Is Red" (demo with extra lyrics): unreleased
5. "Debaser" (demo version): seven-inch release (1997)
6. "Down To The Well" (original demo version 1986): Rare Pixies French promo CD (1996)
7. "Hang On To Your Ego" (Beach Boys cover): unreleased
8. "Here Comes Your Man" (original demo version 1986): unreleased
9. "I Can't Forget" (Leonard Cohen cover): *I'm Your Fan* tribute album
10. "In Heaven" (live version in German): unreleased

10 Pixies promotional objects to look for
1. *Doolittle* posters set (1989, U.K.)
2. *Doolittle* postcards set (1989, U.K.)
3. Pixies candy stix (1989, USA)
4. Get Pixielated badge (unknown)
5. *Bossanova* metal pin (1990, USA)
6. Eyeball key ring (1991, France)
7. Pixies watch (unknown date, Canada)
8. *Death to the Pixies* beer mats (1997, U.K.)
9. *Death to the Pixies* candles (1997, U.K.)
10. *Death to the Pixies* matchboxes (1997, U.K.)

Released Pixies covers and unreleased live covers

"Alec Eiffel"
The Get-Up Kids: *Where Is My Mind?* tribute album (1999)
An April March: *Pixies Fuckin' Die* tribute album (1999)
Drumkan: *Tribute To The Pixies* (2000)
Also played live by Compulsion

"Allison"
Garageland: *No Empty* EP (1999) and *Pixies Fuckin' Die* tribute album (1999)
Eve 6: *Where Is My Mind?* tribute album (1999)
Happy Pills (Polish Band): *Happy Pills Meet Schneider* (2000)

The Fastbacks: *Answer The Phone, Dummy* tour single and *Waste Of Time* promo CD

"Ana"
Drake Tungsten (a.k.a. Britt Daniel from Spoon): self-released tape

"Bird Dream Of Olympus Mons"
Radius: *La La Love You Pixies!* tribute album (2004)
The String Quartet: *The String Quartet Tribute To Pixies* (2004)

"Bone Machine"
Hard Candy: *Pixies Fuckin' Die* tribute album (1999)
Cowpers: *Tribute To The Pixies* (2000)
Laakso: *La La Love You Pixies!* tribute album (2004)

"Broken Face"
Quit Your Dayjob: *La La Love You Pixies!* tribute album (2004)

"Cactus"
David Bowie: *Heathen* (2002)
The String Quartet: *The String Quartet Tribute To Pixies* (2004)
Also played live by the Frames and Foo Fighters

"Caribou"
Sense Field: *Where Is My Mind?* tribute album (1999)
The String Quartet: *The String Quartet Tribute To Pixies* (2004)

"Dead"
Twinkie: *Pixies Fuckin' Die* tribute album (1999)
Radio Active: *Tribute To The Pixies* (2000)

"Debaser"
Kerbdog: *Dummy Crusher* single (1994)
Beat Crusaders: *Tribute To The Pixies* (2000)
Feed: *Tribute To The Pixies* (2000)
Loud Family: live on *From Ritual To Romance* (2002)
Radon: live on *We Bare All* (2003)
Dirt Bike Annie: *It Ain't Easy Bein' Single* (2003)
The String Quartet: *The String Quartet Tribute To Pixies* (2004)

Also played live by the Frames, Ash, David Bowie & Tin Machine, the Wrens, and Coldplay (at least at sound checks)

"Distance Equals Rate Times Time"
J Stroke featuring La Loba: *Pixies Fuckin' Die* tribute album (1999)
Doktor Kosmos: *La La Love You Pixies!* tribute album (2004)

"Ed Is Dead"
Melon: *Pixies Fuckin' Die* tribute album (1999)

"Gigantic"
Orange: *Thurtene 4AD* tribute album (1993)
Ladies Who Lunch (Josephine Wiggs): *Kims We Love* seven-inch (1995)
The Low Road: *Fidelity* (1996)
Pixels: *Death To The Pixies We're Better* tribute album (1997)
Brotherhood Foundation: *Death To The Pixies We're Better* tribute album (1997)
Reel Big Fish: *Where Is My Mind?* tribute album (1999)
Allison With One: *Pixies Fuckin' Die* tribute album (1999)
Silent Films: *Her Space Holiday* EP (2000)
[Japanese name]: *Tribute To The Pixies* (2000)
Hello Goodbye: *La La Love You Pixies!* tribute album (2004)
The String Quartet: *The String Quartet Tribute To Pixies* (2004)

Also played live by Pavement and Belle & Sebastian

"Gouge Away"
Hayden: *Mild And Hazy* seven-inch (1994)
Promise Ring: *Where Is My Mind?* tribute album (1999)
Bethany Curve: *Pixies Fuckin' Die* tribute album (1999)
Papa Roach : *Lovehatetragedy* (2002)
Jacques Lu Cont: *Fabriclive.09* (2003)
The String Quartet: *The String Quartet Tribute To Pixies* (2004)

Also played live by Castaways and Letters to Cleo

"Here Comes Your Man"
Zea: *Death To The Pixies We're Better* tribute album (1997)
Samiam: *Where Is My Mind?* tribute album (1999)
Penpals: *Tribute To The Pixies* (2000)

Teenage Fanclub: *I Need Direction* single (2000)
Alice Wonders: *Mod Tea Diary* (2002)
Mattias Alkberg BD: *La La Love You Pixies!* tribute album
(2004)
The String Quartet: *The String Quartet Tribute To Pixies* (2004)

"Hey"
Telefunk: *Death To The Pixies We're Better* tribute album (1997)
Ramona The Pest: *Contrary Sanctuary album* (2003)

Also played live by dEUS

"I Bleed"
Rise And Fall Of A Decade (French band): *Mistake* EP (1995)
Giant Ant Farm: *The Clapper on Dressed In Milk* EP (1996)
Homer: *Death To The Pixies We're Better* tribute album (1997)

"Into The White"
Drekka: *Pixies Fuckin' Die* tribute album (1999)

"Isla De Encanta"
Persil: *Death To The Pixies We're Better* tribute album (1997)

"Is She Weird"
Seedling: *Death To The Pixies We're Better* tribute album (1997)

"I've Been Tired"
Jonus: *Death To The Pixies We're Better* tribute album (1997)
Also played live by Pearl Jam

"La La Love You"
Weston: *Where Is My Mind?* tribute album (1999)

"Levitate Me"
Weaklazyliars: *Yesterday Night* (unlisted) (1999)
Seafood: *Tribute To The Pixies* (2000)

"Manta Ray"
Man. . . Or Astroman?: *Project Infinity* (1995)
Man. . . Or Astroman?: live version on *Live Transmissions From Uranus* (1995)
Teen Heroes: *Where Is My Mind?* tribute album (1999)

"Mr. Grieves"
TV on the Radio: *Young Liars* EP (hidden track)

"Monkey Gone To Heaven"
Deep Sweden (Czech band): *Maiden Prague* (1997)
Far: *Where Is My Mind?* tribute album (1999)
Bonfire Madigan: *Pixies Fuckin' Die* tribute album (1999)
Hamell On Trial: *La La Love You Pixies!* tribute album (2004)
The String Quartet: *The String Quartet Tribute To Pixies* (2004)

Also played live by Pearl Jam and Paul Westerberg

"Motorway To Roswell"
Played live by the Jesus And Mary Chain

"No. 13 Baby"
Moth Wranglers: *Pixies Fuckin' Die* tribute album (1999)

"Planet Of Sound"
Face To Face: *Standards & Practices* (1999)
Mo'Some Tonebender: *Tribute To The Pixies* (2000)
Honky Mofo: *Honky Mofo* (2002)
Also played live by the Divine Comedy

"River Euphrates"
The Interstellars: *Pixies Fuckin' Die* tribute album (1999)

"Silver"
Bluebottle Kiss: *Pixies Fuckin' Die* tribute album (1999)

"Subbacultcha"
Engine: *Pixies Fuckin' Die* tribute album (1999)

"Tame"
Local H: *Where Is My Mind?* tribute album (1999)
Jarboe And The Trepaners: *Pixies Fuckin' Die* tribute album
(1999)
Milemarker: *Changing Caring Humans 1997–1999—A
Collection of Singles and Compilation Songs* (2000)
Song Of Zarathustra: *A View From High Tides* (2002)

"The Happening"
The Ottomen: *Robin The Indian* single (self released)
It's A Trick, It's A Trick!: *La La Love You Pixies!* tribute album (2004)

"The Holiday Song"
The Siren Six!: *Where Is My Mind?* tribute album (1999)
Glass Candle Grenade: *Pixies Fuckin' Die* tribute album (1999)
Hell On Wheels: *La La Love You Pixies!* tribute album (2004)

"Trompe Le Monde"
Braid: *Where Is My Mind?* tribute album (1999)
Ca-p: *Tribute To The Pixies* (2000)

"U-Mass"
Mollycuddle: *Pixies Fuckin' Die* tribute album (1999)
The Ottomen: *Adventures At The Shore* (self released)

Also played at least once and at least partly by Radiohead

"Velouria"
Weezer: *Where Is My Mind?* tribute album (1999)
Twelve24: *Pixies Fuckin' Die* tribute album (1999) and *All In Focus* EP (1999)
The Bad Plus: *Give* (2004)
Nathan Larsson: *La La Love You Pixies!* tribute album (2004)
The String Quartet: *The String Quartet Tribute To Pixies* (2004)

Also played live by 3 Colours Red, Grandaddy and Bob Nanna from Braid

"Wave Of Mutilation"
Number Girl (Japanese band): *Toomei Shoojo (Invisible Girl)* single (1999)
Superdrag: *Where Is My Mind?* tribute album (1999)
No Wings Fins Or Fuselage: *Pixies Fuckin' Die* tribute album (1999)
Naht: *Tribute To The Pixies* (2000)
David Fridlund & Sara Culler: *La La Love You Pixies!* tribute album (2004)
The String Quartet: *The String Quartet Tribute To Pixies* (2004)
Kristin Hersh: *High School Reunion* compilation (2005)

Also played live by Grant Lee Phillips and The Unbelievable Truth

"Where Is My Mind?"
The Gosh Guys: *Thurtene 4AD* tribute album (1993)
Crackity Jones: *Death To The Pixies We're Better* tribute album (1997)
Koos Kreuk: *Death To The Pixies We're Better* tribute album (1997)
Miss Universe: *Death To The Pixies We're Better* tribute album (1997)
House Of Wires: *You Are Obsolete* (1998)
Orbit: *I Wanna Make You* EP (1998)
Raz Ohara: *Realtime Voyeur* (1999)
Ghoti Hook: *Songs We Didn't Write* (1998), *Retrospective* (2002)
Nada Surf: *Where Is My Mind?* tribute album (1999)
Underwater: *Pixies Fuckin' Die* tribute album (1999)
Roadsaw: Roadsaw/Blackrock split single *The Boston Sherwood Tapes* (2001)
The Toadies: live on *Best of Toadies—Live From Paradise* (2002)
Ghoti Hook: live on *R.I.P.* (2003)
Placebo: XFM Live Version on *This Picture* single (2003)
Placebo: live with Frank Black on DVD *Soulmates Never Die: Live in Paris 2003* (2004)
Stereotyperider: *Under The Influence* (2004)
Leit Motif (Mexican band): *Strange Sounds From The Past* (unknown)
Hey (Polish Band): *Koncertowy* (2003)
The String Quartet: *The String Quartet Tribute To Pixies* (2004)

Also played live by Pavement, the Frames and Coldplay (at least at sound checks)

Tribute albums to Pixies
Death To The Pixies, We're Better!
(Pias Benelux, 444.0005.29, Netherlands, 1998)

The project started with a Pixies covers contest launched by the magazine *Oor*, the radio station VPRO, and the Play It Again Sam (PIAS) label in October 1997.

Eleven bands were selected, playing grunge, new wave, new age, techno, or Dutch folk versions of Pixies songs. They were all invited to play live at the Paradiso in December 1997. The compilation was released in February 1998.

Pixies Fuckin' Die! (a tribute)
(LifeLike Records, USA, 1999)

LifeLike Records and Bedazzled Records (from D.C.) released a 100% indie Pixies tribute album in May 1999. The 19 track compilation focuses on the 4AD/quirky pop side of Pixies.

Where Is My Mind?: A Tribute to the Pixies
(Glue Factory Records, USA, 1999)

Major labels honored the Pixies' legacy, too. Through their Glue Factory Records subsidiary, Warner Bros. initiated a 15-track Pixies tribute compilation in May 1999.

Tribute To The Pixies (Invisible Records, 2000)

Tribute made by Japanese experimental and punk bands.

Hey—A Pixies Tribute
(FrankBlack.net, 2003)

This download-only album compiles Pixies covers recorded by 22 FrankBlack.net members. A "B-sides" download-only album (compiling songs which weren't selected for the original album) is also in progress.

La La Love You Pixies! A Tribute
(Dusseldorf Recordings, Sweden, 2004)

Tribute made by mostly Swedish bands (and a couple of Americans, too).

The String Quartet Tribute To Pixies
(Vitamin Records, USA, 2004)

One in a series of instrumental tribute albums.

A NOTE ON SOURCES

The authors wish to acknowledge the following individuals for granting permission to reproduce unpublished excerpts from original interviews:

Johnny Angel interview by Marc Spitz. Additional Kim Deal, Marc Geiger, Joe Harvard, David Lovering, Joey Santiago, and Charles Thompson interviews by Marc Spitz (used with permission)

Steve Albini, Jeff Craft, Robin Hurley, Ben Marts, and Paul Tollett interviews by Carrie Borzillo-Vrenna. Additional Chas Banks, Kurt St. Thomas, and Ivo Watts-Russell interviews by Carrie Borzillo-Vrenna (used with permission)

Additional Kristin Hersh, Gary Smith, and Charles Thompson interviews by Andrew Beaujon (used with permission)

Additional Joey Santiago and Charles Thompson interviews by Brian Raftery (used with permission)

Additional Paul Kolderie and Sean Slade interviews by Tom Kielty (used with permission)

Bono interview by Chuck Klosterman (used with permission)

Courtney Love interview by Phoebe Reilly (used with permission)

Billy Corgan interview and additional Charles Thompson interview by Kyle Anderson (used with permission)

SOURCE NOTES

1   "No Time Wasters!" *Q*, No. 48, September 1990
2   "Life to the Pixies," By Marc Spitz, *Spin*, September 2004
3   "Pixies Cast Their Spell," By David Fricke, *Rolling Stone*, June 15, 1989
4   "Life to the Pixies," By Marc Spitz, *Spin*, September 2004
5   "They Don't Call Him the Martin Hannett of the '90s For Nothing (Eyewitness Record Reviews" By Steve Albini, *Forced Exposure*, #17, 1991
6   "Life to the Pixies," By Marc Spitz, *Spin*, September 2004
7   "Life to the Pixies," By Marc Spitz, *Spin*, September 2004
8   "Life to the Pixies," By Marc Spitz, *Spin*, September 2004
9   "Here and There and Everywhere," by Marlene Goldman, *Alternative Press* Vol IV, No. 22, September 1989
10 "Life to the Pixies," By Marc Spitz, *Spin*, September 2004
11 "Los Gringos Locos," By David Cavanagh, *Mojo*, January 18, 2001
12 "Here and There and Everywhere," by Marlene Goldman. *Alternative Press* Vol IV, No. 22, September 1989
13 "Here and There and Everywhere," by Marlene Goldman. *Alternative Press* Vol IV, No. 22, September 1989
14 "Los Gringos Locos," By David Cavanagh, *Mojo*, January 18, 2001
15 "Life to the Pixies," By Marc Spitz, *Spin*, September 2004
16 "Animal Farm," By Jim Greer, *Spin*, July 1992
17 "Life to the Pixies," By Marc Spitz, *Spin*, September 2004
18 "Life to the Pixies," By Marc Spitz, *Spin*, September 2004
19 "Life to the Pixies," By Marc Spitz, *Spin*, September 2004
20 "Pixies Return To Hit Markets They Missed," By Jill Kipnis, *Billboard*, May 14, 2005

ACKNOWLEDGEMENTS

JOSH FRANK WOULD LIKE TO THANK:

Creative counterparts:

Heather Zicko, who has been my partner/co-producer on developing the musical for the last three years, rain or shine, and who made the trek with me to Dayton, Ohio, what seems like many winters ago to meet and interview Kim, Kelley and their leaning dog—you are my anchor in this mad world of creation. Michael Harriot, if you had not answered the phone this book would not exist. Andrea Somberg, Celeste Fine, and David Vigliano. Michael Connor at St. Martins and Eleanor Maxfield, Stuart Slater, and Stuart Evers at Virgin UK. Ashley Mathews, my one-time publicist for six months, who enabled everything that has transpired over the last three years. Brannon Wiles and Snug Harbor Productions, our patient and generous general managers for the "musical." And of course, Caryn my co-writer for jumping in head-first, embracing the playwright in me while teaching me how to talk rock.

Family:

Steve, my dad, best friend, and copyeditor of my early years, Marcia, my mom, my sister Rachel and my soon to be brother-in-law Jaime Carlson, Shirley, my Grandmother(s), Joe Frank, the grandfather, Dennis and fam, and the Rosen clan.

Inspirations:

Steven Appleby and Simon Larbalestier for the honor of being able to use your wonderful work. Chas Banks for the forward and inspiration. Gary Smith for help and encouragement from the get-go, Charles and his management, Kim, David, and Joey for letting me hear your stories when you did, I am forever inspired. 4AD, Vaughan Oliver and v23, and everyone else who took a little time from Boston to New Mexico, Los Angeles to London, Manchester to Maryland. Joshua Weiss, the biggest Frank Black fan, advocate of my projects over the last few years, website manager and friend. Charlie Buckholtz, my brother in Israel, a brilliant short story writer who makes my messes seem cleaner, a creative partner and the guy who I first listened to *Bossanova* with. Amy and Terri Gilliam for a bit of inspiration when it was much needed. Same goes for Jonathan Richman and in Texas, Kinky Friedman, who was meanwhile back at the ranch. Werner Herzog, for giving me my first chance to adapt a brilliant seldom-seen film into a play. Eric Nederlander, the beat-you-up-when-mom's-not-looking-but-still-loves-you big brother I never had. Amy Nederlander, a tough love mentor, and sport for giving me work when there was none at the beginning of this journey.

Friends:

Kevin Fay, my high school friend and rock bandmate, and his older brother Owen who took pity on me and first introduced me to Pixies a long time ago at a high school far far away. Didier Gertsch, Greg Nodler, David and Rachel Wyatt, Isaac Levy, Steve Shapiro, Brian Roff, Dalia and Paz, Clint McCown, Russ Roten, Mel Rodriguez, Abigail Revasch, Conrad Choucroun, Vanessa at BHV. Extra special thanks to Jodi Bart who got me in with the Vig.

Other book help:

Jean-Michel Biel and Christophe Gourraud for fun facts help, Andy Barding for *Rock A My Soul* zine and Alison Hale for pictures, Marc Mazz, Ted Mico, John Murphy for Boston connections and historical memorabilia, and Lars Ingebrigtsen for discography help.

Caryn Ganz would like to thank:

Everyone who made time to talk to us on the record for this book—in many ways, you *are* the book and the project could not exist without your recollections, commentaries, contacts, and honesty. I'm greatly indebted to the writers who donated their own interviews to the cause: Marc Spitz (your advice and advocacy is greatly appreciated), Carrie Borzillo-Vrenna, Andrew Beaujon, and Brian Raftery, as well as Kyle Anderson and Tom Kielty—your contributions are invaluable. Desiree Flores (my motivator) and my family, Jerilyn, Eli, and Melissa Ganz.

Stuart Evers, Eleanor Maxfield, Stuart Slater and everyone at Virgin Books, and Michael Connor and everyone at St. Martin's Press. Michael Harriot, Andrea Somberg, and Celeste Fine at Vigliano Associates. Sia Michel and the staff of *Spin* magazine, especially Phoebe Reilly, Jon Dolan, Chuck Klosterman, and Bethany Mezick. My encouraging friends who've probably heard more about Pixies than they'd ever dreamed possible: Marian Barragan, Greg Chow, Nicholas Fonseca, Emily Haines, Nate Harris, Rebecca Sears, Katey Wood, and anyone else who's heard me utter the phrase "As soon as I finish the book..." in the past year (I know there's a lot of you). Ari Burd, Ross Raihala for the good start, Sophy Grimshaw for the good efforts, Rob Sheffield, Andy Greenwald, Ellen Carpenter, Tracey Pepper, and Elaine Garza. And Steven Warner, a true rock 'n' roll character who will always be in my thoughts.

I'm very grateful for the extremely helpful folks who sent me off in the right directions and made the interviews happen: Fernando Aguilar at Vagrant, Nils Bernstein at Matador, Jennie Boddy at Interscope, Brendan Bourke at Tag Team, Bobbie Gale at Capitol, Lisa Gottheil at Beggars, Alexandra Greenberg at MSO, Martin Hall at Merge, Sonya Kolowrat at Beggars, Owen Levin at Stick Figure, Billy O'Connell, John Reid at JPR, Sherry Ring, Jason Roth at Capitol, Brian Schwartz, Nick Stern at Atlantic, Stacey Studebaker at Shout Factory, and Alison Zero at Girlie Action. I'd also like to thank Heidi Ellen Robinson Fitzgerald for her continued kindness and helpfulness.

Josh Frank for his unending energy and enthusiasm. John Murphy, Gary Smith, Andy Barding, and T Max for digging into their personal archives. Broken Social Scene for their inspiring, magnificent set when they opened for Pixies at New York City's Hammerstein Ballroom in December, 2004. And Pixies for making music that, even after a million spins while I worked on this oral history, still sounds brilliant and fresh to me every time.

INDEX